AT THE
BRIGHT HEM
OF GOD

Praise for *At the Bright Hem of God*

Radnorshire boasts more than 100 peaks exceeding 1500 feet. Literary peaks abound, too: poets and writers who were born here, sojourned here, or just dreamed of visiting. Conradi weaves them all into Radnorshire's warp to create a stunning tapestry, injecting familiar names with fresh insights...Kilvert is Radnorshire's supreme ambassador, caught marvellously by Conradi. '

– David Wilbourne, *Church Times*, 2009

"Conradi writes thoughtfully and non-judgementally even when dealing with contentious matters of Welsh politics and cultural identity. He is glad to quote Bidgood's declaration that she did not come to this area to escape the world: 'This is the world.' Completed by Simon Dorrell's exquisite pen-and-ink miniatures, it is the perfect primer to this quiet stretch of Wales."

– Nicholas Murray, *Independent*, 28 July 2009

"Mr Conradi is a Londoner, but loves this area more deeply than any other, and has had a cottage here since 1965. 'Its very name,' he says, 'like the glimpse of a lover, has the thrilling power to stop the mind'. He brings the passion of the incomer, the curiosity about every detail, the longing to belong... Like anyone in love with remote and marginal places, Mr Conradi disputes the dismissive adjectives. This is not the edge; it is the forgotten centre.... 'You never enjoy the world aright,' [Thomas] Traherne wrote, 'till the sea itself floweth in your veins, till you are clothed with the heavens and crowned with the stars, and perceive yourself to be the sole heir of the whole world.' And, one might add, till you know that Radnorshire matters."

– Adam Nicolson, *Country Life*, 5 August, 2009

"The title of this book comes from R.S. Thomas, about whom Peter Conradi writes with some daring, leaving us with a kind of last portrait. In a brilliant early chapter, he reminds us that 'Wales' comes from the Old English adjective *wealh* – foreigner, which he interprets as 'other.'...*At the Bright Hem of God* is a scholarly, lyrical, autobiographical guide to the March. Conradi is witty, dreamy and gossipy by turn. 'Houses fall into ruin and die. So do poets. The landscape of good poetry itself recalls mid-Wales, each time depopulated when the old voices 'go down' like houses. Later new talents invade and colonise.' He is one of them."

– Ronald Blythe, *Times Literary Supplement*, 14 August 2009

AT THE BRIGHT HEM OF GOD

RADNORSHIRE PASTORAL

Peter J. Conradi

Illustrated by
Simon Dorrell

SEREN

Seren is the book imprint of
Poetry Wales Press Ltd
Nolton Street, Bridgend, Wales
www.serenbooks.com
Facebook: facebook.com/SerenBooks
Twitter: @SerenBooks

Text © Peter J Conradi, 2009
Drawings © Simon Dorrell, 2009

First published in 2009
Reprinted in 2009, 2019

The right of Peter J Conradi to be identified
as the Author of this Work
has been asserted in accordance with the
Copyright, Designs and Patents Act, 1988.

ISBN 978-1-85411-490-7

A CIP record for this title is available from
the British Library

The publisher works with the financial assistance
of the Welsh Books Council

Cover Photography: The River Wye at Gamallt by Barry Needle

Printed by 4Edge Ltd, Hockley

Contents

List of Illustrations

For Dick Shannon and Cascob neighbours

I'r estron, os myn,
Boed hawl tros y glyn;
I ninnau boed byw
Yn ymyl gwisg Duw
Yn y grug, yn y grug

Let the stranger, if he will,
Have his way with the glen;
But give us to live
At the bright hem of God
In the heather, in the heather.

Anonymous folk stanza tr. R.S. Thomas

PART ONE
THE MARCH

1965

In spring 1929 the grandmother of a college friend of Welsh descent rode her motor-bike down to the Great Wilderness, where fireplaces sometimes still burnt peat, and Baptist farmers' wives scurried shyly indoors in their head-scarves on her approach, and found a remarkable upland cottage at fifteen hundred feet, two miles from any road, and empty for many years. So this story was first picturesquely told me. She rented it for £8 per year, of which three pounds was named as buying her the right to burn oak from the surrounding woods, and, since her husband was killed at sea in 1940, the patriotic Welsh farmer who owned it never had the heart to put this rental up.

The small cottage windows, deep-set to resist the weather, looked out upon Wales's Empty Quarter – also known both as the Green Desert, and as "miles and miles of bugger all". The differently dramatic, steep shapes of the Cambrian mountains – Gamriw, Gorllwyn, Drum Ddu and far-off Drygarn Fawr – held your attention. On 3 September 1939, the day that war broke out, the motorcyclist's daughter left the cottage to climb the Drygarn, and from its stylish cairn on top – it was a notably clear day – she could see out to the island of Bardsey in the Irish Sea on which are improbably reported to be buried 20,000 saints. Gazing at this view, she found, diluted her foreboding.

In this same cottage I stayed for the first time in the summer of 1965, having hitch-hiked from London. It was my first taste of the colossal, timeless, golden silence of the hills. Nobody passed the small house. There were whole days of peace. Company consisted after one week of a beautiful, spirited, unpredictable girlfriend, rampant house-mice feeding off and shredding blankets, golden plover, curlew, buzzard, and wild pony. Wandering about the fern-filled small sessile oak-woods – Welsh oak, I learnt, are 'sessile', English 'pedunculate' – full of dappled sunlight, was novel. The oaks were not the only items that were different here. An emotion whose name I looked for but could not find ran through those days.

I did not think on that first visit to Wales that I had ever visited a place of such transcendent magic. It was quite other than where I had grown up, in the green good manners of the South-English parkscape. The summer was hot, the air clear, no rain fell on this wild area encompassing the big reservoirs created after 1890 to carry water to Birmingham. It comprises one border of the old kingdom of Ceredigion and divides the largely anglophone East from the Welsh-speaking coastal region.

Here were sublime views over the ancient hills, the shock of silence, and then the surprise of a new feeling compounded of exhilaration, trust, and peace-of-mind. Anxiety and restlessness had slipped away. Much later, I recognised a description of Rousseau's:

> There is something magical and supernatural in hill landscape, which entrances the mind and the senses. *One forgets every-thing, one forgets one's own being, one ceases to know where one stands.*[1]

It took some days to recognise this condition as happiness: I had fallen unreasonably and ignorantly in love. I was young and twenty and shamefully unaware, for example, of the grim extent of upland depopulation over the previous century, a topic eloquently addressed by Ruth Bidgood's local history and poetry alike: more of these, in a later chapter. The space and solitude that awed me were, like all landscape, haunted by absence and by loss.

Meanwhile the very county name of 'Radnorshire' – like the glimpse of a lover – had the thrilling power to stop the mind. A place you love, like a person, has many faces: it presents as an elsewhere, a mystery which might one day be unlocked. While living for five years abroad (a kibbutz; Colorado; Krakow) my dreams concerned mid-Wales, never London. I equated the county name with wellbeing; and want in writing about it to explore this equation.

Up in the silence of these hills in 1965 I read the four interminable volumes of Samuel Richardson's *Clarissa* – at night by hurricane-lamp – in preparation for Lorna Sage's first seminar that autumn at UEA: a novel even longer than the Bible. You have to wait for three volumes for Lovelace finally to manage to rape Clarissa, which, to add to its capacity to irritate, is accomplished within one paragraph, after which, during a whole final volume as I remember it, she mainly knits her shroud. Lorna Sage, who was born in the Welsh March, re-enters this story a little later.

*

The night before we found our house we slept in another of those remote upper moorland cottages miles from any road, used for centuries – as do the peasants of the Cevennes, or, for that matter, of Tibet – for 'transhumance', the family decamping each summer to graze their sheep on the high grass-lands. These summer cottages were known in Welsh as *hafodydd* or *hafotai*. This one had been left uninhabited since the Second World War, and had some largish holes in the roof. We found it after two hours, carrying amongst much else a paraffin heater, during a night rapidly turning to swirling snow-blizzard: snow caught in torch-light came slanting wildly out of nowhere. Davy, a lonely shepherd wearing fertiliser bags tied by rough twine as leggings, rescued us. Wet through, partly from falling over, we found out how to create make-shift warm and dry footwear from old newspapers bound to the sole with wire manipulated from coat-hangers.

The following night we were guests in a big Gothic mansion re-designed around 1820 by Humphrey Repton, later rented out to the TV company adapting Tom Sharpe's *Blott on the Landscape*. The chatelaine of this crenellated house, in her sixties, moved to this part of Radnorshire around 1933; then a wide-eyed beauty, she knew Wilfrid Thesiger, who grew up in the dower-house and was thus Radnorshire-bred, before his departure alone to Nuristan and, twice, to cross the Empty Quarter of Arabia. She had also known some who remembered Kilvert, always with affection. Kilvert, too, returns in this story, later.

On the day in between these two adventures, we found the school: a sign on a tree invited the interested to turn up a cul-de-sac valley for two or three miles to a hamlet described in 1700 as "*O bobtu 5 o dai*" (about 5 houses) – still accurate today[2]. Around us is a huge quadrilateral or rhombus lying on its side, called the Radnor Forest ('forest' as originally denoting wild common, rather than woodland) or – its ancient, correct Welsh name – *Fforest Clud*, comprising about one hundred square miles with no through-road inside it, lonely, alarming, where the legendary red dragon of Wales was defeated by St Michael; our St Michael's church is one of ten in Radnorshire. The March has many secrets. A small four-acre estate lost two and a half miles up a very narrow single-track lane that leads nowhere, our home has by definition no through-traffic, and is situated at the elbow of a cul-de-sac valley inside one of the larger wildernesses on the edge of southern England. At this elbow the valley swings around from north-south to east-west, by a simple church built around 1300 on a knoll.

Our garden borders this church and churchyard, about which Iris Murdoch, whose official biography I wrote, asked "Do you know many of the dead people there?" Increasingly, we do, and in winter when the hedges are bare you can see gravestones from the house. To live by a graveyard is a happy stimulus to reflection, meditation, and, to a Buddhist, an aid to retreat. John Bayley wrote of our Welsh house in his *Iris: A Memoir*; our blue-eyed collie-bitch, whom Iris Murdoch wrote into *The Green Knight*, came from this valley, and lived much of her life here, like her successors. And Iris swam often with us here between 1996 and her death in 1999. We also walked the hills together.

Hill-walking, in almost any weather, dispels or ventilates care and anxiety, putting them into a bigger perspective, beyond the ordinary experience of time, restoring the spirit. Its exhilaration rarely fails: so I was shocked in 1970 when a Dutch boy-friend confessed after a weekend that hills made him sea-sick. Not for him any living truth in Psalm 121: "I will lift up my eyes unto the hills, from whence cometh my help": the magical beauty of the hills, the swift skies, the glimpses of wildness, affording a healing experience of elsewhere.

Even higher mountain country rises up two miles to the West like a bare, windy whale. It's easy to get lost up here in the loneliest and highest land in the county among the prominent hill slopes covered in bracken and gorse, and the long, bare slopes of peat and heather rising more than two thousand feet above sea level: "*i flaen hoywfro Maelienydd*" (the bright uplands of Maelienydd). On the summit is mist-driven moorland from which the red grouse startled you by exploding into wings and air and a bad-tempered freakish flight just before you stepped on them, like harmless land-mines. Here in the early seventeenth century three shepherd-brothers tending their flock were found in one another's arms frozen to death: as locals say, this area 'gets a lot of weather'. Clud was always treeless pasturage and hunting country – "foggy and moorish" says the Domesday Book. According to an inquest in the year 1565, the only trees in the forest were "VIII acres of lowe shrubs and bushes of smalle hazill and thornes". The jurors said that the tenants of the parishes around the forest had "free common of pasture there tyme out of minde in the said forrest"[3]. And over all, the enchantment of ever-changing light and colour...

Nowadays the Eastern valley-sides are wooded, and fields well irrigated by trout-streams beneath – one of these flows along the border of our field. The place astonished us. Great vistas to be found on the wild bare hill-tops combined with a gentle, fertile valley-bottom so that the valley itself seemed intimately to cradle you, as if within an immense tea-cup. Towards the bottom of this cup, on a knoll, sat, by themselves, the gothic school and thirteenth-century church and a cottage, a mini-Camelot. Near the school three-hundred-year-old oak and ash-trees lined a ridge-walk, outside a courtyard. Electricity and running water alike had arrived a short time before. That both R.S. Thomas and Roland Mathias, two of the greatest Welsh poets recently writing in English, had each written a poem about this tiny hamlet we did not then know.

In this valley flourished William Jenkins Rees, rector of Cascob for some fifty years, notable among the *hen bersoniaid llengar* – that group of Church of England clergymen who fostered Welsh culture in the first half of the nineteenth century, often in the face of apathy or opposition from the bishops of the established church.[4] His Rectory must have been a kind of Welsh Abbotsford, and he played a key role in helping Jonathan Williams's county history see the light of day.

"But where is the village?" visitors ask, forgetful that Wales favours 'scattered' rather than nuclear hamlets. Church, mill cottage and schoolhouse are the only centre here. The various farmhouses, some eighteenth century, a few earlier, many distin-guished, sit back a few hundred yards from both the road and the little brook that soon feeds the Lugg. One cottage was in 1860 a Baptist chapel, others earlier housed a blacksmith and a cobbler.

Only one farm boasted a telephone. The old red kiosk outside our house even today houses a stool so that the incum-bent can make seated business-calls. Television was rare, and one neighbour had – impressively – decided not to have one. This seemed independent-minded: here was a valley that had decided stubbornly to belong to itself.

An impression of local autonomy was somehow compounded by the fact that the misleadingly named Great Road to Aberystwyth, which once went through our valley, had been re-routed in 1767, when the Turnpike Trust moved it to the north. It is not hard to see why. The lane it once went through, known as the Cwm, is narrow, steep in gradient for a mile, and sunk between very high wooded banks; there are primroses and wood-violets in spring, bluebells soon afterwards. This road cannot have been passable in the mud of winter, and must have been dust-clouded in a dry summer. It can, despite its name, have taken pack-horses only, as a recent TV programme by Terry Jones showed: it was at best a speculative enterprise hoping to profit from the future export of coastally-mined silver to the capital. Small wonder it was soon re-routed, leaving us a remote backwater, by-passed and forgotten.

★

But this condition of retreat mirrors Wales as a whole. Old Welsh being the original language of our island, the arrival of the Saxons heralded – at least in popular myth – a long withdrawal: the Welsh leaving the land of summer for the western fastnesses[5]. Saint Beuno (545-640) is said once to have heard a voice on the far side of the river Severn, inciting hounds to chase a hare in a strange language. Beuno told his disciples to pack and leave, prophesying that the hunter's nation would soon colonise. He retreated to Merioneth.

Living in a forgotten backwater has its own benefits. Shakespeare with typical acuity makes Henry of Monmouth comment on Fluellen,

> Though it appear a little out of fashion,
> There is much care and valour in this Welshman.
> (*Henry V* Act 4 Scene 1)

Being a little out of fashion has sometimes suited Wales, which stayed loyal to Edward II when he was beleaguered by enemies in England, to Richard II after Bolingbroke's usurpation, to Catholicism long into the Reformation and to King Charles long into the Civil War. Even the tall black hats of Welsh folk-costume turn out to be Calvinist hats worn in London around 1610: the message that these appeared a little out of fashion did not reach Wales.

The writer Byron Rogers recently described a North Wales housewife pulling away at the walls of her ancient barn to find to her astonishment first mullioned windows, then the outline of two great arches attesting that her barn enshrined the gatehouse of the last native prince of Wales. Such surprising glimpses of the past seemed to belong to local magic. At the end of Tom Bullough's 2007 novel, *The Claude Glass*, set today, a Radnorshire shepherd's boy, brought up rough to eat scraps under the table with the sheep-dogs, opens an unused farm-house door to discover a once-elegant room in decay from the time it was enlivened by Wordsworth's conversation two centuries before; even the chandelier, though dusty, is intact.

The blue-covered *Transactions of the Radnorshire Society* had articles on the distribution of local bats, of Victorian encaustic tiles, and a series by the novelist Anthony Powell proudly tracing his Radnorshire antecedents back to a chieftain flourishing at the time of Roman Emperor Magnus Maximus – *Macsen Wledig* to the Welsh – in the year 388 AD.

Few parts of Wales seemed as out-of-time as Radnorshire, ignored or forgotten by the English as too remote and by the Welsh as too English[6]. The geography of the county is relevant to its history: each of the county's river-valleys opens up towards England – Teme, Arrow, Lugg, Wye. As an ancient rhyme about the thirteen old Welsh counties has it "*Ond wfft i Sir Faesyfed,/ hen Saesnes rhonc yw hi*" (But forget about Radnorshire,/ She's an old Englishwoman). This calumny reflects the common misconception of Radnorshire as no more than the most anglicised Welsh county.

One neighbour, pondering anxiously what clothes to take for a day out with her son seventeen miles away in Herefordshire, said, "The problem is I never know how the weather is going to be, in England...". Sometimes the weather-systems differ visibly. On a hill walk around January 1989 a freezing fog visibly and dramatically followed the line of the border itself. Seen from above, this heavy blanket of fog, under which England lay concealed, was striking, a great pall of sheep's wool; Heathrow was closed while in Wales we gloried in a brilliant winter sunshine.

*

Each year after 1980 another 40,000 or so English people bought homes in Wales. Those puzzled by Welsh nationalism might try to imagine how it would feel if the USA directly bordered England, and five million Americans bought weekend homes there over twenty years – roughly the proportion of English buying houses in Wales. The fear of being overwhelmed by a huge powerful neighbour, with alien speech, shallow culture, and a habit of ignorant condescension would arouse bitter resentment, as it began to during the Second World War. And the Welsh are undefended by any Atlantic against the English, who out-number them 25 to 1.

The first wave, to which we belonged, were hippies and dreamers, sometimes yurt- or teepee-dwellers, seeking a parallel universe, a quest traceable back to Romanticism. Neighbours were forgiving. One spoke kindly of the English as "South-of-Britain people". (That was a Victorian Unionist coinage: when Miss Ivors charges Gabriel Conroy in Joyce's 'The Dead' with being a "West Briton", she means a flunkey to the English.) We were often beholden to neighbours. After nearly one year of waiting for the bill for a car service carried out in a local farm-house, I made enquiries, and was asked, "What's the hurry?" Little monetary accounting happened between valley-born neighbours, who considered it ill-bred.

Having traversed a different border, I and my partner were

as a same-sex couple outsiders from another point-of-view, but if eyebrows rose at this, no one objected. We were not the only such couple hereabouts. The border with Wales has for centuries seemed also a border with the unexpected, as the two Ladies of Llangollen found in the eighteenth century. These two well-bred and well-read ladies, popularly thought to be lovers, were much visited.

There are – by many factors – more sheep than people. One recent spring, trying to get my car filled, the petrol attendant arrived, a Macbeth after murdering Duncan, tired, panicky and guilty, sleeves rolled up and fore-arms well blooded, begging me through the driver's window to get out and "help him draw a difficult lamb". I was a sentimental Londoner, squeamish about reports of a farmer in a distant valley who regularly let his bitch whelp and drowned the litter rather than pay to have her spayed; and had watched another pour detergent over his right hand and arm to lubricate it for the turning of a lamb – how did the sensitive mucous membrane of the sheep's vagina cope with this stinging liquid? I explained how little use I felt I should be.

Living nowadays literally in a cul-de-sac, without newpapers or television, among these ancient hills, it is easy to forget the day of the week. I can still see the Boss leaning on one of the hazel switches he carefully cut for himself, thumb hooked at chin-height over its high V, communing in quietness with other old boys. He pronounced the 'a' in father like the 'a' in May. He fed his sheep-dogs of a morning, they sitting patiently to be given, each in strict order, a ritual morsel of bread. He had left school one year early, at thirteen, as his walk to school and back was fourteen miles, and was first hired for five shillings a week (25p) for looking after a pony. He was amazed when that sum doubled for looking after and 'baiting' (feeding) four cart-horses. Hiring happened at the Knighton May Fair, where the plant you wore in your hat signified your preferred task, and where a shilling or two would be pressed into your hand as 'earnest money'. There were fights, not all with gypsies, and once a murder.

It took time to guess from which decade of his long life a reminiscence came. He always praised the folk 'up-country' near Abbeycwmhir, where he had lived, whose kindness and open-handedness were unequalled. Visits, usually without notice, were always rewarded by gifts like home-made jam as a token of hospitality (a custom continued by one ninety-year-old today: it induced embarrassment until I learnt always to arrive with a home-made bottle myself).

The arrival of a telephone in his house in 1980 baffled him comically: when there was a 'wrong number' he detained the caller and, if he was from the area, was generally able, after up to half an hour, to work out their kinship and exchange news. He was a contented, stately, courteous man, unpuzzled by great thoughts, too young to have fought in the Great War, too old for the second. In 1953, he helped the local landlord plant a lime-tree in the churchyard for a coronation, he couldn't recall whose, but was bothered that such landlords had largely departed: "Where be the big folk to plant for the future now?"

He liked wild-life. Hares still box in March on the hills until, as he put it with unconscious poetry, speaking a dialect Shakespeare would have followed, "they ups and goes to another country"(country = county). And he liked the extraordinary aerobatic winter freedom of the raven, tumbling with one wing in-folded in parachute-style mating display, while in other seasons the steady, rhythmic thrash of its wing-beat is uncannily audible even when it flies high at a thousand feet. On the stream are curtseying dipper who fly off low down the brook like phantoms; and on the hills buzzard, goshawk, hen harrier, and now red kite, merlin and peregrine.

I last saw him travelling happily past in a trailer with his son, their legs stretched out like two Guy Fawkes, the tractor driven by his grandson, all three waving and smiling gap-toothily. He thrived on his daily, exclusive diet of bacon and eggs until, nearing ninety, his parts, as his family put it, like those of a motor-car, 'wore out', and he died.

During icy weather his grandson took bread, milk and

newspapers on his tractor to the upland cottages, and wrote comic doggerel about the neighbours he found there. Poetry and mutual aid were both Welsh.

★

The historian Gwyn A. Williams identifies and opposes two Wales's, nearly as different as "the Serbs are from the Croats", essentially a single people set tragically at odds by history and geography. One is fortress Wales, *Pura Wallia*, the Wild Wales to be found still in the West and (especially) the North, conquered with difficulty by Edward I, proudly Welsh by language and custom. The other is the March, 'planted' by the Normans with folk from many countries – Gascon, Flemish, by no means only English – and always assumed to be more anglicised.

This is the classic and simple view, but it needs modifying. In fact Edward I's conquest of Wales in 1284 put *only* the far North and West – known as the Principality – under the direct rule of the crown. The March or Marches, the long North-South border, stayed fully independent for a further three hundred years. So for five hundred long years in all it was outside the king's rule, with a make-up unique in Europe.

The March consisted of a group of forty or so fiefdoms administered as huge private mini-states or feudal demesnes by individual Marcher Lords, rebellious military adventurers who could establish local parliaments and courts, create forests, confiscate estates at will, maintain private gaols and gallows. Marcher Lords could even build castles, elsewhere a jealously guarded royal privilege, and mint their own coins. Indeed, they could wage private wars, against the Welsh and also against one another. They were miniature kings, administering laws, establishing market-towns, maintaining chanceries. Only when there was no heir did royal writ obtain, for the lordship then reverted to the Crown. Even on the Anglo-Scottish border, a line agreed by 1157, there were no equivalent Marcher lordships. The Welsh Marchers believed (falsely) their liberties derived from William the Conqueror's royal grant.

'Fortress Wales' in the far North has long posed as the truest Wales, where ancient custom and language prevail. Yet these mongrel borders are even stranger: exactly how strange I did not understand until starting to write this book. This land lying between England and Wales was governed by neither. Its separate status was endorsed in the Magna Carta, which stated that disputes might be settled in any of three ways according to location: by the laws of Wales, by those of England, and lastly according to the law of the March. Lawyers found the legal claims of Marcher barons to independence from the King's over-lordship "breath-taking", guarding as they did the right to treasure trove, wreck, mines and royal fish and total exemption from royal taxation. No-one else in the kingdom enjoyed the same exemptions. The status of the March, says one historian, was "in every possible way anomalous – archaic in its militarism and feudal ethos".

In the March the king of England had few powers. When in 1230 Richard Marshall Earl of Pembroke led a rebellion against the crown, Henry III swore he would have no peace with that earl until he came before him with a rope about his neck begging forgiveness; twenty years later the Lord Clifford, stung by receiving a peremptory letter from Henry III, forced the messenger to eat both the letter and the royal seal.

Small wonder that the March of Wales had one of the greatest castle densities in all Europe, for it also contained a uniquely unstable balkanisation of power. A law-case from Clun (where only Welsh was spoken) involving Knighton men was deferred until it was learnt how Clun men were treated in Knighton courts – a distance of six miles! Men from the next neighbourhood were known as *extranei* or aliens and treated thus. A criminal's paradise, a land of multiple bolt-holes and loop-holes, you could steal cattle in one lordship and fly to safety in another. Even those outlawed within the March could escape to a neighbouring lordship, or to England, or simply hide by day. So-called Days of the March or love days were established when criminals and stolen cattle alike could be exchanged between different Marcher lordships. Such Days were sanctioned even by Edward I and suspension of them was next to a declaration of war.

Here was the Wild West, where lordship was won and maintained by war. No single public authority existed to impose any unity whatsoever. And this five-hundred-year history of anarchic local autonomy influences the area even today, in both its marked individualism and its concern for locality and kinship.

The *OED* defines March as "Boundary, frontiers, (often pl., esp. of borderland between England & Scotland or Wales); tract of (*often debatable*) land between two countries". Debatable boundaries of all kinds are part of my argument. I could not easily imagine living in the North; I loved the hybrid East.

★

It is no accident that Bruce Chatwin, drawn elsewhere to Patagonia, Dahomey, the Australian dream-time and the Franconia/Bohemian border, set his first novel in Radnorshire. The Welsh March was exotic too, because so little mapped. Compare it to the Scottish Border, hymned by Sir Walter Scott, who collected one quarter of its ballads, its history and geography feeding the whole European Romantic Revival. The much longer Welsh Marches constitute, by contrast, and despite an equally weighty cultural history, a relatively unknown, still hidden border-line.

It is hard to imagine a Welsh equivalent to Donizetti's *Lucia di Lammermoor*: the March lacks the famous profiling the Scottish borders have long enjoyed, and Radnorshire is indeed the least populated of all counties south of the Highlands. In 1970 the county population only just topped 18,000 – scarcely more than in 1640 – and its then capital town, Presteigne, had a mere 1,200 citizens. There were only two roundabouts and no traffic lights in the county, whose weekly *Mid-Wales Journal* has a circulation of 5,000; few towns, and only five villages more substantial than the 'scattered hamlets' so typical of Wales:

hamlets which have no nucleus apart from church or chapel plus a few widely separated farms. In one remote hamlet the schoolmaster also cut hair: the nearest professional barber was too far off for anyone to bother with the journey. An ambulance hereabouts is often a red helicopter rather than a van.

Radnorshire has been called Britain's best-kept secret. Jonathan Williams, who spent more than a decade writing his great pioneering history of the county, never received enough subscriptions from the gentry and clergy to enable him to publish during his lifetime. He died bitter and disappointed in 1829, and his history was first printed in its entirety only in 1905. Mona Morgan, born near Gladestry in 1916, recorded that there were folk in neighbouring Herefordshire who had never even heard of Radnorshire, whose domestic routines and farming methods lagged so many decades behind those of Southern England. Yet the Welsh Marches, of which Radnorshire is a central part, have arguably as much interest as the Scottish Borders. The writers Geraint Goodwin and Margiad Evans spent periods in England but were pulled back to the March by an old sense of belonging. The Shropshire March alone inspired A.E. Housman to place here his land of *hiraeth* and lost content, P.G. Wodehouse to create his Lord Emsworth in love with an enormous black sow, and Mary Webb her doom-ridden idylls: each a different never-never-land.

Radnorshire is small and mountainous – in only 470 square miles there are one hundred hills over 1,500 feet; it is also so under-populated, and apparently anglicised, that it is often either forgotten or sidelined. Yet it has played a noble part in the history of Wales. A hand-written annotation on the margin of a manuscript in the Bodleian Library, Oxford, tells a relevant and strange tale. These notes are by the poet Lewys [Llywelyn] Glyn Cothi (*fl.* 1447-1489). What Lewys read with his patron he identifies as 'Gwion' – aka Taliesin. This *Book of Taliesin* is one of the famous 'Four Ancient Books of Wales'.

And the book on whose margins Lewys has written his comments is another of Wales's 'Ancient Books': *The Red Book*

of Hergest – source of the *Mabinogion*. These two cycles –
Taliesin and *Mabinogion* – were thus both found locally and are
major sources for the Arthurian legends we inherit today. A
distinguished scholar of medieval Welsh once day-dreamed to
me that if a new, fifth, Ancient Book of Wales were one day ever
to come to light, it would come as no surprise if this were to
happen in Radnorshire, rather than anywhere else: so numinous
because centrally important to past history did the county
seem, and so little-explored today.

A Herefordshire friend says he could in the 1940s at once
distinguish a farmer out of Radnorshire from one who had
travelled from Monmouthshire or elsewhere, by his poetical
combination of unworldliness and quick wits, qualities bred by
the isolated lives they led. It may be that a certain reclusiveness
links natives and incomers hereabouts. At any rate Kilvert in
1870 noticed and appreciated the *silence* of Radnorshire: he
could walk for a day and meet no one. You still can today.

Until you learn how to listen for it, the past itself is silent
here. And this is, unsurprisingly, a Welsh past. In Radnorshire –
most anglicised of all Welsh counties apart from South
Pembrokeshire – when neighbours learn Welsh in evening class,
they complain of finding few to converse in it with. This never
deterred Ffransis Payne (1900-92), born in Kington in
England, only half Welsh, who taught himself Welsh and wrote a
cultural history of Radnorshire in Welsh in two volumes: he
lived on the south side of the Radnor Forest, in Llandegley. The
Welsh past he elegised is still visible. Within our church chest
around 1800 an Elizabethan Bible in the Welsh language was
found, and the Welsh names of fields and farmhouses recall a
lost past that the silence has even now not entirely obscured,
though the traces are hard to decrypt: 'Redborough' near
Newchurch comes from *Ar hyd y fro*, (across country)[7].

So far from being 'marginal', remote, little-known
Radnorshire is Wales's true forgotten centre: where Henry III
encamped at Painscastle for the summer of 1231 with his whole
apparatus of government, issuing 180 decrees; where the

headless trunk of Prince Llywellyn II (the Last Prince) was secretly buried by Cistercian monks at Abbeycwmhir in 1282 – while his head was paraded in London; where Owain Glyndŵr won the last battle for Wales at Pilleth; where the family of Elizabeth I's court magician John Dee came from; where Vavasor Powell in Knucklas and elsewhere helped move Wales from the Anglican to the Puritan cause[8]; and where early Quakers, those un-peaceful persons[9], placed the very first Meeting House in Wales – the Pales – in 1717.

The arrangement of this book is shamelessly personal. Firstly the area explored corresponds – very roughly – with that signified in Welsh by *Fferegs* – an old name covering Greater Radnorshire and including adjoining areas such as southern Montgomeryshire, west Herefordshire and so on. Simplicity, solitude and retreat have marked human lives hereabouts for centuries, said to be essential food for the inward life. Secondly 'snapshots' of this part of the Marches are explored, showing how artists and contemplatives have sought very different versions here of a world-beyond-time, over successive periods of change and upheaval.

From Giraldus Cambrensis taking the Cross at New Radnor for the Third Crusade, to Alfred Watkins discovering ley-lines in the Radnor Forest, many pilgrims have visited Greater Radnorshire with strange agenda. Any selection has to be subjective, if only because of the abundance of choice. Most visitors came, like me, from East of Offa's Dyke. Which is why this essay adopts – of necessity – the same angle of vision.

'Psycho-geography'

The *Sunday Times* on 21 April 2002 launched the term 'Psycho-geography' for what it claimed was a new-ish genre. "Space," the reviewer hyped, is the "new paradigm". Citing two writers, W.G. Sebald, who features in this chapter, and Ian Sinclair, the reviewer described a new literary genre, heir to the traditional travel book, a form given to drifting off into essay and memoir, now re-discovering the exotic in the backyard instead of in Tuscany or Tibet. Genuinely innovative because so accommodating, this new form, claimed the *ST*, could hold together "recondite art criticism, social history, gossip and farce".

In fact, multiple and sometimes apparently discursive narratives about the sense of place, each finding its own unique unity and coherence, have long flourished: Peter Levi's *Flutes of Autumn*, Sebald's spiritually desolate and politically radical *Rings of Saturn*, Blythe's *Akenfield*, Adam Nicholson's *Sea-Room*, Claudio Magris's *Danube*, Neal Ascherson's *Black Sea*, David Thomson's *Woodbrook*.

A number of these – Levi, Sebald, Thomson – make room within the narrative for their author's subjective response to and feeling for place; and maybe this inclusion of the subjective is innovative. I want to tell stories of the March and some of their writers, framed within an over-arching narrative that is personal, discursive and sometimes autobiographical. What has the past, indeed, to teach the present? I notice that my old college teachers, each a parent-surrogate, keep appearing in this essay, and not accidentally. How do we learn from the past, if at all? And what can *a place* in and of itself teach us, if anything?

Around 1980 my teacher and friend Lorna Sage was writing *Bad Blood*, which is of course set in distinctly Marches country – Hanmer in "Flintshire detached", where her father was vicar, and R.S. Thomas (though she never learnt this) was his curate. She visited us in Radnorshire, wanting only to chain-smoke, drink and talk, all three prodigiously. She detested the country-side, English and Welsh, with quite impartial venom. A good Marxist and an adoptive child-of-the-city, she thought that idylls exist, but that it is generally somebody else, poorer and more wretched than you, who secretly pays for your holiday. The only unpoisoned idyll for her was Marxist Cuba, where she and her second husband liked to spend Christmas. The very idea of living-in-the-country seemed to her faintly ridiculous: violence was as endemic to country life as tedium, feuding, TB, incest and what Karl Marx termed "rural idiocy". Lorna's own place of retreat was accordingly the *piano nobile* of a Renaissance flat in Fiesole, outside Forence. She and I both, meanwhile, loved London.

The whole point of Lorna Sage's *Bad Blood* is that she saw the Marches, not as I did – roughly as H.D. Thoreau saw Walden – as some sort of guide to living the classical ideal of a good life[1] – but as a hell-hole worth doing anything at all to get out of, a place of stagnant inequality, provincial bigotry and hypocrisy. So she shows no loyalty to the kindred who, after all, helped make her all that she became. I took, from an over-privi-leged standpoint, a different view. Hers was an escape *from* the

Marches, as a harsh workplace; mine an escape *to* them, as a soft playground. Between those for whom the countryside is a workplace, and those for whom it is a playground, there is a gulf fixed.

Pastoral straddles this borderline. It is, in part, literary fantasy written about the former, for the selfish pleasure of the latter: pastoral is often a townsman's view of the country. And this essay will often be concerned with the experience of the easy-livers, summerfolk, incomers and outsiders: the soft seekers after pastoral, rather than those hard-workers about whom pastoral gets written.

Lorna Sage taught me to love William Empson's *Some Versions of Pastoral* with its witty celebration of the different ways we employ pastoral and I liked Empson's passing, easy acknowledgement of the pain of life, that no 'pastoral' can escape: "the feeling that life is essentially inadequate to the human spirit, and yet a good life must avoid saying so" – and also "the waste even in a fortunate life, the isolation even in a life rich in intimacy, cannot but be felt deeply, and is the central feeling of tragedy". No golden age, no golden elsewhere, says Empson. But dreams, including literary dreams, matter, and have their own results.

Lorna's own dream of escape is bodied forth in *Bad Blood*, which has sold half a million copies. She compared the task of composition to a conjuror pulling out silken handkerchiefs from his sleeve: all you needed, she maintained, was to get a grip on and have trust in *a first memory*, and then you would find that that first memory unexpectedly had a second one attached to its tail, a process which slowly elicited an infinite and brightly-coloured series: this still seems a good way to proceed. If indeed, as she believed, someone else, poorer and more wretched than us, had paid in the past for our happiness today, I wanted to find out who they were, and how they lived. One part of my quest in this essay.

★

My old teacher Angus Wilson explored the pains of existence. He had created as his own retreat a notable cottage garden within an ancient wild Suffolk coppiced wood to write in, but visited us in Radnorshire in 1976, advising us on choosing climbing roses – and told us Dickens intended Little Nell in *The Old Curiosity Shop* to die, pursued by the evil dwarf Quilp, five miles away, in Presteigne, something I have never checked. In his novel *The Old Men at the Zoo* (1961), he imagined the Anglo-Welsh March – echoing Gerald of Wales – converted into an enormous wild game reserve.

Angus wrote, famously, of modern man being split between the twin hells of loneliness on the one hand, and 'other people' on the other. Listening from mid-Wales during different winters to the news of the imposition in the snowy December 1981 of martial law in Poland (where I went to live for two years, from 1990 to 1992 and in *Cold War: Common Pursuit* co-edited essays about); of the Christmas car-bombing of Harrods (17 December 1983); then of 9/11, I often thought of Wilson's view of the matter and decided that I loved him but could not agree: why not the twin *joys* of being sociable and of being-on-one's-own?

And Wilson's pessimism is far outdone by that of his colleague W.G. Sebald, praised by the *Sunday Times* for uncovering in *The Rings of Saturn* connexions between East Anglian landscape and grief. Few other recent writers have been so attuned to the sorrowful menace of modern existence, or more adventurously registered the traces within a landscape of the effects of class-war, nationalistic conflict, genocide, exploitation and loss. Wherever he looked Sebald found an opening to hell. Nobody writes as bravely as does Sebald about the occasional terror of modern life, and its pervasive sense of anxiety. His vision is close to that of classical tragedy. I admire and yet disagree with him.

Unsurprising that *Private Eye* took to nick-naming him 'Eeyore', with whom he shares Teutonic gloom and the satisfying certainty that things will turn out as badly as we fear, and generally worse. Grief is one essential part of the picture, one wants to tell him. A famous story from Buddhist scripture: grieving the loss of her only child, a bitterly weeping mother approaches the Buddha for consolation, and is told that he will help her only after she has collected a herb from the garden of any one house in the village that has never known a death. Of course she fails, and of course she learns, as the Buddha had intended, that loss is universal.

Sebald knows this too and his motto might be 'After such knowledge, what forgiveness', where knowledge of loss means the special case of the Holocaust, which, born as he was in a quiet corner of the Catholic Allgäu in Bavaria in 1944, he did not directly experience. Me neither. Reading Victor Klemperer's wonderful, terrifying diary of Dresden under the Nazis, *To the Bitter End*, a text Sebald admired and cited, I was startled recently to learn that Klemperer knew and was surprised to like a Professor Conradi who, on Easter Sunday 1943, aged 66, was arrested and then gassed for buying radishes, a food-stuff which, in order to safe-guard this rare provision for Aryans, Jews had that year been forbidden by a new law to purchase.

My great-grandfather Henry Conradi was born in Dresden in 1838, a Jewish civil engineer who married and lived in Paris, whence he was kicked out in 1870 when the Prussians invaded, moving in a single day, it was said, to Golden Square in London. Many of his family stayed put in Dresden and were still there when the Second World War started, a time when other cousins found themselves in the occupied cities of Rotterdam and Thessaloniki. I knew that the letters 'KZ' appearing against Dresden names on one family tree, always together with a Cross, signified death in a *Konzentrations Anlage* or Concentration Camp. And also that most of the fifty Dresden Jews who survived the fire-bombing in February 1945 made it to the end of the war, like, most notably, Klemperer himself. The papers identifying you as Aryan or non-Aryan, after that destruction, could not be expected to be carried or possessed by anyone with a Dresden accent.

As Sebald depicts them, expatriates are generally tragic victims of history: his wonderful *The Emigrants* traces the alienation, madness and despair of an unrelated group of German-born survivors, mainly Jewish, whom history has beached, abroad. In summer 1940, by contrast, another remote and gallant cousin, immediately before the Germans invaded Holland and, in three short May days, bombed ancient gabled Rotterdam to pieces, sailed his yacht across the North Sea from the Hook. He had been deputed to parley, without success as it turned out, with the invading Germans from, as he judged it, the neutrality of a railway carriage that had originated in Uruguay and therefore seemed to him a kind of no-man's-land. He was now, as he sailed across the North Sea wearing his tennis whites, and alighting eventually in Frinton in Essex exactly as he had intended, readying himself to challenge his Anglo-Dutch cousins living there, who included my Great-Aunt Katie, to a game.

This insouciant family folklore raises many questions: how this youngish man braved the vigilant German and then the British port authorities; how many tennis courts were left when we were all 'digging for victory'; how the family happened to be at home when, to pre-empt invasion, their coastal houses were being requisitioned for Army use. It is a story told among a group who had every reason for wanting to distance themselves as much as possible from the scarcely imaginable sufferings of the *Ost-Juden*. As my assimilated Anglo-Jewish mother put it, fresh from having being 'finished' in Lausanne in 1936, "we opened our homes to these refugees; not our hearts".

Yet the moral of the story of the Dutch refugee remains symbolically true: wealth did help save a few surviving emigrants from alienation. Luck and a happy temperament helped others. Some found in these shores not purgatory but retreat. Some found safety, a generous welcome, or joy in sociability and solitude. And some writers find their needs met. An account of life anywhere that excludes happiness seems incomplete. After the war this cousin, returned to Holland, was Dutch

Minister of Defence at The Hague.

Though we had gentrified cousins, including one who hunted in the 1930s with a smart pack, I found their squirearchical pose unconvincing. As the first of Howard Jacobson's comically Jewish anti-heroes put the matter succinctly, in panic at the prospect of a weekend in the country: "But Jews don't have Wellington boots". The alternative pose of staying an outsider – for good – seems entirely satisfying. Outsidership seemed to me a good locality from which to start trying to understand a place in Wales where people really have belonged for millennia, where families are extended and some larger farmhouses had within them, in 1970, three generations living together, often in conditions of strain, and where ties of kinship can easily be traced across the entire county and into surrounding counties too. One way you can tell the gardens of the Radnorshire-born from those of incomers is that the former cut their hedges low, sacrificing privacy for neighbourliness; for the incomer priorities are reversed, and the hedges accordingly high.

I often wonder how claustrophobic such clannish community life, with its strong senses of conformity and genealogy, in which the respect of your neighbours meant everything, must sometimes have felt. I recall how my mother in 1946 fled Hampstead, where some hundred cousins supported one another and minded each other's business, how it was always a leading question at any family event "whether or not to invite the great-aunts". If you asked one, you had, to avoid offence, to invite all nine, none of them especially touchy, yet who might feel justly offended if left out. In both of these different communities marriage within the kinship group was traditional, and marrying 'out' looked on askance.

Being Jewish recalls being Welsh: you suffer a sense of difference that is a badge of pride or shame, struggle with the desire to get on or get out, blessed and cursed by strong ties of family on whom you stay dependent beyond childhood. Family sanction or censure counts for much. And knowledge of cousinship and pedigree, even to the ninth degree, matters to both, funerals being very well-attended. Both have important diasporas in London. I once discovered three second and third cousins named like me, to honour the same uncle shot down and killed during his final flight as trainee-navigator off the Lincolnshire coast in November 1941, weeks short of his twentieth birthday. His parents did not recover: my grandma wore his 'wings', made up as a marcasite brooch, for her remaining days of good works, bridge and whisky.

Even the surface-area of Israel, pre-1967, was the same as Wales. And the Old Testament chronicles a pastoral economy together with a patriarchal family life which idealised filial piety: all familiar to the mid-Welsh. So at least observed Alwyn D. Rees, to whose work we now move.

★

Kingsley Amis in *Lucky Jim* exploded the fiction that there had ever been a Merrie England. But was there ever a Merrie Wales? Did Wales ever live in the land of summer, experiencing real community, in what Shakespeare called "the time of good neighbours"? The classic study of a mid-Welsh hamlet by Alwyn D. Rees, *Life in a Welsh Countryside*, published in 1950, is back in print. This wonderful, pioneering book explores Llanfihangel-yng-Ngwynfa, in Montgomeryshire, or northern Powys, around 1942. Here was a culture retaining many ancient characteristics. Here you spoke always in Welsh to your cattle (named Penwen, Frochwen, Cochen), but in English to your horses (Captain, Prince or Duke): since Anglo-Normans taught the Welsh horse-management, as Gerald of Wales pointed out, these animals belonged to a foreign tradition of chivalry.

Recreation and entertainment were home-produced. At an annual 'Fools' Fair' (*Ffair Ffyliaid*, held on the first Tuesday in May), with no economic importance – which is to say no hiring – there appeared, even during the war and the blackout year of 1940, between six and eight hundred people. An annual festival of carols was held on the second Sunday in January, nowadays imitated elsewhere in Wales, in which each family jealously guarded its own traditional songs. Some of these carols were pre-Reformation.

The countryman from the Marches, Rees notes, had continued to live in a world of his own, the standards of which differed from those of modern industrial society. Bonds of kinship, connection with chapel or church, the individual's status among neighbours, all tied him to the locality and made life elsewhere seem incomplete: a cohesion of kindred, family and neighbours gave the individual a sense of belonging. Much was transacted without thought of payment. To appear concerned about profit was 'not done': religious observance, writing for the local eisteddfod, giving time to neighbourliness, mattered too. If there was a high evaluation of money there was also a low evaluation of the luxuries and ephemeral pleasures it might buy.

The average age at marriage was over thirty, with the result that some children stayed psychologically and economically dependent on their parents until middle-life. Sexual intimacy before marriage and illegitimacy were both common: troth-plight – found in Shakespeare and Hardy – was still common here[2]. In this the Border lands may be more traditional, hazards Rees, than the *notionally* more Welsh areas to the north where Methodism, with its strict disciplinary action against sexual transgressions, bit more deeply.

The class configuration of upland Wales differed markedly from that of lowland England with its squires-landlords, capitalist farmers and landless labourers. The English had a manorial and feudal system; the tribal Welsh were – or at least saw themselves as – freemen, a vision helped on by the defection of squires to England and to Englishness, and the sale of many of their estates. It was helped, too, by the fact that the Welsh language, which has distinct regional varieties, possesses no class dialects. You cannot speak Welsh 'in an upper-class accent'.

This vision of the Welsh as less class-bound than their English neighbours received endorsement from a Royal Commissioner in 1867 who noted with interest that the line of demarcation between farmer and labourer did not exist in Wales

as it did in England. "The farm servant on a Welsh farm lives
and eats with his master and mistress, and is treated in every
respect on a footing of equality"[3]: Welsh farm servants were
then well paid and often in time able to set up themselves as
independent farmers. The line between these 'English' and
'Welsh' forms of service ran along the border itself from the
Begwns and Clyro hills across the Radnor Forest and out to
Bailey Hill. Even now you can hear the phrase 'a gentleman's
fool' used of an old boy gently mocked for forelock-tugging.
(Such egalitarian sentiment did not prevent pride in lineage:
Mrs Cadwallader in George Eliot's *Middlemarch* and Mrs
Woodcourt in Dickens's *Bleak House* are both pedigree-
obsessed Welsh curiosities, the latter interestingly omitted from
Andrew Davies's recent television adaptation.)

Viewed from the outside, Llanfihangel-yng-Ngwynfa
appeared a place caught in a time-warp, a quaint and archaic
survival from a pastoral and tribal past. Judged on its own
terms, it was by contrast a society in full decline. For twenty
years there had been a measurable falling off of religious observance. In a culture traditionally hostile to gambling,
card-playing, dancing and drinking – nearing a pub you could
distinguish a chapel- from a church-goer by the former's wary
glance-over-his-shoulder before entering – whist-drives were
growing in popularity. Schooling meant that children were
taught to value towns as sources of learning and culture.
Farmers' wives preferred to shop in Oswestry in England than
locally in Llanfyllin. There was less time now than hitherto for
entertaining and visiting. Moreover, changes in farming –
mechanisation and pastoralism – meant that fewer 'hands' were
now needed for farm-work. Many left for mining, quarrying,
dock and transport work, for opportunities in the USA,
England, or the Dominions. Alwyn D. Rees's testing of the idea
of a close community of freemen lends his *Life in a Welsh
Countryside* much of its charm and interest.

There are wider and more mythical resonances at work in
Rees's study, too. One important early school of Welsh studies,

based in Aberystwyth where Alwyn D. Rees studied, and later taught in the Extramural Department, saw the heart, soul and centre of Wales as belonging in the great upland plateau on whose edge Llanfihangel yng Ngwynfa stands. Here, according to this narrative, are the true bearers of the identity and values of the Welsh past. This vision casually dismissed or diminished the experience of more than half of the population of Wales: the South, after all, acted both as laboratory and as coal-and-steel fired power-house of the biggest and earliest industrial revolution on the planet. But it is a narrative that rightly includes Radnorshire, albeit most anglicised of all Welsh counties.

The writer Meic Stephens, partly of Radnorshire descent, in his enchanting and discursive journal with memoirs *A Semester in Zion*, tells a story illustrating this county's remoteness. There was to be a new vicar of Pantydwr and St Harmon, near Rhaeadr. A public meeting was held to determine in which tiny village the vicarage should be sited, neither with more than a few hundred inhabitants. After much debate it was decided the vicar should live in St Harmon, the lower of the two villages. An old man who had voted in favour of his native Pantydwr rose to his feet to say "Very well, so be it. But mark my words: give a man a taste of town life and he'll never be up in the hills again": a typically Radnorshire roundabout way of conveying a point. The story jokes about the strong local loyalties of the hill people as about upland simplicities. An undertow of course recalls depopulation, as hill-farmers' children steadily left for the big cities of South Wales and England[4].

R.S. Thomas, in his war-time essay 'The Depopulation of the Welsh Hill Country', echoes and adds to this potent mythologisation. On the hills he imagines he hears the curlew mourning the people who have passed away, and dreams of the *Calan Mai* and the summer-cottages or *hafotai*, the days when the Welsh went to the high pastures to live for the summer. Thomas translated an anonymous and beautiful Welsh folk stanza, "At the bright hem of God/ In the heather, in the heather"[5]. He comments: "Time stands still in these areas, and it is easy to forget the contemporary world. After a day in them, I return to my house in the valley like a stranger". On one such day Thomas records meeting a hill-poet who has written of the searchlights during a German air-raid on Liverpool[6], but who remains inwardly at peace, belonging only to himself and to the hills. This hill-poet can smell the sea today, and remarks contentedly that he often thinks there is more interest in the hills than anywhere else.

This poet-figure belongs intimately within the conventional idealisation of the uplands where, as the poet Harri Webb put it, you are as far away as you will ever get from the world's madness. A war-time essay put the matter thus: "These are the only Welsh; they will always exist, if left alone. They are of magic"[7]. Thomas imagines shepherds and their familes in the past "swapping *englynion* over the peat cutting". The *englyn*, oldest recorded of Welsh poetical forms, is highly intricate, dating from the ninth century, but this image of the poet-shepherd persists into recent literature. Rees recounts farmers proficient in the form in 1940. Robert Graves once met a Welsh poet with a hayrake, while Elizabeth Clarke in *The Valley* in 1968 attributed the silence of one shepherd thirty years earlier to his inwardly composing his *englynion* "according to the complicated rules".

This is, perhaps, close to the heart of one kind of myth of Welshness: English poets use the idea of the shepherd as a romantic artifice to idealise one another (Milton's *Lycidas*, Shelley's lament for Keats, *Adonais*). Some Welsh shepherds – by contrast – combined the two trades in one. Here was a vision of the poet not as an alienated, marginal figure, but at the community's centre, giving voice to its values, the creator of cultural coherence and of communality. It stunned George Borrow in *Wild Wales* (1862) that in Wales it was possible to be working-class and cultured at the same time.

*

The impassability of central Wales is important. This geography keeps Wales internally divided, as well as cut off from the outside world. The mountainous physical structure of the country abounds in internal and external barriers. The Romans set up the only roads, skirting this central heartland, or driving through without pause or bifurcation: the population was so sparse that diversion wasn't worthwhile. The austere North remained thus cut off from – and mutually suspicious of – the garrulous South; and equally the secretive March from the coast. As recently as the last world war the old road from Rhaeadr to Aberystwyth was problematic. A friend recalls her mother getting out of their 1933 vintage Austin 12 saloon that resembled a packing-case, its radiator boiling vigorously, and having to walk up the hair-pin bends that had defeated her car-engine: above the top dam, the old road to Aberystwyth went through Cwmystwyth and the old lead mines and past Hafod. Such a heartland acts as a barrier rather than as a focus for regions surrounding it[8]. And living close to subsistence, the communities of mid-Wales were "tenacious of their ancient ways and suspicious of innovation".

Such conditions made for strong local ties to the *gwlad* or region which survive into our day. They were unpropitious for creating a unified kingdom, a default with serious consequences. The heartland is stubbornly conservative, dreaming vitally of the past.

★

The broadcaster and commentator on Welsh affairs Denis Balsom proposed a 'Three Wales Model', dividing the country into 'British Wales' (Vale of Glamorgan, Cardiff, Gwent, Powys and all the way up to the north-east coast, as well as south Pembrokeshire); 'Welsh Wales' (the industrial areas from Carmarthen to Pontypool); and *Y Fro Gymraeg* (Ceredigion, Meirionnydd, Gwynedd and Anglesey). This division seems to be generally accepted now, especially when it comes to voting patterns[9]. Yet the extension of the huge central wilderness nearly from the coast to (in places) the English border, over-riding the division of languages, qualifies this perspective.

Another curious record of life over the past two centuries in exactly this great wilderness, dividing the dour North Welsh from their talkative Southern cousins, comes in a book by Erwyd Howells, a Cardiganshire sheep-farmer, published at his own expense in 2005. It has sold well. At the age of seven he knew only one English word ('Yes') and he still finds the Saxon-descended dialect older Radnorshire farmers use as exotic as the latter find Welsh. A neighbour warned him early, "You'll have a job to understand these Radnorshire people, who'll ask after a gathering, 'how bist ye boy, have you any ship for we?' " (How are you boy, have you any sheep for us?).

Howells urges no claims to literary merit, and you don't read a vernacular record for polish. There used, he tells us, to be two kinds of pudding made from pig's blood. The first was called blood pudding. The second was also called blood pudding. But this second pudding was sweet, with spices added. What is lacking in gloss is more than made up for in colour and detail.

Howells is a passionate chronicler of mid-Welsh life, anxious that it be recorded and known about in the inhospitable future that threatens it. There are chapters on those features of upland life that mattered most – on snow-storms, pigs and postmen, on sheep-dogs (both Welsh and the cannier, more recently intro-duced Border Scots), on the gathering, ear-marking and shearing of sheep, and on the huge and essential endeavour of feeding the shearers.

A chapter on quarrels indicates a moral willingness to give a rounded picture, to present rough with smooth, dark as well as light. He tells of shepherds who mutilated the teats of straying stock so that such ewes could never suckle wandering progeny: other persistent strays, or their lambs, were killed or drowned. Boundary disputes were common. There were paupers who until the nineteenth century still built overnight clod-walled dwellings on common land: if you had smoke coming through the chimney by the morning, the law gave you the right to remain. The livestock of such new settlers was sometimes destroyed by established farmers. He describes, too, the killing by otherwise squeamish shepherds of a rogue sheep-dog that kept eating precious human supplies, by tying to its tail and lighting a stick of explosive.

There were other predators worse than rogue dogs. Foxes decapitated lambs, taking their blood, and were identifable from their habit of killing on alternate nights. Human urine was poured over lambs to safeguard them. Badgers rarely took lambs but Howells is alarmed that today both they and the foxes increasingly take the eggs and chicks of ground-nesting birds.

He also tells of a shrewish wife who out of jealous spite poisoned her hag-ridden husband's sheep-dog, and who, the further to torment him, would periodically threaten to hang herself, until she one day happened to overhear a neighbour friendly to the husband offering to assist her in this enterprise. The prevalence of fleas is hinted at; the deaths of three children playing with a World War Two mortar described. A two-year old burns to death when her clothes catch fire.

One disturbing story tells of a man who killed himself 'due to being mocked'. No moral is drawn therefrom. But here was a world in which peer-approval and support were essential, and hence also in which peer-pressure, doubtless mediated also through the chapel, played a crucial, if under-stated role. "Keeping an eye on the neighbours is the most important leisure-pursuit", remarks one Carmarthenshire-bred writer, who argues that the mothers of west Wales out-did the KGB in intelligence-gathering[10]. A culture intimately shared by so many could not help but be conservative, slow to change, if not with an actively backward-looking regard. A culture with strong conventions and thus a limited regard for difference, tenacious of ancient practice, suspicious of novelty.

You can learn from Howells how to castrate a lamb using your teeth, and be warned against excessive intake of beer beforehand, for your own sake as well as that of the lamb; as well as how to wield a knife and green ointment for the same purpose. Shearing parties nine months earlier in July were accompanied not only by the vigorous exchange of jokes, some of them practical – like pretending that mustard, hitherto unknown to one shepherd, was a pudding – but by sexual favours too. Thus the volume of human births in the hills each following April is explained.

Their humour, he explains, was unique to upland people, differing from sea-level joking, and necessary to hill-farmers to attenuate the harshness of life and lend a sense of proportion. This was a place of limited diet, of mutton, butter-milk, dripping; where the summoning of the doctor was a major and protracted drama – by the time he received the call, the patient might have died; where the role of postmen and postwomen was to bring comfort and local news as much as mail; where shopping was often by mail-order, and, if in person, happened once a month, and was a service you provided for your neighbours also; where reading happened by candle-light or pressure-lamp; if a windmill was installed, strong gales helped build up a usable current.

There is more to his story than this. A character in a 1910 E.M. Forster novel demanded to know what on earth the new and terrible "civilisation of luggage" is coming to, if a person might no longer die in the room that they were born in. Howells describes people who often live and die in one place, and who, moreover, know who they and their neighbours *are*. One shepherd knows the provenance of every farm from Aberystwyth to Brecon – over sixty miles – and can itemise their inhabitants and narrate their lives and histories in detail too. Howells admires and honours above all such powers of observation and of memory and exhibits them himself, and over a long period. It is at first disconcerting to find his tales roaming over more than two centuries, so that you are not always sure, until he tells you, which epoch he is recounting. Some superstitions lasted centuries: pregnant women were not allowed to salt a pig; nor was a sow-on-heat ever butchered since its meat was thought not to keep. The effect is that of the chronicling of a dream-time, just outside or before our own.

The preciousness of the individuals who make up this way

of life is his burden, and chapters narrating the simple and unremarkable lives of his neighbours are often eulogistic. "Rest in Peace… for you did a very good day's work", he salutes a tirelessly hospitable friend. He records a world in which no stranger passed without being invited in for tea and a bite to eat, where shopping could take hours, depending on whom you met en route: you had naturally to exchange news. There was time in the world, and neighbourliness.

The pedigree of people, as of animals, interests him: the talent to minimise losses among your stock runs, he believes, in families. So does generosity among the poor. And he has that special sense of timelessness that belongs to a poetic and religious sensibility. Peat-fires, which gave adequate heat, were kept going through the summer months, this being thought auspicious. Alwyn D. Rees noted that his community belonged to a 'hearth' rather than an 'oven' culture: you ate by the fire, as in earlier days, not at table.

Howells depicts the same world. A fire at Wenffrwd was said to have been alight for a hundred years. If you moved, this fire was carried in a bucket to consecrate, in effect, the new home. Indeed putting clocks forwards and backwards in spring and autumn was little honoured in the wilderness, so that hill-folk were often caught out by appearing one hour early or late for functions. They were often unaware of what day it was, let alone what hour, and he recounts a family who habitually arrived for chapel on Saturdays, a day early, and then waited out the extra time with no fuss.

Yet he knows that all is subject to time, too. Although he believes that Welsh sheep-dogs are mentioned in the Laws of Hywel Dda, c. tenth century, he also knows that the tasks they must then have been allotted had to do with rounding up cattle, the predominant stock before 1750. As for today, he deplores the bureaucratisation of farming, and the cult of post-traumatic stress alike, which betoken respectively the stupidity, and then the softness, of the present age.

Dogs provide continuity, and he has much to say of them.

He has studied dogs, believing they repay that effort: his first dog hung himself and he quickly learnt to tether a dog better. They were at their best from four years old, and bitches allowed to litter were often more eager to work. There were children who took their sheep-dogs to school, tying them up for the day before helping someone with their stock in the evenings. Dogs attended church so often that some churches had wooden dog-tongs to drag fighting curs outside. One dog could, when needed, fetch a peat-turf; another (his) could both climb a ladder and then open the hatch-door above. And – movingly – he tells of a dying shepherd who, asked by the pastor for his final wish, opted to "see a good dog". Only this, he knew, might now cheer him up.

PART TWO
THEN

1176: Summer

This chapter concerns the border between the English and the Welsh upon which Radnorshire sits. Before the Union in 1536-43 the nations that confronted one another here, often bloodily, differed profoundly one from another. No better witness to their differences survives than the writings of the Norman-Welsh Gerald of Wales, arch-deacon of Brecon, a child of both peoples, who therefore experienced their warfare within himself, as well as recording the historical struggle. He is among the earliest eyewitnesses to have berated the Welsh for being 'out-of-sync with modernity', a persistent theme in this book. This chapter also emphasises the anchorite tradition in Welsh Christianity: a way of life Gerald praised and thought especially honoured in Wales.

In the summer of 1176 Gerald paid an unwelcome visit to the lands of Elfael and Maelienydd – roughly today's Radnorshire. Successive local attempts were staged to prevent this visit from happening. First the local rural dean sent clerics as he was about to set out, urging him not to conduct the visit in person but to act, like his predecessors, through messengers. Gerald foreswore any such "sloth and cowardice". While the rural dean was offering his own good offices as messenger, the local clergy held up a crucifix to bar Gerald's passage. The next ruse was to claim that Gerald should, for his own safety, meet clerics within a great forest through which he was obliged to pass, but where – or so they claimed – his life might be in danger from triggering the revival of an ancient family feud. There were, they warned, chiefs lying in wait for him.

Gerald, unimpressed and playing down his followers' fears, proceeded on the forest journey, eventually arriving at Llanbadarn Fawr – two miles north-east of the present town of Llandrindod Wells – where he intended to hold an assembly. The progress of his entourage, which he had sent on ahead of him, was held up by showers of spears and arrows. Finding no other shelter, Gerald spent the night within the church itself, effectively besieged. He at once sent out messengers to the prince of Maelienydd, Cadwallon ap Madog, to whom he was related. Cadwallon provided food, and, threatening vengeance, came in person the following day to liberate the Archdeacon. One tradition maintains that Cadwallon founded the Abbey at Cwmhir[1].

This arch-deacon, Giraldus Cambrensis, or Gerald of Wales (1146-1223), one of the most colourful characters and best writers of his age, gives us an early and in-depth picture of the Welsh only a century after the Normans arrived. He was tall, handsome, with thick eyebrows, bustling, energetic, fearless, a magnificent horseman, self-admiring, highly critical of others and therefore quarrelsome, and a mean enemy. Every detail of contemporary life interested him – history, diet, gossip, mythology, ethnography, folklore, etymology, tales of supernatural agency, tales of every kind…. Language fascinated him, and he noted – accurately – that Wallia and Walensis came from the English adjective *wealh*, meaning simply foreign (and therefore analogous – though Giraldus doesn't say so – to the words *Wallachian, Walloon, Gaul, Gael, Galician,* and to the canton of *Vallis* in Switzerland: all lands of the 'other', the foreigner).

Since he was one quarter Welsh and three-quarters Norman, he embodied the Border within his own being: he was therefore well-placed to record how different were the peoples on each opposing side of it. He was related to the grandees of Wales and England alike and remarked bitterly that "Both peoples regard me as a stranger". His uncle was the Norman Bishop of St David's, but he was also first cousin once removed of the Lord Rhys, greatest of contemporary Welsh princes, respected by Henry II, who kept peace with him. Maelgwn ap Cadwallon, Prince of Maelienydd (north Radnorshire today), was another kinsman, son of that Cadwallon who rescued him in 1176 and who was three years later murdered – despite being on his way back from court and so carrying Henry II's royal safe-conduct – by Roger Mortimer, a local Marcher lord[2]; while Maelgwn's middle son – Owain Cascob – was murdered at nearby Ednol. As Gerald often boasts, he was "kinsman to all the princes and most of the great men" of Wales.

Henry I had carried away Gerald's grandmother, the famously beautiful Princess Nest, the so-called Helen of Wales, who had much charm and many lovers and in 1109 was duly abducted like the Greek Helen. Nest was grandmother to a number of knights who would accompany Strongbow on his invasion of Ireland – Gerald among them. He was thus Norman – indeed a Fitzgerald – as well as Welsh, his perceptions sharpened by inhabiting a divided society, and by inheriting that dividedness within himself. He accordingly despised the English, wrote disobligingly about the Normans and had dramatically mixed feelings about the Welsh, on whom he heaped praise and censure in equal measure.

The English he dismisses as mere slaves and subjects to the Normans, coldly reserved, ungiving in speech, servile in manner, and gluttonous alike for food, drink and profit. He has an aristocrat's contempt for these faithless minions who, even in

Wales, cleaned the sewers and were artisans, cobblers, skinners, ploughmen and shepherds – "most worthless of all peoples under heaven". It is indeed extraordinary that while it took the Normans more than two centuries to conquer obdurate and brave Wales, a mere five years sufficed for them to subjugate the English. Normans were accordingly the upper class; the English menial workers, a division still reflected in the double code of words today for animals herded as distinct from animals cooked. 'Swine', 'deer', 'sheep' and 'cow' are roughly what Saxon herdsmen called these animals, while their French-speaking Norman overlords ate at table 'pork', 'venison', 'mutton', 'veal' and 'beef' [porc/venison/ mouton/veau/boeuf].

But the Anglo-Normans don't fare much better. They were, writes Gerald, debauched, boastful, blasphemous, arrogant and militarily remiss, violent and vindictive, committing inhuman slaughter and bloodthirsty outrages, unjust against the people whom even Henry I acknowledges as rightful heirs to their own land: the Welsh. He dislikes those clients of the Normans in South Pembrokeshire, the Flemish, whose maltreatment of the Welsh was, like that of their bosses, "cruel and shameful". He also despises the Plantaganet kings the Normans have imported to London, being hostile, like so many Marchers, to strong and centralised royal power. As court chaplain over some years, he had observed this power at close quarters. And he wrote a curious and malicious denunciation of Henry II, whom he knew well.

Of the Welsh he has two views, and his *The Description of Wales* (*Descriptio Cambriae*) famously sets up a disputation between them. "You will never find anyone worse than a bad Welshman, nor anyone better than a good one": the Welsh are given to extremes. Inconstant, unstable, rarely keeping their word, living by plunder, theft and brigandage, they look fierce, but run in battle. Lazy, backward and sexually immoral, they disrespect boundaries and are faithless and treacherous. They should be swept away, uprooted, moved out: a Wales emptied of the Welsh might be converted into a game reserve.

This is not the whole story. The Welsh were also shrewd, hospitable, and music-loving – then as now they sang in choral part-harmony – were witty, ready in repartee, given to prophecy and soothsaying, keenly respectful of noble birth – fierce but devoted tribespeople. Gerald praises Welsh hospitality, the laws of which meant that anybody giving up their weapons was taken in, offered water to wash their feet and entertained, with a period of grace during which no questions were asked of this new guest for the first three days: blood-feuds probably meant that it was safer not to question your guest! They wore their hair long, shaved their faces but not their moustaches, and cleaned their teeth with green hazel twigs. They favoured communal beds.

The Welsh, he sometimes seems to feel, were, unlike the English, worthy adversaries. Even though fascinated by geneal-ogy and so un-egalitarian, a great proportion of them were none the less free. Unlike the servile English, the Welsh were bold, warlike, noble, generous and free-spoken. And so he objected to the violence of imposition of Norman rule, in ecclesiastic as in secular matters.

Gerald was born in Manorbier Castle in Pembrokeshire, and wrote with a loving local patriotism about this part of Wales. His mother-tongue was French and his occupational tongue Latin. The consensus is that he must also have known Welsh; exactly how much is disputed, but he felt able to pass comment on the standard of Welsh (praising the speech of Ceredigion, for instance) and was able to appreciate the verbal wit of its speak-ers[3]. He wrote on occasion of "we Welshmen", and called himself, after all, by the name Cambrensis (The Welshman). He was suspected at times of subversive Welsh sympathies. He famously wrote that "no other race or language [i.e. than Welsh] will answer to God on the day of judgement". If only the Welsh were inseparable they would be insuperable. But, he laments, they had no single King. In this frontier-society he appeared too Welsh for the Normans and too Norman for the Welsh.

*

What was the purpose of Gerald's pugnacious 1176 march into Llanbadarn? He had just returned from his first of two periods of living in Paris, zealous for the new Church reforms that were starting to unify Europe. What St Bernard wrote of the Irish – that they were Christian only in name, and pagan in fact – was a common complaint of European colonisers faced with strange usages. Wales, too, differed from England, and some of these differences, innocent by virtue of ancient custom, were nonetheless conveniently construed as 'barbarian', to justify the bullying interventions of a powerful neighbour.

There was the tradition of partible inheritance which dictated that all land be apportioned among heirs rather than given to the eldest son. This continued in Kent and elsewhere in England for two hundred years after the Conquest, where it was known as *gavelkind*. It lasted much longer in Wales where it seemed the ruin of the country, contributing as it did to a remorseless fragmentation of estates and therefore also both of power and of collective responsibility: *Cyfran* (its name in Welsh) was still being cited by Radnorshire freeholders as late as 1618. It affected princely families too. When Madog ap Maredudd the Lord of Powys – 'paradise of Wales' – died in 1160 his lands were dismembered between five quarrelling male heirs, and later yet further sub-division followed. In Gwynedd ten years later an eldest heir was murdered by his half-brothers. Such jealous strife contributed to what Tony Conran wittily termed the "miseries of a heroic age".

Welsh marriage customs also differed significantly. Bastard children had full legal status, divorce was provided for in Welsh law, and Gerald, who disapproved and believed the Welsh sexually immoral, claimed that girls might be purchased 'on trial' and that 'incest' – by which he meant alliance within the prohibited degrees of cousinhood – was common. Certainly cohabitation before marriage was common: the traditional troth-plight noted by Alwyn D. Rees in 1940, and known in England as 'bundling' or hand-fasting, meant that a sworn engagement had some of the binding force of marriage itself. In the first paragraph of his own autobiographical writing Gerald twice uses the word 'lawful' – first of his parents' marriage, and then of his own legitimate birth, showing awareness that transgression abounded. Cadwallon, the Welsh cousin who saved him from the besieged church, had, as one motive for helping, a fear of exposure of the status of his marriage to his wife and close cousin Efa. Gerald ignores the fact that such marriage within prohibited degrees had the useful function of helping to patch up feuds within the kindred. This same strong sense of insider/outsidership survives in the March today.

Sexual irregularity extended into church practice. Gerald found Jordan, the aged Archdeacon of Brecon, living contentedly with his mistress, and, to Jordan's fury, promptly suspended him. It was as a result of this that Archbishop Richard appointed Gerald in Jordan's place. He also objected to, and reported, non-payment of tithes.

But the custom of married clergy, and of sexual laxity in general among priests, especially offended him. Many local clergy married, passing on benefices to their children, had minimal spiritual duties, and aimed at being left alone. Gerald believed – perhaps rightly – that benefice-inheritance was an ancient characteristic of the British or Celtic church and was found among the Bretons too, a survival of what is today called Celtic Christianity. (Though he objected to benefices being passed on within the family, this neither stopped his accepting the post from his own uncle, nor arranging later for its transfer to his own nephew...)

He was not alone in noting laxity. Dafydd ap Gwilym (*fl.* 1320-70), greatest of Welsh poets, wrote a mischievous and teasing defence of priestly amours, just as his near-contemporary Iolo Goch (1320-98) wittily demolished the arguments for clerical celibacy. As late as 1536 clergy from the diocese of Bangor petitioned Thomas Cromwell to be allowed to keep their 'hearth-companions' or concubines in accordance with tradition. A good deal of evidence survives to suggest that the Welsh at this time had a healthy and good-humoured tolerance in such matters. No-one accused Gerald of sharing it. Undoubtedly the clergy of Llanbadarn Fawr, and of Elfael generally, wanted to be left alone to continue with local practice and local loyalties, unmolested by an interfering priest with new-fangled ideas from elsewhere.

★

Gerald never states exactly why, in 1187, Henry II asked Baldwin, his ageing and frail Archbishop of Canterbury, to spend arduous months riding around Wales, rather than any other destination, whipping up enthusiasm for a Third Crusade[4]. Henry II had a double motivation. He admired Welsh soldiers and wished to recruit them. He also wished to use the Church as an instrument to further the Anglo-Norman subjugation of Wales, which entailed much violence committed on both sides.

Wales was a soldier-breeding mountain country like Scotland, Switzerland, Castile, and Gerald's aspersions against Welsh flightiness in battle need qualification. The first military uniform recorded in Europe – a coat and hat in chequered green and white – was worn by the roughly five thousand Welsh long-bow men fighting for the English at the battle of Crécy in 1346, some of whom had served the Crown at Flanders (1297) and Falkirk (1298): the poet Iolo Goch addressed a celebration of this victory to Edward III. A military career had irresistible appeal for innumerable Welshmen, who were employed by English kings for service in France and Scotland as well as against their own countrymen. A Welsh archer was paid twice as much as a day labourer. Gerald notes how expertly the South Welsh made their long bows out of rock-elm, and also notes admiringly that this was an entire country familiar with taking up arms and training for battle, not only the nobility. They had, after all, had many bitter centuries of experience in fighting the English, as well as, on occasion, one another.

Vengeance – including blinding and castration – lived cheek-by-jowl with piety, and churches in such a world must have been havens of peace. The writer Patrick Thomas documents a constant tension in this period in mid-Wales between heroism and holiness, or between military and spiritual bravery. The scent of "dead saints and dead heroes inextricably intermingled"[5]. The church itself had adopted some of the values and assumptions of a heroic and violent society, its saints provided with genealogies proving their noble descent, and depicted as sacred heroes performing wondrous acts of spiritual valour. The right of vengeance might be jealously upheld in the name of the saint[6]: indeed Gerald claimed that Irish and Welsh saints were more vindictive than others!

A crusade, therefore, with its strange mixture of military zeal and religious pretext, might seem well-adapted equally to Welsh talents, and to Welsh other-worldliness. Gerald's contemporary, fellow-cleric and friend Walter Map (c.1140-c.1209) depicts the Welshman as extreme in his devotion and abstinence and as savage in his delight in battle and bloodshed[7]. Gerald echoes this judgement. By the end of the Tour of Wales Gerald and the Archbishop Baldwin between them had recruited three thousand Welsh soldiers for the Third Crusade, on which Baldwin himself was to die. Upon pledging either to reach Jerusalem or die in the attempt, pilgrims marked their clothes with a sown-on cross. It is somehow typical of Gerald both that he was the first man to take the Cross at New Radnor, and also that he never left for the Crusade.

There is implicit in Gerald's observations an argument about historical progress that reads as uncannily contemporary. Like T.E. Lawrence admiring the Bedouin, Gerald stressed the pastoral and nomadic, that is transhumant, aspects of Welsh life, aware that this represented an earlier stage of historical development than that of town-bred Anglo-Normans. Pastoralism, Gerald recorded, was "the first mode of living", the order of mankind progressing "from the woods to the fields and from fields to towns and gatherings of citizens"[8]. The Welsh, like the Irish, had spurned the hard work of farming, or for that matter, creating orchards, or living in townships or castles. He wrongly believed the Welsh did not garden[9]. He claims that they ate meat but little bread. The "Welsh clung to the woods like hermits". They practised no trade or industry and were thus free from the material greed that degraded the English.

The Welsh had "simple tastes" and Gerald at times idealises the primitive. Here, then, is an heroic and a pastoral society, an historical survival inhabiting what modern parlance terms a time-warp. And this is of course classic colonial mapping: seeing the Welsh as inhabiting an ancient past from which we have redeemed ourselves by becoming modern. It has been used for millennia to justify meddling and oppression; the theme is still palpable in the work of Kilvert and Chatwin.

Thus the Welsh declined to unite under a single ruler, as the English so precociously had under King Athelstan in 927. It took a further five centuries before France united, and nearly one thousand years before the world, to its cost, saw a united Germany. The king of England, uniquely, could arrange terms binding on all subjects; no-one in Wales could so promise. One single Welsh Prince would have made the Welsh easier and less capricious to deal with. "If only the Welsh were inseparable they would be insuperable" as Gerald taunts. Yet when Wales threatened to unite, as towards the end of Gerald's life under Llywelyn the Great, or again under his grandson Llywelyn ap Gruffudd, conflict with England intensified. One part of Gerald wishes to bring the Welsh into the 'modern' i.e. Anglo-Norman world. Another half secretly admires the way their mode-of-being criticises 'modernity'. It sometimes seems as if he only just falls short of calling them Noble Savages. Here is the inner division that echoes what the border divides.

A second motive for the journey in 1188 was for Baldwin to celebrate mass in each of the four cathedral churches of Wales. No previous Archbishop of Canterbury had done so. Indeed the first Bishop of Bangor to be consecrated by an Archbishop of Canterbury, in 1092, was intruded by force and then subsequently driven out by the Welsh. This set a pattern. For the Archbishop to celebrate mass successively in Bangor, St Asaph,

St David's and Llandaff would be to assert the symbolic supremacy of England over Wales. This Baldwin achieved, even though at Llandaff on 15 March the English and the Welsh were separated into two hostile and mutually uncomprehending national cohorts, from each of which, separately, recruits for the Crusade took the Cross.

Gerald was not alone in sincerely cherishing the (false) belief that St David's had once possessed the ancient dignity of a metropolitan seat, which would mean that it was answerable directly to Rome, without mediation from Canterbury. The Scottish church had an independent relationship with Rome; so did the Irish. The English King used the archbishop as a way of extending his influence, his church an instrument of conquest.

Gerald later came to represent his whole life as a quest to be granted the Bishopric of St David's and to liberate it from the see of Canterbury and the English[10]. St David's was the holy grail. It was vacant in 1176, when Gerald's uncle David Fitzgerald, the then Bishop, died, but went to a rival candidate, Peter de Leia. Gerald feared that this was because he was suspected of pro-Welsh sympathies[11].

When Peter died in 1198, Gerald again hoped to be elected, and travelled to France to canvas King John, who was favourable to his cause. At St David's Gerald was elected by the full chapter, who directed him to go to Rome to be consecrated by Pope Innocent III, most powerful and canniest of the medieval Popes. He accordingly made at least three journeys to Rome to win Pope Innocent's favour, journeys that took five years, and are told at length and in detail in his autobiography.

He wanted both to purge the Welsh Church of disorders and establish its independence from Canterbury. He expended much time and energy pleading this case, at one point spending a day and night locked up without food or money in a prison in Châtillon-sur-Seine. He protested to the Pope about injustices committed against the Welsh Church, and championed the Welsh cause. In 1198 the Welsh besieged Painscastle in southern Radnorshire and were excommunicated, before three thousand of them were slaughtered in a single day – a disaster Sir Walter Scott later wrote up in *The Betrothed*. This castle, Gerald pointed out, was constructed by the English for the express purpose of depriving the Welsh of their lands. And Gerald objected to this misuse of excommunication by the Church: it was a "political abuse of a spiritual weapon for a political end". (This, too, was a weapon Gerald, when it suited him, was happy to exploit: he and the Bishop of St Asaph once raced to be the one to excommunicate the other first – like cowboys in a Western shoot-out – a story at which Henry II laughed out loud.)

He wanted Welsh-speaking bishops. A priest who spoke no Welsh could neither preach a sermon nor take confession without an interpreter; (that Gerald's own speeches during the Welsh recruiting tour of 1188 were in French or Latin he overlooked).

Gerald was disappointed yet again. Welsh-speaking bishops were never appointed; he never became St David's bishop; and the subjugation of Wales by England accelerated in the century following his death. He passed his last days in "humble circumstances among his books, confessing his sins in the dim recesses of churches"[12]. Among those sins, we might add, was a new shrillness in his denunciations of the Welsh. In 1223, and at nearly eighty years of age, Gerald died.

The Anglo-Norman conquest of Wales, which Gerald chronicled and played his small part in, took five hundred years. "Beware of Walys, Christ Jesu must us keep/ that it make not our childe's child to weep" ran one saying[13]: they again and again rose up against the English, spurred on by a tradition prophesying their recovery of England itself. Since the English already outnumbered the Welsh by some 12:1, you could say that reality has never been a strong point in Wales[14]. Indeed the English spoke in this connexion of Welsh 'light-headedness'. Or you could more generously call this belief in triumph against the odds quixotic, and sympathise with the sense of disinheritance fuelling it.

★

Gerald demonstrated plenty of evidence of Welsh superstition. His tour of Wales starts in Radnorshire, where he recorded many signs and wonders, and much evidence of supernatural agency: omens, prodigies, occult prognostications, and chimaeras. There was the Lord of Radnor who went blind after kennelling his dogs in a church; the rich St Curig's crozier held at St Harmon which cured tumours on payment of exactly one penny; and at Glascwm a handbell exhibiting "most miraculous powers". Elsewhere a bitch has puppies sired by a monkey; a woman sews with her feet; a Breconshire knight gives birth after three years of very painful pregnancy to a calf; and a magnanimous and conscience-stricken weasel cleverly saves a human family from poisoning.

He also described the details of Welsh devotion. The Welsh held their right hands out when taking an oath, gave the first corner of each loaf to the poor, sat to eat in threes to honour the Trinity, and loved going on pilgrimages, especially to Rome. There were 143 chapels in Wales dedicated to the Virgin Mary. More especially, he wrote that nowhere do you find anchorites of greater abstinence, commitment and spirituality than in Wales, which he ascribes to the Welsh temperament, and their tendency always to go to extremes. Lay Welsh people dwelt in the woods like hermits and clung to this seclusion, as if they shared a sympathy for the hermit's way of life. And Welsh hermits were indeed famous, some living in communities, and even accorded special status in Welsh law[15].

Perhaps this was why Cistercians succeeded in Wales. Their monks favoured remote places for their monasteries – Strata Florida, Cwm-hir, Tintern – the simplicity of whose architecture, combined with their grandeur of conception, is still both beautiful and moving: Cwm-hir's nave, is where the body of Llywelyn, the last Prince of Wales, lies. Such churches provided venues for assemblies as well as royal mausolea. They belong to an order that tapped into the strong reclusive and heroic elements in local tradition. Thus they caught the imagination of the Welsh who shared, in Gerald's view, the Cistercian lusts for solitude and asceticism.

Local Welsh dynasties as much as Anglo-Normans favoured these monks, who tried to reproduce or out-do the austerity of monastic life as it had been in earlier times. Their most striking reform was the return to manual labour, especially to field-work. Here were the great farmers of the Middle Ages, who simplified the divine office, renouncing all extraneous sources of income, depending for their income wholly on the land, albeit worked by lay brothers. They pioneered selective breeding and introduced new strains of sheep – initially emphasising the highly lucrative export of wool rather than the production of mutton. Soon Flemish and Italian wool-merchants visited and traded. Especially in the March they became very rich[16] and, while praising their virtues, Gerald also thought them sometimes covetous. His view of their growing and aggressive entrepreneurialism is shared by some recent scholars.

Gerald accordingly favoured the Augustinians, "more content than any of the others with a humble and modest way of life", and championing the church reforms Gerald backed. It is striking that a hand-book – probably Augustinian – and in any case one of the great pieces of medieval devotional English prose, designed for women-hermits or anchoresses, survives from Gerald's time; and that this was moreover written on the Welsh borders, and for people living there[17].

The anonymous *Ancrene Wisse* or *Ancrene Riwle* (the Guide for Anchoresses) was written not long after 1230, read throughout the Middle Ages, adapted several times for different audiences, much translated and exchanged, quoted and copied for three centuries, and survives in seventeen manuscripts. It may have helped inspire, a century later, the famous Welsh anthology known as the *Book of the Anchorite of Llanddewibrefi*[18]. The *Ancrene Wisse*'s inclusion of two Welsh words has helped to locate its writing within the March, possibly at Wigmore Abbey. Its original audience consisted of three lay women of noble birth who had withdrawn from the world to live in perpetual seclusion.

Such recluses were regarded as living the highest form of Christian life, something to which women, with few other options for religious life, were particularly drawn.

These anchor-holds were a familiar feature of the medieval landscape. Usually attached to parish churches or religious houses, they could be anything from a single room to a small compound with courtyard and garden. The building envisaged in *Ancrene Wisse* was probably at the larger end of the scale, attached to a church, with a window allowing the anchoress to see the altar. The cell itself was divided into a secluded area and a reception area, where the anchoress's maids guarded her privacy. The anchoress has one window communicating with this area and one communicating with the outside world, for food and waste to pass. Very few anchor-holds survive today. In Chester-le-Street, near Durham, a rare surviving late medieval anchor-hold consists of two large rooms, one on top of the other, built into the northwest side of the church. The upper room has a squint or small window offering the anchorite a view of the side altar reserved for public use.

Early desert fathers like St Anthony, who sought to subdue the flesh in life retreat, had a continuing appeal in Wales. And for many solitaries entering the anchor-hold must have recalled stepping into the desert landscape: a leading commentator on desert spirituality believes its lure lay in its promise of "recapturing paradise and restoring fallen human bodies to their Edenic state"[19]. The ceremony of Enclosure usually included receiving last rites, having the Office of the Dead said over you, entering your cell, and finally being bricked in, each stage accompanied by appropriate prayers.

Today this sounds austere to the point of derangement. Why were increasing numbers of women, as well as men, once drawn to this life of perpetual enclosure? Although Tibetan Buddhists today still sometimes enter immurement and life retreat, and commonly leave the world for three years, the idea that inner freedom and joy might be purchased at such expense is offensive to many. But if a life of retreat seems strange to us, perhaps people of that age would have been just as perplexed by our modern separation of – and opposition between – secular and sacred; perhaps we are wrong to assume that we always have the truth of the matter. Inner freedom and joy are indeed what the climactic seventh chapter of the *Ancrene Wisse* describes, maintaining that divine love and happiness, not pain or penance, are the highest goals of the inner life of the recluse, and likening the love of Christ to that of a knight whose recalcitrant mistress – the recluse – refuses his advances.

The most famous anchoress is Dame Julian of Norwich (c.1342-1416), among the greatest of Christian mystics, walled like all anchorites into her church during prayers for the dead. Known during her lifetime as a counsellor, whose advice combined spiritual insight with common sense, many came to speak with her. Even today her *Revelations of Divine Love* is a well-loved work to which many turn for help. Her waking vision of Christ therein, to whom she poses the eternal question, still speaks potently to us: "What is the meaning of sin and suffering?". She receives the wonderful, mysterious reply: "All shall be well: and all shall be well: and all manner of thing shall be well: and sin is behovely"; which seems to mean that sin and frailty too have their place in the great pattern. Christ then hands her a hazel-nut. "What's this?" she asks. "The cosmos." "And is it so small?" "Yes."

Dame Julian was not alone in withdrawing from the world, only to find herself thereby of greater spiritual use to her peers. Here was a world in which a village anchorite was a feature of religious life "both commonplace and awe-inspiring"[20]. Thus the *Ancrene Wisse*'s author advises anchoresses not to keep valuables in their anchor-holds, run a school, send, receive or write letters. The author further warns his readers that the anchor-hold should never become a source of news or gossip. Such prohibitions offer a tantalizing glimpse of the social functions of the typical anchoress. At least some anchor-holds, it seems, became "the centre of village life, acting as a sort of bank, post office, school house, shop, and newspaper – services which today are provided mainly by public and quasi-public institutions". That these activities are proscribed points to the fact that many anchorites became, like Dame Julian, celebrities, and a focus for the communal religious life of the village.

What has a treatise on the life of a retreatant around 1230 to do with us today? Well, the tradition of retreat in the Marches continues into the twentieth century, beyond the collapse of organised religion, and into the era of new age spirituality. The noted Welsh border novelist Margiad Evans began her autobiography in 1943 with a chapter entitled 'A Little Journal of Being Alone'.

22 June 1402: The Great Century

In the next valley, but visible from atop the hill, is the sloping site of a battle, the final moment in history when the Welsh, united under a single leader, defeated the English. That was the battle of Pilleth. The date was 22 June 1402, feast of St Alban's, and the story is recounted in the first scene of *Henry the Fourth Part One* where Westmoreland tells King Henry that, not merely have the English lost to "wild Glendower", but the corpses of one thousand of them, badly mutilated, had "such beastly transformation... done as may not be/Without much shame re-told or spoken of". Welshwomen castrated the English soldiers, then stuffed their open mouths with their privates. One contemporary – Adam of Usk – puts the total number of dead much higher: "with woeful slaughter even to eight thousand souls, the victory being with Owain".

Owen Glendower – in Welsh, Owain Glyndŵr – was the wealthiest of Welsh squires, nobly descended, a man of breeding and education speaking several languages, who had lived in the

Inns of Court in London and fought on the English side against the Scots. His rebellion started as a feud with a neighbour and grew into an international event. A consummate leader, a man of dignity and vision, Shakespeare paints him as in touch with mysterious powers, and indeed in 1401 when writing to the King of the Scots Glyndŵr referred to ancient prophecies. Also, he was in 1402 encouraged by the appearance of a comet, and was later influenced by a bardic soothsayer.

This moment is as pivotal to Wales as Bonnie Prince Charlie and Culloden to the Scots. It says something of English provincialism that while we at least know of 1745, the equally momentous Great Rebellion in Wales sometimes escapes our notice. By contrast, every modern Welsh poet of any importance has written about Glyndŵr. His was the defining moment, when Welsh nationhood seemed within an ace of realisation.

Adam noted that Wales yielded £60,000 each year to the coffers of the English kings: Wales was both exploited and oppressed. His account nonetheless emphasises the treachery of the Welsh, who "burned on all sides the towns wherein the English dwelt amongst them, pillaging them and driving out the English", as well as the cruelty of the English, who hung, drew and quartered Welsh rebels of rank, utterly laying waste large parts of Wales and "ravaging them with fire, famine and sword, [leaving] them a desert, not even sparing children and churches". They used the church of Strata Florida – where Dafydd ap Gwilym, greatest of all Welsh poets, is said to be buried – and its choir, even up to the high altar, as a stable, pillaging even the silver patens; and carried away into England, Adam claims, more than one thousand children to be their servants. At the same time, he notes, the same Owain did "no small hurt to the English, slaying many of them, and carrying off the arms, horses, and tents of the king's eldest son, the prince of Wales... to the mountain fastnesses of Snowdon".

This Welsh rebellion lasted fifteen years, during which Welsh students at Oxford left their studies for Owain. The number of Welsh students after 1170 was one in forty, and there had been ugly anti-Welsh riots in Oxford as recently as 1395: "kill, kill the Welsh dogs", yelled the English students. Welsh labourers and craftsmen too were abandoning their employers and returning to Wales in droves. The Cistercians provided some of his advisors; some disaffected English joined forces too. Glyndŵr's wife, Margaret Hanmer, was of English origins. The Marcher lords, high-handed and ungovernable as ever, refused to obey royal commands to cooperate in quelling the rebellion.

This was essentially a guerilla war, at first brilliantly fought by Glyndŵr, with many skirmishes and much violence. The battle of Pilleth in 1402 was followed by Glyndŵr's sacking the churches at Cascob, Bleddfa, Old and New Radnor, while at the castle of New Radnor he hanged the entire garrison of sixty soldiers from the battlements. Towns and castles, both being mostly English, were principal targets. Presteigne was so destroyed by rebel fire that the income of its lordship fell to £3.7s. Soon came the years of glory, when Glyndŵr convened a Welsh Parliament at Machynlleth, where tradition maintains that he was crowned Prince of Wales in the presence of envoys from France, Castile and Scotland. The noble seal on his letter to King Charles VI of France, with whom he had concluded a formal alliance, and who sent a fleet from Brest, shows him crowned, with a dragon on his helmet and four lions on his shield. His standard, Adam noted, was "a golden dragon on a white ground"; others record this dragon, more traditionally, as red. On 29 March 1406 he wrote to Pope Benedict XIII, the rival Avignonese Pope favoured by France and Scotland, pleading, like Gerald before him, that priests in Wales should "speak our language". He also wanted two Welsh universities established, north and south, King Henry IV to be excommunicated, and those opposing him to receive full remission of sins.

The rebellion was never crushed: over the following years "it simply petered out". In time Glyndŵr was offered a 'pardon' but no record survives of his reply; or of his death. One Welsh annalist famously and poetically put it that "Very many say that he died; the seers maintain that he did not". In other words, like

King Arthur, Glyndŵr sleeps in a cave, awaiting the Welsh nation's next call to arms.

Meanwhile, in 1409, his two daughters, three grand-daughters and beloved wife were all carried away to captivity in London, and the English Parliament enacted penal laws against the Welsh. Henceforth the Welsh could – at least in theory – neither gather together; gain office; carry arms; nor dwell in fortified towns. They were disinherited and disenfranchised, exiles in their own lands. Englishmen with Welsh wives underwent the same strictures: and as late as 1433 Owain Glyndŵr's English son-in-law John Scudamore was dismissed from office because his wife was Welsh. No chief office in Wales was held by a Welshman before 1461, and no Welshman again became a bishop until 1496.

If he wished earnestly enough to hold office a Welshman had to petition Parliament to become English, with how great a charge of bitterness and ambivalence may be imagined. Many did and were granted this new nationality as a result: the way to get on with the English was to become less Welsh, a phenomenon variously repeated over the next six centuries: as Dylan Thomas facetiously remarked: "Land of my Fathers? My fathers can keep it". If, as has been argued, to be Welsh has sometimes meant to fight a sense of inferiority, then the harshness of these terms of surrender may have contributed. These laws were renewed in 1431, 1433 and 1477 and only removed from the statute book in 1624. Small surprise that Welsh literature after 1415 was more nationalistic than before or since.

Not long ago in Harlech castle, where Glyndŵr had held court for five years and had even plotted the partition of England, a small horse-brass with the four lions of the house of Aberffraw was discovered in the dust. A solitary memento of the meteoric career of the last native-born Prince of Wales.

★

It seems at first paradoxical that the fifteenth century, starting thus, should nonetheless have been Wales's so-called 'great century'[1]. The penal laws, despite being on the statute book, were not always enforced and were gradually forgotten. Henry V on his accession in 1413 – like his father before him – offered pardons and exemptions that helped recruit him soldiers for Agincourt. Soon the Yorkist faction, who controlled the March (Lancaster ruling in the Principality), cultivated the Welsh by acting as patrons to many Welsh poets: encouraging Welsh poetry was another way to gain Welsh support. Ambitious Englishmen moreover, while anxious for new titles and land in Wales, were often absentees, delegating duties to the Welsh squires, who thus filled a power vacuum. "Native gentlemen had to be given a chance of office"; even rebels were on occasion restored to their possessions and tasks.

The age of the Welsh princes was over. That of the Marcher Lords, some of whose estates were taken over by the crown, was also slowly coming to an end. The age of Welsh gentry – of the squires – was starting. Wales enjoyed far more peace and prosperity at this time than Ireland or Scotland. Castles were out-dated. New houses, cruck-framed, half-timbered, with chimneys, started going up especially in east Wales and the middle March in particular. Here were the first great un-fortified hall-houses built for a new age of peace: some are still there.

Radnorshire was accordingly chosen in the 1980s by the Royal Commission on the Ancient and Historical Monuments of Wales for six years of research into its hundreds of timber-built houses – a project to balance against their earlier study of the stone-built houses of Glamorgan and Caernarfon. Late medieval cruck-trussed building in the Radnorshire uplands, they revealed, was particularly strong. The resulting book is full of secret splendours and endorses the sense that Radnorshire has been overlooked. The largest single surviving medieval house in all Wales, Bryndraenog, survives along the Teme valley in Radnorshire, not far from Knighton, still a prosperous farmhouse and virtually complete. Richard Suggett's *Houses and History in the March of Wales 1400-1600* is a book to delight Radnorshire-lovers everywhere. The picture on its front cover is of the hall-house of Ciliau in the Wye valley, white-washed as we know it would have been half a millenium ago. Ciliau has never been modernised and is privately lived in today, by its owner's decree, without contemporary amenities. Llowes Hall in southern Radnorshire also survives intact.

The exquisitely detailed rood-screens of isolated Marcher churches (Partrishow – which has dragons – and Llananno – with wyverns – the knot-work and twining stalks on both recalling Celtic-Viking work from the Dark Ages, and Llanwnog) date from this time, the fifteenth century, too. Each is a marvel of detail. Nobody knows how they survived the puritan iconoclasms: that each church is little, lonely, and remote must have helped. A fine 2006 book on the rood-screens of the March notes how many remain unvisited and unknown in this "secretive, folded land-scape"[2]. Both such superb churches and ambitious hall-houses prove the existence of highly-skilled local workmen, and of their wealthy patrons in the fifteenth century.

The discovery that Radnorshire is rich in this way would not have surprised the late Ffransis Payne. He visited Bryndraenog in 1964, informed that it dated from the seventeenth century. This he declined to believe. He felt an intuitive certainty that the present Bryndraenog was identical to that black-and-white house praised by the poet Ieuan ap Hywel Swrdwal from Newtown who flourished between 1430 and 1470, and who in one poem compared the house to the appearance of a new star on the horizon, a "proud maiden of lime and timber framing", its whiteness dazzling even at night. Its great roof-trusses impressed the poet, who duly compares it with the affluence and high fashion of Cheapside in London, with the great ecclesiastical buildings of Rome and St David's, and with Celliwig, court of King Arthur himself in Cornwall. Even Richard Duke of York, heir to the vast Mortimer estates and houses, could not, claims the poet, compete.

Such houses had a public function as meeting places where agreements were made and financial transactions occurred, as well as courts, where poets recited and sang. And since the age

– and the March – were still sometimes given to lawlessness, the safety and bounty alike of a local hall-house must have been the more welcome. We now know the precise felling-date for the timbers: Bryndraenog was built around 1436. Its owner, as Payne surmised, was indeed Llewelyn Fychan (in Welsh, where it means 'short' or 'younger') a surname soon rendered into English as Vaughan.

Of course poets were paid to flatter, a convention understood by all parties. Among the six extant praise poems to Owain Glyndŵr is a famous verse by Iolo Goch around 1390 celebrating Sycharth, Glyndŵr's main house in neighbouring Montgomeryshire, as a baronial court, a place of fine manners where many poets came, and where life was good. Iolo details the moat with its bridge, the wide portal, belfry, gold chancel, nine matching wardrobes and four lofts where minstrels slept, bakehouse, orchard, mill, dovecot, fishpond with pike and splendid whiting, and park-lands adorned with peacocks, rabbits and deer. Here was an "open house" serving beer, wine and honey-mead, a "bard's haven". Sycharth was destroyed in a punitive raid by the future Henry V in 1403 and never re-built. Yet recent excavations uncannily endorse Iolo's description: the remains of the fishpond and moat were discovered, the outlines of five wooden houses on top of the green hill traced. The main house was 13 metres by 5.5 with an outbuilding measuring 3 metres by 3. All Wales, wrote Lewys Glyn Cothi, was in Glyndŵr's council.

★

To be a poet in Wales has always been different. The Welsh for poet, *bardd* – which gives us the English 'bard' – connotes both a 'remembrancer' and a seer or prophet, two roles specially valued in a conquered people. No accident that Edward I, after his long bloody conquest, took action – ineffectively – against the poets of Wales. Although the tale that he burnt at the stake five hundred Welsh bards for refusing to praise him is unfounded, it points to an underlying reality: Welsh poetry meant subversion, and kept alive an alternative reality, constituting the sole available form of nationhood[3].

Every Welsh court and many a sub-court had its official *pencerdd* or master-poet who was seated next to the prince's heir in hall, and also its *bardd teulu* or household poet. The latter seems to have been perhaps a permanent retainer, while the *pencerdd*, 'chief of song', may have been more exalted, head of the bardic guild of the region, with more autonomy and freedom. There was probably a long apprenticeship which must have covered a wealth of native learning, judging by the density of allusions to characters of story, myth and legend presented in the Welsh Triads. It may be that, as in Ireland, aspiring poets were required to be familiar with hundreds of tales before they could qualify. And you could combine being a poet in Wales – both then and now – with many other trades: there were drover-poets, outlaw-poets, soldier-poets, priest-poets, farmer-poets and combinations of these: *bardd gwlad* is the generic name for a rural poet.

Many of the great poets, who lived by their art, exacted a fixed charge for it, writing to a formula that required references to its subject's ancestors, generosity, house, wife and importance to society. The bard's duty was to celebrate the exploits of his patron, lament his death, record his pedigree and so on. With the loss of Welsh independence, the descendants of the old princely lines preserved in their houses a faint reflection of the modes of the courts of their ancestors. Experts in genealogy, complex metrical form, song, copying, and history, such poets were essential to their culture. A great part of this literature still exists and has been said to constitute one of the great literatures of medieval Europe. Moreover, wherever the poets sang in Welsh, a virtual Welsh commonwealth came into existence[5]. This is the world Payne explored. Although it "may appear to be a strange little inner world of make-believe"[6] its very conventionality betokened the economic and political vitality of the world it celebrated. It is mainly because of this literary flowering that the fifteenth has, as we have seen, been called Wales's 'great century'.

By 1400 poets travelled from squire-patron to patron, household to household (including the wealthy Cistercian houses). Nothing quite like this relationship between squire and bard existed elsewhere, or has survived into modern Europe (unless one counts Ceaucescu's bards, praising him as "bear of the Carpathians" and so on). It bespeaks an ancient world[7]. As comparatively recently as 1694 one wealthy Welsh family still kept a hired poet as a member of the household: poetry was declaimed or sung to the assembled company.

A relationship of patronage has inevitable constraints, and poets, being paid to praise their patron's generosity, could appear superficial, servile or mendacious. They had literally to sing for their supper. Small wonder that Welshness and eloquence, like Welshness and poetry, have long been associated. This courtly culture – most famously represented at Sycharth – flourished alike in Radnorshire, where Ffransis Payne must be accounted its chief discoverer.

Payne's story belongs here. Born of mostly Welsh parentage in 1901 he was brought up in a draper's shop just over the border in Kington in Herefordshire – a place and a time that he later lovingly evoked. He was to tell his story mainly in Welsh, a language he taught himself on his travels after the First World War, together with Latin and Greek. In 1941, taking his finals in Welsh at Cardiff, he was asked to criticise a passage he had himself written in his super-correct Welsh and published shortly before: his writing had early gained a cult-following[8].

His awakening happened on the north side of the chancel of Kington church where he practised as a choir-boy four times a week. Never a devout Christian, but like many writers a devout day-dreamer, he would watch the colours of the long narrow window above the altar gradually going cold and disappearing in the darkness outside. He would also gaze across the chancel to the shadows of the chapel of the Vaughans where an armed soldier and his noble wife lay side-by-side "in the white splendour of cold alabaster", their dog at their feet.

He knew that here were images of Tomas ap Rhoser of

Hergest, and of his wife Elen Gethin. Tomas was killed just
before the battle of Banbury in 1469. Bored by sermons, Payne
wove romantic and childish stories about this couple instead.
One day when he was about fourteen, he read a translation of a
fifteenth century poem describing that very tomb[9] and even
detailing the gold helmet on which Tomas rests. Hearing this
voice from the Middle Ages describing something he saw every
day electrified him. History, he suddenly saw, was alive. The
past was far more challengingly intimate than he had understood: he glimpsed for the first time "the unity of history and
literature and locality".

The people of the past were once not mere funerary statues
but "living, moving beings"; a realisation that led him, fifty
years later, to write in Welsh about Radnorshire. Payne started
a 1938 essay by observing that it is commonplace to assert that
Radnorshire alone among the Welsh counties has contributed
nothing to Welsh literature as if it were "some sort of desert
devoid of history or tradition or anything distinctive". Payne, by
contrast, thought the neglect of Radnorshire – Wales's true
centre whose learning and culture was inseparable from that of
Wales itself – was both strange and impoverishing. He found
that Radnorshire, just as it had among the highest proportion of
timber-built medieval buildings of all Wales, and for that matter
of church bells cast before 1600, had a rich tradition of praise-
poems too.

At fifteen Payne left school, the uneventful happy bustle of
Kington, and the distant and enclosed world of his youth for
jobs in the iron furnaces of the South as check-weigher and later
as coal-truck repairer, as a clerk in Glasgow, and as a World War
One RAF wireless operator. After the Great War he was also an
apprentice farm-hand at various Welsh farms and an itinerant
book-seller on a bike with an official pedlar's certificate from
the police, a job he recalled with qualified joy. Sometimes at
night he bivouacked outside. It is hard not to see distant paral-
lels between Payne the vagabond book-seller struggling to bring
gladness to outlying farms in Ceredigion, and the itinerant

fifteenth century bards he came to love, moving from hall-house to hall-house with poetical wares for sale.

★

Payne discovered more than forty Welsh poets who had visited Radnorshire, and wrote about them in *Crwydro Sir Faesyfed* (*Exploring Radnorshire*) in 1964-6, a book to which this chapter is greatly indebted, and which is at last being translated into English[10]. One hundred and sixty poems survive, written between 1400 and 1600 in the area that is after 1536 called Radnorshire, to which a further 28 poems, addressed to the extensive Vaughan family at two of their houses just over the border in Bredwardine and Hergest, need to be added, making a grand total of 188. Payne felt that the welcome recovery of this lost literature healed a break with the past of which many Radnorshire folk were conscious. This break was occasioned by the loss of their old language.

Consisting of four separate ambles around the county, past and present, Payne's is a passionate, sometimes moody book, its irritability stemming from what it cherishes. For example the big and important Royal Welsh (Agricultural) Show happens every year near Builth at Llanelwedd, lazily believed to be in Breconshire, though in fact – being East of the Wye – still within Radnorshire. Payne enjoys reproving errors, and humorously suggests Radnorians spit at the bridge over the Wye to signal depth of local feeling.

Payne is a poetic soul, who can classify the different styles of silence, who praises windows as aids to recollection rather than means for looking out of and avows *hiraeth* (yearning) for lost worlds that will never return. He is an intelligent and melancholy romantic: he loves the combination of wildness and fertility that constitutes Radnorshire's special magic. The sense it gives of solitude as well as community.

The county, he feels, is best approached from the East, whence, from the flatlands of England, the swelling hill-scapes, the warmer accents of men's voices, the unrulier sheep and ruder shepherds alike lift the spirit in anticipation. I feel this still, after forty years; it does not fade or fail. That there are no traffic lights in the county and only two roundabouts: this pleases him. The only villages in the entire county comparable with those elsewhere are New Radnor, Glasbury, Newbridge-on-Wye, Llangynllo and Clyro. "If it is a Welsh characteristic for houses of a parish to be scattered over its acres like sheep, then there is no county more Welsh than this one." Those who love Radnorshire – for example Kilvert, "a saint", and Iolo Goch, who in another poem commended southern Radnorshire (Elfael) as "blest" – win his approval.

He loves Radnorshire hall-houses. Many burnt down. Some lost whole wings and came down in the world to function as ordinary farmhouses or even barns. A frisson of ghostly or spiritual disturbance can, it seems, follow, and this compels his imagination. Hergest Court has 'Black Vaughan', who was bewitched and shrunk to the size of a blue-bottle, entrapped in a snuff-box and then thrown into the Arrow; it also has a large black spirit-dog that probably inspired Conan Doyle's *Hound of the Baskervilles* (a local name). At Llanddewi Ystradenni is another ancient barn disturbed by spirits; while at old Llinwent deaths were portended by spine-chilling sounds of the arrival of men on horseback, who then passed audibly through the house.

Whether such spirits are 'real' or imagined we could still say that Payne in the truest sense believes in ghosts: his Radnorshire is everywhere actively haunted by its past; and civilisation itself appears to him essentially a conversation between the living and the dead. He communes more effectively with spirits than John Dee. Llinwent is the great house where Dafydd Fychan lived and was killed. Revenge came quickly. His sister Elen Gethin (= the terrible) – the wife on the Kington tomb – went to an archery contest disguised as a man and shot her brother's murderer though the heart.

On a quest one day to find the site of Llinwent, visited by Iolo Goch, inhabited by "people of high authority and wonderfully hospitable", Payne finds *"mieri lle bu mawredd"*[11] (brambles where once was greatness). At the cold hearth with the mists descending down the hillside he is despondent trying to imagine what their opinion would have been of the life of the area today. Most of the mansion was pulled down in 1782, and what was left burnt to the ground in 1919. What would Dafydd Fychan, grandson of Iolo Goch's patron, think of the unpopulated wilderness there now? Payne cheers up on discovering, within a corrugated iron barn, old oak posts, joists and cross-beams – and a floor of huge slates. Here after all is some continuity.

But he seeks in vain for Gweston on the Lugg, and for once-famous Gardd Faelog, gathering-place for bards over three centuries[12]. And the site of the long-lost hall of Philip ap Rhys, son-in-law of Owain Glyndŵr, at Cefn Cenarth, which attracted Lewys Glyn Cothi "as the north drew a compass needle", eludes him too. The old mansions are vanishing, leaving only the odd relic in the soil to perplex those who know nothing of the history of their own parish.

Payne loves to show how neighbouring parts of Herefordshire were also part of Wales's history, the overwhelming majority of their inhabitants, though they no longer wish to remember this, Welsh by blood. He loved the ancient riddle: "How many miles, how many / 'Twixt Leominster and Llanllieni?" Answer: none, since Llanllieni is the Welsh for Leominster. Yet each year saw Llanllieni retreat further into the past. Welsh poets visited Bredwardine as late as 1550. Cwrt Llangain, known as Kentchurch Court, is still today home of the Scudamore family, believed to have been patrons to the poet Siôn Cent and to Owain Glyndŵr himself. Both are thought to have found refuge there at the end of their lives.

Lewys Glyn Cothi (*fl.* 1447-1489), who described the tomb in the poem that electrified Payne, wrote nearly a third of surviving Radnorshire praise-poems, with more patrons in Radnorshire even than in his native Carmarthenshire: Radnorshire was wealthier, and he loved it and its thirteen saints. He wrote many poems there in the new manor-houses that were evidently both urbane and civilised. We know a lot about his travels. He also frequented Harpton Court near New Radnor, then known as Plas Mawr yn Nhre'rdelyn, and left a mouth-watering list of its fish, poultry, eight tables of pastries, herbs, white sugar and honey-wine. His best-known work is a heart-piercing elegy on the death of his five-year-old son Siôn.

There were cases of real friendship between poet and patron, and one authentic constant in all their songs: resentment of the English. It is thought that Lewys suffered under the anti-Welsh laws and may therefore have spent time as an outlaw. In one poem he describes days spent on the run, resting in a lair in a hollow oak, and making for a patron's home for supper and bed. He longed for the day when no Englishman would hold office in Wales and considered the battle of Banbury during the Wars of the Roses a national calamity, so great were the Welsh losses.

Lewys records sitting with another local patron – an Old Radnor squire called Dafydd ap Rhys ap Meurig – reading together a subversive work of literature. We know Lewys liked his food and drink and had a discriminating palate, and can imagine that they drank together on this occasion, as they read, *metheglin* (Welsh honey-wine or mead), or *bragget* (spiced ale) - maybe from Weobley – drinks he liked to praise. They were reading an old book about 'Gwion' a.k.a. Taliesin.

We know for certain that *The Book of Taliesin*, one of the famous 'Four Ancient Books of Wales'[13], was in Radnorshire in the sixteenth century when it belonged first to Hugh Myles of Evenjobb and then to the antiquary and historian John Lewis of Llynwene, barrister and author of a *History of Great Britain*, born at Harpton of a Vaughan mother. But it seems already to have been in the Old Radnor area in the fifteenth century.

The book on which Lewys has written his comments is another of the Four Ancient Books, *The Red Book of Hergest*, a huge and valuable portable library of texts, including some pre-Norman poetry, a vast collection of verse from the period 1100-1400 and the *Mabinogion* prose tales, our source for stories of the Welsh King Arthur. There was also once a *White Book of Hergest*, destroyed by a fire in a bindery in Covent Garden in 1808, though copies of part of it have survived, and probably also written by Lewys Glyn Cothi at Hergest Cwrt (Court). This house, a short distance into Herefordshire, was once much grander than today: Payne chronicles how it has diminished. In the passage of 740 years it has only changed hands once for money. And in 1422 Tomas ap Rhoser, the Vaughan depicted on the Kington tomb and owner also of *The Red Book of Hergest*, rebuilt it.

That two of the Four Ancient Books were found in Radnorshire is very striking. The two story cycles they contain – *Taliesin* and *Mabinogion* – are major sources for the Arthurian legends we inherit today. Arthurian romance has been called the most potent story-cycle in the world, offering a parallel universe, a Celtic otherworld outside time and space, and a rich, mythical compulsive history ending with a prophecy of redemption ('King Arthur returns...').

King Arthur prompted poetry wars. Edward I, zealous in stealing Welsh icons, had celebrated his victory over the Welsh by holding an Arthurian Round Table at the old princely court of Nefyn, where the floor gave way under the weight of festivities. He had a Saxon tomb in Glastonbury opened up and declared the bones officially to be those of Arthur and Guinevere: the Archbishop of Canterbury conducted a rite of re-interment during which Edward carried Arthur's relics and his wife Eleanor carried what was left of Guinevere.[14] He similarly removed from Wales a fragment of the True Cross (*y Groes Naid*), with its authenticating 'mana' or power, for his own use. Welsh mysteries were gradually co-opted to the English cause. King Arthur was even by the year 1180 already a hero in the states of Antioch and Palestine, as much as in Wales, France and Flanders – the Flemings took the stories wherever they traded. But the Frenchified, chivalric – and familiar – English Arthur hid the original, sturdy, rougher Welsh Arthur honoured in the Radnorshire texts.

Payne quarrels with those well-heeled English who argue that
east Radnorshire has for centuries spoken English. The traveller
Benjamin Malkin noted in 1803 that while Presteigne is English,
the Welsh language is "partially known to all or most in the
places five or six miles to the westward"[15]. Indeed in 1826 a
reporter in the *Gwyliedydd* (Observer) wrote that "Radnorshire
can be proud of its vernacular as one of the most excellent
dialects of Wales. It seems that various refinements of Powys
(North-east Wales) and Deheubarth (South Wales) meet in this
estimable dialect". And Payne is a determined optimist: "A
couple of English people come here to live, and Welsh dies. A
Welshman or two buys a farm and the language revives".
Despite the fact that when the last speaker of Welsh in Glascwm
died in 1867 she had no-one to speak it to, he mainly dates the
loss of Radnorshire bilingualism to 1840-70[16]. By 1891 one in
sixteen Radnorians spoke Welsh. In every town and village he
details the Welsh-speakers listed in the 1961 census: few of them
native-born. He deplores the anglicizing 'cancer' corrupting
Welsh place names, so that Graig Pwll Du becomes Grapple
Dee.

Anglican clergy sometimes discouraged Welsh so that
English priests got the livings. But the Puritan sects in this
county were worse. Payne blames Nonconformity – so important in Welsh life over the past three hundred years – for the loss
of the language. For the Nonconformity of Radnorshire, unlike
that of any other Welsh county, was largely imported by the
English. When Englishmen brought the 'full salvation' to
Radnorshire this, unsurprisingly perhaps, turned out to entail
speaking English. Radnorshire was the field of work of self-
satisfied missionaries with no love for Welsh[17] who indeed
regarded it as a hindrance to salvation. Payne accordingly
enjoys some good jokes at the expense of Nonconformity,
reporting one local explaining of the closed doors of a Quaker
meeting-house: "Well, they do say it's to keep the devil out…
but, I do say it's to keep the blighter in".

Payne catches local speech well. One old boy, of the generation Payne records as dressing in knee breeches, polished
leather leggings, tweed jacket and felt hat, is asked, "Are you
Mr. Williams?" After a silence Payne hears the traditional
watchful answer, "Well, – maybe". Followed by the usual
perplexing confession, "And if not, who I wonder?" None of
the old people claim their name without cautious pronounce-
ment first. And asking another countryman if he knows who
Twm Bach was he hears the typical figurative understatement:
"Well, he was a bit before my time".

He is not entirely a Luddite. True he detested the sterility,
poverty and rootlessness of the Ebbw Vale lodgings he rented in
1916, missing the happy bustle of colourful, unsophisticated
Kington, where he knew nearly two thousand people. And
modernisers are his enemies: Victorian worshippers of
pinewood and varnish who vandalised medieval churches; roads
designed to connect a far-off factory to some invisible port:
roads should be for meeting in and exchanging gossip. He hates
"the wizardry of the TV box", transistor radios, petrol stations,
car parks; and also the closing of schools, smithies, workshops,
churches, chapels and pubs. Without these, community dies.

He hates ruins, discerning in them only "failure and sadness
and death". He sees the need equally for council houses, refor-
estation and modern roads, but wishes they could be less ugly,
and look as if they belonged where they are planted. He approves
of tractors. Above all else he despairs at the disappearance of a
world in which people had time for one another, and in which
stories and memories were shared and lasted for centuries. Only
such a lived sense of the past gives meaning to the present. Loss
of memory, for him, was real death. Payne was very struck that
a Radnorshire man called Pritchard was around 1870 able to
recount one entire day in the life of King Charles two centuries
before, from his breakfast in Brecon to his bed in Old Radnor.

> He pointed out in detail the length and size of the king's
> retinue of horsemen as they came in pairs through the parish.

The retinue stretched from Pen-faen farm in Cwm Milw down over this bridge and up the hill as afar as Blaencerdyn. It was a hot day in August, and the king was tired. So a chair was put out for him in Bryncerin farmyard so he could rest a little and the wife of the house, Mary Bayliss by name, brought out a jug of milk for him.

Payne was impressed that the chair and jug were still in the house, as he was also by the fact that at the beginning of the First World War you could still hear the same story in all its details. But by 1963 the old community had completely unravelled and, as in every other place through the country, people stayed by their own hearths, gazing fixedly at the television. His point is less the charm of the story itself, more the shock of losing a world in which shared stories survived for centuries. Without such a mutually valued past (which for Payne meant an idealised rural past) he felt that we have lost our way.

A fastidious man with a passionate and scholarly interest in tracing the history of rural Welsh folk-culture, he worked from 1936 for the National Museum of Wales, and after the war for the new Folk Museum. After retirement, he lived with his family at Llandegley on the southern side of the Radnor Forest. He rejoiced that the first and only National Eisteddfod ever to be held in Radnorshire was scheduled for 1993, though he died the year before. Through Payne's work some of the spirit of Glyndŵr's 'great century' may be said to live on.

1593-1695: The Paradise Within

For five centuries from Giraldus Cambrensis on, commentators noted the exceptional willingness of the Welsh to attend church. They thought nothing of travelling three or four miles or more in each direction on foot to attend public prayers, the need for devotion sometimes over-riding even the question of the style or denomination through which it was expressed.

This was still true in the seventeenth century: a golden age of spiritual writing with many poets exploring very different meanings within retreat – finding a quiet haven, escaping the enemy, living by religious discipline, and waiting for secret inner change. It remains a mystery that three great spiritual poets – Herbert, Vaughan and Traherne – flourished close to one another within the central Welsh March at this time, two Welsh, one English.

Speculating about this coincidence is hazardous. What influence being born within sight of the unruly English-Welsh border and close to one another might have had on Herbert,

Vaughan and Traherne is indeterminable: each presents a vision of human life as potentially harmonious, to contrast with worldly disorder. Each opposes to the world of change and suffering a vision of timeless joy and is concerned to show how to uncover "the paradise within". Their different journeys still have something to teach us. But to understand them we need to go back a century. The coming to power in London of the Tudors was greeted at first as a victory for Wales; and its long-term significance only later grasped more accurately, as a species of disaster.

★

The success of a Welsh dynasty in 1485 was taken by many as fulfilling ancient Arthurian prophecy and thus as ending history itself. A Venetian emissary wrote home that "the Welsh had regained their former freedom: the most wise and fortunate Henry VII is a Welshman", a view echoed by observers from both France and Scotland. Henry Tudor had spent fourteen childhood years in Wales, had a Welsh nurse called Joan, and liked when melancholy to be cheered by "Welsh rhymesters". His preferred written language being French, we have no evidence about how much Welsh he understood. Accounts show that those currying his favour sent him Welsh cheese and *metheglin*; he also kept Welsh harpists and bards whom he may have commissioned to seek out his pedigree. He raised Welsh troops for the battle of Bosworth Field by promising to deliver them from "miserable servitude". "Nowhere celebrated his accession with more joy [than Wales] in 1485, nor mourned his death more sincerely in 1509"[1]. That he celebrated St David's Day and named his oldest child Arthur did his case in Wales no harm at all: nor that he fought under the banner of the Red Dragon of Cadwaladr, which re-appeared soon after in the chapel of Kings College, Cambridge, the shrine to Tudor myth he founded. He soon used the same dragon prancing as supporter for the royal coat-of-arms.

All this provides the context for Ellis Gruffudd (c. 1490-c.

1556), Welsh chronicler of Tudor times and soldier living at Calais, who recounts an interesting legend of Owain Glyndŵr. Walking one morning on the Berwyn mountains, Glyndŵr meets the Abbot of Valle Crucis and greets him: "You are up betimes, Master Abbot"; to be answered, "Nay, Sire, it is you who have risen too soon: by one hundred years": the cause championed by Glyndŵr, purportedly sleeping in his cave awaiting the next call to arms, had – so it at first seemed – belatedly triumphed at Bosworth.

Henry was later believed (not necessarily reliably) to have charged his son and heir Henry VIII to take special care of 'his people' (i.e. the Welsh). In reality, as John Davies quips, Henry VIII and *his* children probably thought as much about their Welsh ancestry as Elizabeth II today reflects often on *her* descent from the house of Saxe-Coburg Gotha: such amnesia about origins is a feature, too, of the ambitious Welsh magnates who followed Henry and succeeded in London like him. The poet Lewys Glyn Cothi, possibly disillusioned with Henry VII, wrote "Life is still sad. The world is still hard".

Most saw the matter differently. Despite anti-Welsh laws staying on the statute book until 1624, Henry rewarded many kinsmen with high office. Welsh origins were now a commendation, not a source of suspicion, and the Welsh flocked to London, the court and the professions: so much so that the poet John Skelton quipped that you could quieten heaven, where everyone was being driven mad by the incessant babble of the newly-arrived Welsh, by having someone outside call out *Caws pobi* (toasted cheese or Welsh rarebit in Welsh) and then watch your new companions rush out to taste their favourite food and lock the doors behind them.

Presently Wales was 'shired', with twenty-seven new Welsh MPs making the journey to Westminster – it would be good to hear more of their pioneer experiences. The administration of Wales, as John Davies puts this, was being given back to the Welsh gentry to whose interests the Union was "vastly favourable". Soon the newly Reformed Church of England needed the old Celtic church of Wales, claimed to have been founded by Joseph of Arimathea, as a legal precedent for a British Christianity independent of Rome. A famous translation of the Bible into Welsh was accordingly commissioned. Its importance for the survival of the language and the literacy of the Welsh people cannot be over-estimated.

Wales had new uses. One anglicised Welshman was John Dee (1527-1609) – seer, scientist, astrologer and alchemist. Only a few hundred yards from Owain Glyndŵr's battle-site is the gabled house where Dee's father – Rowland Bedo before he changed his surname to Dee – was born.[2] The themes of magic and the occult run right through the story of the Marches, and Dee has been named as the original of Shakespeare's white magician Prospero in *The Tempest*. Certainly Dee, despite his dislike of being thought a 'conjuror', was, among other professions, another Welsh magician: his Mortlake house was raided after he conversed with the spirits he sighted in an obsidian Aztec sacrificial mirror. Dee was useful as Arthurian theorist of British empire, writing to Elizabeth I – to justify her claims on Newfoundland – about the voyages King Arthur made in 530 AD towards the North Pole.

Shakespeare shows the Welsh in the roles of hot-headed yet impressive warrior claiming magical powers (Glendower), garrulous good-hearted soldier (Fluellen, a mis-hearing of Llywelyn) and pedagogical parson of eager simplicity and hot-headed goodness (Sir Hugh Evans in *The Merry Wives*), though not as school-master or lawyer, professions they also soon excelled at in London. Many Welsh distinguished themselves as courtiers: Elizabeth's Welsh lady-in-waiting Blanche Parry – cousin to John Dee – is buried in the Golden Valley. It is notable how sympathetically Shakespeare portrays Glyndŵr – "a worthy gentleman; exceedingly well-read... valiant as a lion and wondrous affable, and as bountiful as mines in India"[3]. This was a period when many Welsh gentry, like the English, learnt to speak in public of Glyndŵr as a traitor and a rebel[4]. There may have been understandable schizophrenia: Ben Jonson in 1618 reported that Welsh friends in private regarded Glyndŵr as a great hero.

Shakespeare's friendliness towards his Welsh characters is shared by others. A minor Jacobean play called *The Valiant Welshman* had it "...faire Wales her happy union had/Blest union that such happiness did bring". A remarkable study of stage representation of Celts – *Teague, Shenkin and Sawney* – demonstrates that most of thirty plays containing Welsh characters, written between 1592 and 1659, show an underlying kindliness towards and interest in the Welsh – unlike the Scots and Irish – at least on the London stage. The Welsh were the "most remote and strange of provincials" and simultaneously the "nearest and most intimate of foreigners". Represented as hot-headed or choleric, excitable and emotional, voluble, with much national and family pride as well as pride in gentlemanliness or caste, the Welsh in this period were liked, and not just by Shakespeare, all of whose Welsh characters (including the Welsh captain in *Richard III*) are sympathetic, individualised and never stock. And Ben Jonson, with the help of Welsh-speaking friends, as also of Rhys's *Welsh Grammar* (1592) learnt Welsh and put Welsh speeches into his masque *For The Honour Of Wales* (1618). A few plays by others also contain spoken Welsh.

*

Wales had become an 'internal colony', tolerated on condition it stayed subservient. The 'cause' of Wales, as of other small countries with powerful neighbours, flourishes in adversity. A period of assimilation like this was also a time of deliberate amnesia about local culture. If the Welsh at last were given a voice and vote in London this was at the cost of Welsh squires defecting to the English side and forgetting their own: for which the modern poet R.S. Thomas coined the eloquent phrase "Bosworth-blind". The gentry sped along the road to anglicisation; their hearths soon went cold towards those poets who continued to write in Welsh. Although he did find one last new poem in Welsh from Radnorshire as recently as 1826, Payne notes that the singing for the most part here fell silent by 1631. Of Pilleth Court in the later sixteenth century Bedo Hafesb wrote "And we, all we can do is lament/We poets, we go without dignity".

Two grand Elizabethan nobles were Welsh: the Lords Cecil began as Seisyllt, and still took pride in a partially Welsh descent, as did the Herberts or Lords Pembroke. All socially ambitious families are by definition in flight from humble origins, gentility being after all, as George Herbert mordantly observed, "nothing but ancient riches". This need not mean a London family necessarily forgot it came from Wales: John Donne was not alone in boasting a Welsh coat-of-arms, believing his family came from Kidwelly.

But advancement often meant slowly losing touch with Wales itself. The first Lord Pembroke spoke Welsh so well and English so badly that he was suspected of illiteracy. His son the second Earl was also a fluent Welsh speaker with much experience of Wales; indeed, described by a Welsh contemporary as *llygad holl Cymru* (the eye of all Wales). His son the third Lord Pembroke, William Herbert – according to many the dedicatee Mr W.H. of Shakespeare's *Sonnets* – was detested by the Earl of Northampton as a 'Welsh juggler'. Probably a stock insult, rather than imputing fluency in any language but English; but interesting that "Shall I compare thee to a summer's day?" might have been written to a Welsh-speaker....

Glanmor Williams calls these Herberts "the Hapsburgs of Wales", by which he means that they started out as unprincipled thugs. It is all the more striking that they produced in a cadet branch of the family the poet George Herbert (1593-1633), born in Montgomery, greatest of all religious poets of that age, arguably the best devotional poet in English in any age, and famous for a career that saw him first attracted by worldly ambition and vanity before turning away from both.

His admirer Ronald Blythe has written recently of the importance to Herbert of his origins in or near Montgomery Castle, placing emphasis on the Newports, his mother's

Shropshire family whose genealogy, however, also goes straight back to Prince Wenwynwyn of Northern Powys. In the March, writes Blythe, "one can sense Herbert in the air". Moreover, the Herberts kept their links with Montgomeryshire. When not abroad soldiering or conducting diplomacy his elder brother Edward divided his time between Montgomery and London, and indeed the poet John Donne, a family friend, is thought to have written 'Good Friday, 1613: Riding Westward' when on his way to visit Edward at Montgomery Castle.

George Herbert held the living of Llandinam from 1624 until his death; and was also MP for Montgomery in the 1624 parliament, effectively a family seat[5]. This was a parliament much concerned with the doings of the Virginia Company, in which many Herberts had an interest. It would be odd if George, during his time as MP, did not journey home to canvas those he represented: indeed Cambridge University senate released him from his duties as Orator for the relevant six months. But no evidence of him in Montgomeryshire at this time has yet come to light. And neither did the Llandinam living have any residential requirement. For such reasons, perhaps, he does not appear among the many writers of the Welsh March celebrated in Seren's distinguished Borderlines series, doubtless seeming too English.

Certainly the trajectory of his life took him far away from the March, first of all to the chief centres of power in England – Westminster School, where the great Anglican scholar Lancelot Andrewes preached; Trinity College Cambridge, his base from 1609, where King James I regarded Herbert as "the jewel of that University" and where he became Public Orator, giving official speeches in Latin on behalf of the University until 1626. Here Herbert agitated against the draining of the surrounding fens lest this cause the river Cam to dry up: in reality the unhealthy fenland climate shortened his life.

The post of Public Orator commonly led on to preferment, Herbert's two predecessors both becoming secretaries-of-state. Herbert, by contrast, on the return from Spain in war-like humour of Charles, then Prince of Wales, gave a famous and brave speech favouring peace, scuppering his chances. Worldly failure stimulated spiritual insight: Herbert understood that the role of 'gentleman' and that of 'Christian' are in tension one with the other.

So Isaak Walton's *Life* in 1670 famously depicted Herbert renouncing the "painted pleasures of the court" for a life of holiness as a quiet country priest instead. Walton's tale is decked out with picturesque details. Some are moving and convincing, like his love of making music; or Herbert during the long night before ordination glimpsed prostrate with humility in front of the church altar, struggling with his sense of unworthiness. Some of Walton's details, however, are invented and far-fetched, like his depiction of Herbert marrying Jane Danvers "three days after meeting her", when she was a close cousin of the handsome young step-father Herbert had known well for the previous twenty-one years[6].

Ordination took Herbert firmly within the orbit of his fourth cousin Lord Pembroke at Wilton. Belonging to the same great Anglo-Welsh clan they had many links and affiliations. Pembroke was "exceedingly beloved in the court", since unselfishly benign towards others. He was godfather to Herbert's nephew William, the rise of whose father Henry he assisted – Henry was knighted at Wilton, Pembroke's great house. John Aubrey, another engagingly unreliable gossip, says Herbert was one of Pembroke's chaplains: earls were entitled to a statutory five! It is likely that a few weeks before his death Pembroke requested Charles I to offer Herbert the small Bemerton living nearby – "if he think it worth his while", Charles remarked. There, as we know from his letters, he became a friend of Pembroke's sister-in-law Lady Anne Clifford, who wrote that she "gave herself to retiredness... and made good books and virtuous thoughts my companions". Both valued retirement or retreat.

Pembroke was just as much George's patron as Shakespeare's, helping Herbert when he could, donating £50 towards the renovation of Leighton Bromswold church – then doubling the sum when Herbert wrote him a witty and persuasive letter of thanks. (Herbert raised the astonishingly large sum of £2000: the church, still beautiful, is relatively unchanged.) John Donne belonged firmly within this coterie, a friend both to Lady Anne and to Herbert's mother Magdalen, of whose family Donne wrote that he "owed much". Her house was a "court, in the conversation of the best", where she kept a large retinue, and where Francis Bacon and the composer William Byrd might be found. Donne reported that she would exhort her ten children and dozen retainers to prayer saying, "For God's sake let's go". He wrote during her lifetime, "No spring, nor summer beauty hath such grace/As I have seen in one autumnal face" and during his funeral sermon on her life he spoke in praise of her "holy cheerfulness". Walton, happening to be in Chelsea parish church that day, observed Donne weeping.

Although certain critics now react against reading Herbert's life as other-worldly[7] this is partly based on seeing *all* religion as a dressing-up of special interests, nobody ever being any better than he should be. Thus to reduce the human scene diminishes the reader's freedom; and attractive as it might be to see the Herbert cult mainly in terms of nostalgia during the Puritan Commonwealth for the Anglican settlement, the truth is complex. Certainly Charles I, imprisoned in Carisbrooke Castle awaiting execution, read Herbert's *The Temple*. But *The Temple* was admired, too, by the regicide Sir John Danvers, Herbert's step-father, and then recommended too to Oliver Cromwell by his own chaplain!

The testimony of Herbert's peers counts also. His eldest brother Edward noted that Herbert was not exempt from "passion and choler, the infirmities to which all our race is subject", where 'our race' means the Herbert tribe or the Welsh, and probably both. But Edward then proceeds to describe Herbert's "holy and exemplary" final three years at Bemerton as "little less than sainted". Coming from a brother who was the second poet of the family and therefore in competition for laurels, this testimony warrants attention. Barnabas Oley in 1652 similarly wrote that Herbert "lost himself in an humble way".

Walton, who wrote the first life of Herbert, had only seen Herbert and never known him, but none the less had mutual friends in Donne and Wotton, to whom he must have listened. There is further evidence from Herbert's close friend and executor Nicholas Ferrar, who retired with relatives to the small community he founded at Little Gidding, made famous in our day by T.S. Eliot in the *Four Quartets*, and denounced by critics at the time as an "Arminian nunnery". And Herbert's surviving nineteen letters show, as well as a sense of the fragility of life, his concern for others suffering sickness or difficulty. Small wonder Henry Vaughan in 1655 wrote of "the blessed man George Herbert".

In *The Country Parson* Herbert emphasised the parson's humility, charity, prayer and patience, suggesting that sermons be less than one hour long (!), defining the best 'library' as a holy life: "Do well... and let the world sinke". His English poems were published posthumously by Ferrar, going rapidly into six editions. They present "a picture of the many spiritual Conflicts that have passed betwixt God and my Soul", and contain many voices, confident, troubled, mutinous, despairing and acceptant. These debate-poems dramatise exactly such a conflict between rebellion and surrender as Walton identified in Herbert's life. Aldous Huxley called them poems of "inner weather". And Blythe, seeing Herbert as the poet of gratitude, capable of a "terrifying lucidity", notes that, for all their trickery and cleverness, God is always present.

Of the three poets from the March described in this chapter, only Herbert travelled far from his roots to become an official spokesperson of the Church of England. Yet, like Vaughan and Traherne, he too is concerned with the naked travails of the spirit, its subjection to time and its intense longing for rest:

Grief melts away
Like snow in May,

As if there were no such cold thing.
Who would have thought my shrivel'd heart
Could have recover'd greennesse?

('The Flower')

★

Henry Vaughan (1621-95), a radiantly visionary poet, priest
and physician, was both Herbert's cousin and his apprentice.
Both were descended from the daughter of that "Davy Gam
esquire" (Dafydd ap Llewelyn) listed by Shakespeare as among
the dead at Agincourt and long considered a possible model for
Fluellen. She married first Roger Vaughan of Bredwardine, then
William Herbert. Vaughan declared that he owed his inspiration
to "George Herbert whose holy life and verse gained many
pious converts (of whom I am the least)".

Vaughan was born on Trenewydd farm in the parish of
Llansanffraed near Brecon, though his letters and prefaces
favour the English "Newton farm" and "St Bridgets". Since his
twin brother Thomas wrote that "English is a Language the
Author was not born to" and yet we know their father had a
command of English, they were evidently bilingual. Both went
to Jesus College, Oxford, long hospitable to the Welsh, and then
Henry to the Inns of Court. Such periods of study and one of
soldiering apart, Vaughan lived out his life in his native village,
where he is also buried.

Indeed, if Herbert's life can be read as a parable about the
Welsh nobleman in flight from his Marcher origins, Vaughan's
is equally typical of small Welsh gentry who stayed at home
there. The political turbulence of the Commonwealth impacted
on everyone. Radnorshire, where no fewer than five local farms
boast having accommodated the future Charles II, nonetheless
played its part in turning the Royalist Marches toward the
Puritan cause, with Vavasor Powell from Knucklas a key player,
and nearby Lady Brilliana Harley famously holding off the
Royalist troops from her Marcher castle by musket, and alone.

Vaughan lived some forty miles south, in Breconshire, where under Cromwell he had to give up his living as a priest, together with the income from this. He worked as a physician and shared with his twin brother Thomas, also a priest, but one who escaped for the metropolis, an abiding interest in hermetic philosophy. Thomas's eviction from his living is documented by conventional, unreliable charges against him as a "drunkard... swearer, no preacher, a whoremaster and in armes personally against Ye Parliemnt". Henry, in a 1673, letter seems to remember neither whether his brother got the degree of MA nor even where he is buried: the Vaughans were close but quarrelsome. None the less it might not have gratified Henry that his twin was mocked by Samuel Butler in *Hudibras,* nor that he was attacked by Jonathan Swift as a gibberish Welshman writing "most unintelligible fustian".

The Book of Common Prayer was for some years proscribed; so was its table of affinity and notorious prohibition against marrying one's deceased wife's sister. Henry Vaughan, after the death of his first wife Catherine Wise, duly married her sister Elizabeth. His numerous children from each marriage fought as we shall see for love and precedence.

Although Puritan Andrew Marvell wrote verses on the pleasures (sensuous as well as spiritual) of the retired life in pastoral surroundings, 'Retreat' was more often praised by Royalists and criticised by Puritan poets – most famously Milton, who scorned a virtue bred in the cloister and hence untested by life in the world outside[8]. In other words, religion was politics. And, while Herbert's interest in the idea of retreat came after worldly disappointment, retreat in Vaughan's work was a result of being on the losing side of the conflict.

Vaughan fought during the Civil War at the battle of Rowton Heath on the Royalist side (Wales, generally, started out Royalist). And Royalists like him found themselves excluded from office, unemployed. Thus his writings, making a virtue of necessity, idealise retirement. His attitude towards political struggle became one of "epicurean unconcern". He translated

Ovid banished to the Black Sea, and made much of the Horatian theme of gentlemanly contentment in retirement to one's estates. So among the works he translated are to be found *The Praise and Happinesse of the Countrie-Life, The World Contemned* and *The Mount of Olives or Solitary Devotions*.

His alienation from Cromwell's rule also produced his great visionary poetry, in love with silence and with solitude – celebrating the visionary in "I saw eternity the other night/ Like a great ring of pure and endless light" ('The World') and beautifully mourning the dead in "They are all gone into the world of light!/ And I alone sit lingering here / Their very memory is fair and bright/ And my sad thoughts doth clear". He communed with nature and with the unseen, and in him the theme of retirement deepens into the theme of necessary hiddenness.

So in the elegiac poem 'I Walked the Other Day', the poet represents himself as digging in winter in a place where he had once "seen the soil to yield/ A gallant flower,/ And there/ Saw the warm recluse alone to lie/Where fresh and green/He lived of us unseen". In 'The Night', moreover, where he finds within the hidden God Himself "a deep but dazzling darkness", the poet wishes to "live invisible and dim". Hiddenness links in Vaughan to possible future rebirth. His has been aptly called a spiritual response to a political situation, within which he asserts the unity of creation and the value of all creatures: "mustard seeds grow into great trees, or scattered seeds bring forth a hundredfold, in which, that is, hidden and apparently insignificant things grow to a greatness"[9].

"I professe I am no Englishman, neither would I be taken for such, though I love the nation as well as thy self," wrote his brother Thomas. Henry's expression, too, is influenced in various ways by his Welshness. The Usk runs through all his poetry, as Palgrave remarked, "with an undercurrent of peace and music": "Dear Stream! Dear bank, where often I/Have sate, and pleas'd my pensive eye" ('The Waterfall', II, 13-4) and he chose a Latinised version of 'Swan of Usk' as his nom de plume. His use of the word 'white' – *gwyn* in Welsh, where it connotes fair, happy, holy and blessed, and betokens one word for paradise itself – carries Welsh meaning into English. Thus he writes of "a white celestial thought", of "white days" of primeval innocence and "those white designs which children drive". He also uses para-rhyme, alliteration and assonance, mingling the rhythms, sound-patterns and diction of Welsh literature into English.

Among poetic devices particular to Welsh poetry is *dyfalu*, the piling up of sometimes fanciful or riddling analogies and comparisons, the better to concretise what is being evoked. Interestingly George Herbert, who probably had no Welsh, uses *dyfalu* in his well-known poem 'Prayer', a poem with scarcely any verbs or complete sentences, starting "Prayer the Churches banquet, Angels' age,/God's breath in man returning to his birth…" and ending "Church bells beyond the stars heard, the soul's blood,/The land of spices; something understood". And Vaughan's 'The Night' is another perfect example of *dyfalu*: "God's silent, searching flight:/When my Lord's head is fill'd with dew, and all/His locks are wet with the clear drops of night; /His still soft call;/His knocking time; The souls dumb watch, /When Spirits their fair kindred catch"[10].

Vaughan discussed the poetic fury of the Welsh poets in a letter to John Aubrey, telling the story of a poor Welsh foundling boy taken in by a wealthy neighbour, who put him to tending the sheep. One summer day, tired from shepherding, this lad fell asleep and dreamt of a beautiful laurelled stranger who set his hawk to fly into the boy's mouth; terrified and disturbed, he discovered his own poetic gift and soon became "the most famous Bard in the country" – Wales, as always, being a country highly prizing its poets, and this tale mingling poetry with natural magic in a traditionally Welsh manner.

Typical also of seventeenth-century Wales was a tradition of rancorous litigation. A high mortality rate meant second marriages were common, with ensuing tensions between step-siblings and rival heirs. Henry's father had been often in debt and twice arrested for it in the 1650s; and litigations concerning debt and theft also bedevilled his son Henry's seventh decade. His kinsman Aubrey famously described Vaughan as "proud and humorous", where the word 'humorous' takes its ancient meanings of capricious, whimsical, peevish, moody, or bad-tempered. And his long life duly ended in a pitiful and alarming mess of law-suits and family recrimination.

First there was a violent dispute with his eldest son, Thomas, who took possession of the family house in 1689, agreeing in return to provide both a lifelong annuity of £30 to his father, who had decamped to a convenient cottage, and payments of £100 to be divided between his half-brothers and sisters. Thomas, complaining that he had been duped by his step-mother into an arrangement that exploited him, refused to pay, was taken to court, then started proceedings against his own father, whom he accused, *inter alia*, of breaking, entering and stealing documents.

Then the court required Vaughan to pay his daughter Catherine, who had one lame hand burnt in infancy and also a disabled foot, half-a-crown per week through a third party. He preferred to humble her by direct payments himself, as also by occasional non-payments. She understandably filed a suit for maintenance. None of this reads prettily. The "absolute mercy of the poetry", as one of his biographers beautifully puts this, contrasts with the vicious retaliatoriness of Vaughan's actions[11]; or, as W.H. Auden put the matter, the works of poets are often "in better taste than their lives".

At the same time Vaughan's arrogant and puritanical longing for transcendence, his yearning for the better world that his poetry enshrines are perhaps given an unexpected imprimatur of authenticity. And so Sassoon, who wrote the sonnet 'At the Grave of Henry Vaughan', believed devoutly that "above the voiceful windings of a river... faith and mercy, wisdom and humility" still shone.

★

Thomas Traherne (1637-74), the Englishman of this trio, lived out much of his life in Credenhill near Hereford, where both English and Welsh were spoken. As late as 1800 some in the village of Yazor four miles away spoke Welsh. And Traherne would certainly have heard both languages: Nehemiah Wharton, a subaltern in one of the parliamentary forces occupying Hereford during the Civil War, commented that "Many here speake Welsh"; some Welsh speakers in the city were traders visiting the market. Others were residents[12]. The hills of Wales can be seen from the church at Credenhill where Traherne became Rector. Here was another place on the border.

A "radiant if sometimes facile" mystic, alternately reclusive and sociable, whose work is popularly thought to pre-figure Wordsworth's[13], Traherne fought first as an officer in the local Royalist militia, later showing moderate Puritan sympathies and associating with nonconformists[14]. He was "so wonderfully transported with the Love of God to Mankind", one anonymous acquaintance recalled, that "those that would converse with him, were forced to endure some discourse upon these subjects, whether they had any sense of Religion, or no". In other words he could be a bit of a bore. Indeed he noted of his own character that "Too much openness and proneness to Speak are my Disease". His writings, however, are never dull, with their subversive command to enjoy life. And this unique voice was nearly lost to us. That we have it at all is a kind of miracle.

Before 1896 Thomas Traherne was virtually unknown. Since that date no fewer than five manuscripts have surfaced. The first two, consisting of his poems and of *Centuries of Meditation*, were purchased by the same scholar for a few pence from two separate book-barrows, one in Whitechapel, the other on the Farringdon Road, during the same winter of 1896-7, laid aside for investigation "at a more convenient season"[15] and at first mis-ascribed to Vaughan. Then in 1967 the previously unknown *Commentaries of Heaven* was snatched from a burning rubbish tip in south Lancashire. The tight twentieth-century binding had been slightly damaged by fire, but the contents were in perfect condition, legible throughout. In 1997 a long previously unattributed poem of 1800 lines bound in seventeenth-century calf and with the remains of metal clasps, entitled *The Ceremonial Law*, in the Folger Library in Washington DC, turned out unequivocally to be in Traherne's hand.

In the same year – 1997 – another scholar working in the library in Lambeth Palace discovered under an entry marked simply 'Theology' yet another very important manuscript. The title of the second of its five treatises, 'Seeds of Eternity', suggested Traherne's authorship, since corroborated. The following words had been written in an unknown hand on the inside flyleaf: "Why is this soe long detained in a dark manuscript, that if printed would be a light to the World and a uniuseral Blessing?" The words resonate today with new meaning.

Thus has Traherne's very name been snatched from oblivion. It is by any standards an astonishing tale, far stranger than fiction. No doubt other parts of Britain have their own chronicles of manuscripts lost and found. Yet this phenomenon of disappearance beyond the borderline of the discernible is poetically apt in the Marches, where rapid mists alternately obscure and then reveal what was hidden. The miraculous rediscovery of Traherne's poems points to a border between 'lost' and 'found', hidden and revealed, dark and light. And in his extant poetry he expresses at length the wish to be lost, dissolved into God's heaven, thereby crossing the border-line between the here-and-now and the beyond. Perhaps further Traherne manuscripts will come to light in future. It is entirely possible.

Unlike Vaughan, Traherne never yearns for a better world: this one is enough for him. His certainty that happiness can be found in the here-and-now makes him attractive to Buddhists, as to pagans. Even as a child Traherne longed for an "unknown happiness" and complained at Oxford there was no tutor who "did expressly teach felicity". He quotes from Herbert's poetry in his Commonplace Book, and in *Commentaries of Heaven*, where he refers to him as "the Divine poet Herbert". He also copied Herbert's 'To All Angels and Saints' into his *Church's Year-Book*.

Yet Traherne's poetry is quite unlike anyone else's; and the this-worldly joy in his devotional prose works still has much to teach us. Though, too, he celebrates his "angel infancy" and writes of having been taught on growing up "the dirty devices of the world", it is the purity of the world and not its corruptions to which he – again and again – returns. "Never was anything in this world loved too much; but many things have been loved in a false way, and all in too short a measure." That is wonderfully said. Habit, he felt, dulled perception; which, being refreshed, shows us ordinary magic, the miraculous beauty of the everyday; and love itself was the key to unlocking all these secrets. "You never enjoy the world aright till the sea itself floweth in your veins, till you are clothed with the heavens and crowned with the stars, and perceive yourself to be the sole heir of the whole world...."

Of Traherne's part of Herefordshire John Masefield wrote: "Whenever I think of Paradise, I think of parts of this country; for I know no land more full of the beauty and bounty of God". But Thomas Traherne went to London around 1667 and probably never saw Herefordshire again. He became chaplain to Orlando Bridgeman, leading what one observer called a "single and devout life", in his own words "disentangled from all the world". He died in 1674, saying he had not so much but that he could leave it "by word of mouth" – his best hat to his brother in Smyrna, his property on Widemarsh Street to the corporation of Hereford for use as almshouses. He is buried in Teddington.

When the news reached home he was eulogised as "one of the most pious ingenious men" and as "...of a cheerful and sprightly Temper... ready to do all good Offices to his Friends, and Charitable to the Poor almost beyond his ability". And unlike certain eulogies, this one had the ring of truth.

18 January 1766:
Rousseau and Radnorshire

In 1697, just after Traherne's death, Wales was still slandered as "the World's backside, where every Man is born a Gentleman and a Genealogist"[1]. One hundred years later all the Romantic writers except for Keats visited – Southey, Coleridge, Wordsworth, Shelley, de Quincey, Peacock, and Landor fell variously in love with their idea of Wales: it was suddenly fashionable. Wordsworth in 1791 even found himself quarrelling about the respective virtues of the Welsh and English languages with a Welsh pastor, who drew a knife on him. What caused so dramatic a change? Just when Wales starts to serve as crucible of the industrial age, its history and scenery are revalued.[2] The connexion between Scotland and Romanticism is well-known: that with Wales deserves to be.

The crucial figure is Jean-Jacques Rousseau (1712-78), who had followers on both sides of Offa's Dyke. Rousseau invented modern subjectivity; he furthered a new view of landscape and an idealization of the peasant, and he favoured the underdog. Rousseau lies behind the cults of simplicity and of "unchanging backwardness" linked to a radical critique of modernity. He urged nationalism as the cure-all for the troubles of Poland, and what was good for the Poles might also be good for the Welsh. Perhaps it also owes something to Rousseau that the Romantic appropriation of Wales was sometimes so lazy, self-centred and narcissistic.

★

On the 18 January 1766 Jean-Jacques Rousseau received an invitation to settle in Radnorshire. Despite a settled dislike of England and the English, he had just arrived in London, accompanied by his little dog Sultan, and shortly afterwards by his mistress, the Parisian scullery-maid Therese Le Vasseur. He was in flight from absolutist France, where a warrant had been issued for his arrest as an enemy of the state. In his native Geneva the city Council had burned his *The Social Contract* (1762), and, after the local pastor called him Anti-Christ, villagers stoned his house. The Scots philosopher David Hume offered to accompany him from Paris and to share rooms off the Strand. Rousseau arrived wearing a strange furry hat and Armenian kaftan to disguise the fact he went about without breeches: a costume he affected in part because of urological troubles, but which inspired wry comment ("very silly", thought Lady Bunbury).

The invitation to Radnorshire issued from a freedom-loving Tory MP and deputy Lieutenant of the county, Chase Price (1731-77), an admirer of Rousseau who called at Buckingham Street in person to persuade him to settle in the former mansion of the Prices at Monaughty, near Knighton. Price, Receiver of Customs Fines, was involved in many business transactions, some dodgy, and frequently insolvent: a man of quixotic temperament. Hume, concerned about his living so far from 'civilization' in a landscape so remote, without occupation, friends or books, put obstacles in Rousseau's way; but in fact it was wildness, 'savagery' and isolation that attracted Rousseau. "Exactly what I want," he wrote excitedly that day to a friend.[3] The prospect of having nobody to converse with but wild mountain goats – one observer quipped – accorded very well with his philosophy.

The newspapers soon reported that "this learned citizen of Geneva, and writer of several spirited works, is so desirous of retirement that he has prevailed on his friends here, that he may go down to Radnorshire in Wales, to board and lodge with a farmer who lives in a mansion house of a worthy gentleman of that county". Like so many of his English followers with which this chapter is concerned, Rousseau was hungry for Wales.

He partly wanted to escape lionization in London. The Duke of York, the Prince of Brunswick, the Keeper of the Reading Room of the British Museum and many others, all wanted to meet one of the most famous writers and sages of his age. King George III and Queen Charlotte took trouble to arrange to 'quiz' Rousseau at Drury Lane theatre through their eyeglasses; after which the actor Garrick gave a big literary supper. Oliver Goldsmith, who was present, thought Rousseau hated one half of mankind. His list of aversions was indeed generous: theatres, courts, assemblies, books, learned and brilliant women, academies and doctors.

Rousseau, with his ostentatious cult of the simple life that would have such revolutionary and long-lasting impact, longed to escape to the quiet of the country. On 20 January Price wrote that at Monaughty Rousseau would be protected as effectively from the "oppression and prejudice of mankind as from their impertinence and curiosity". Price understood his needs well: solitude, independence and the simplicity of Radnorshire manners would, he promised, atone there for any want of polish and proper cultivation. Price's sitting-tenant, a rich farmer, together with his "clean and industrious" wife, was instructed to "prepare some apartments"[4]. Rousseau was to expect news within a fortnight. He would moreover pay a mere £30 annually for his and Therese's board and lodging, a sum discreetly calculated on his behalf by the careful Hume. In fact Rousseau was skilful at getting to know a long sequence of great patrician landowners wherever he found himself, and procuring favours. But it was part of his philosophy never to show gratitude or to be beholden to anybody. These were matters of high moral principle.

Monaughty, deriving from Mynachdy or monk's house, was once a grange in the Abbey lands of Cwmhir, where the last Abbot may have retired at the time of the Dissolution. The present building – largest and most elaborate of all stone-built manorial hall-houses in Radnorshire – is early Elizabethan. It has wings, storeys, grand fireplaces, and its Great Chamber with impressive floor-plaster ceilings is splendid and lofty: the upper-dais was painted both with the royal coat of arms and the arms of the President of Council of the Marches while its panelled screens bore the arms of the Price family. There was an abundance of ancient armour, helmet, breastplate and twelve nine-foot halberds. A dungeon or condemned hole survived for convicts: the house had served in a judiciary capacity.

The Prices also owned neighbouring Pilleth Court. To get Monaughty ready for Rousseau and Therese evidently involved work and negotiation. Meanwhile Rousseau, weary of the social round and "black vapours" of London, soon moved out to lodge with a grocer in Chiswick, where he began what turned out to be a three-month wait for the forthcoming move to Wales. Boswell tried to interest him in his native Scotland, but, while answering diplomatically, Wales remained the lode-star: three letters from Rousseau to Price communicate the urgency of his desire to escape there. On 16 February Rousseau wrote that he found waiting hard to bear. London bored him to death: "Alas that the years have altered only my features, while inside an aged body I still keep the impatience of a boy". Price apologized for the delay by sending Rousseau a present of *gibier* or hung game, and, since this would feed four, probably amounted to a haunch of venison.

Radnorshire could scarcely have wished for a more distin-guished visitor, or for a more trying one. Rousseau was good at making enemies, even among those who had never met him. Samuel Johnson, who neither knew Rousseau, nor wished to, remarked soon after Rousseau's arrival that he should be deported to the colonies "like a common felon". Voltaire, who also never met Rousseau, claimed that, with Rousseau, God had answered his sole prayer: that his enemies should be made ridiculous. Rousseau was indeed lacking in any sense of humour, subject to soul-storms, to making himself ill with chagrin, and perceived by some as a monster of ingratitude, eaten up by vanity and conceit. His manner was a combination of obsequiousness and effrontery, of craving for sympathy and affection and rejecting either if offered. By October of that same year he and Hume were the deadliest of enemies, denouncing one another in print. Perhaps Rousseau loved solitude in part because he quarrelled with old friends.

In the discarded portion of a 1765 letter Boswell supplied another reason for Rousseau's cult of solitude. He compared Rousseau to a child hiding behind window curtains pretending to be invisible. Boswell meant that all Rousseau did, including renouncing society, was done for effect and badly required the worldly audience that Rousseau affected to hold in contempt: retreat, in other words, was his way of sulking.

Both his *The Social Contract* and his treatise on education – *Emile* – were hugely influential; we live with their legacy today. The turning away from cities, money, manufacture and so-called 'progress', towards an idealization of the Simple Life (Going Back to Nature); the valuing of emotion and sentiment above reality or reason; the assertion of the freedom of the individual (albeit together with a glorification of state power); the nationalism he urged as a panacea, among others, on the Poles; the cult of the Noble Savage and the related rejection of Original Sin: all these are with us yet.

"The good man lives in society; only the wicked live alone", a contemporary wrote[5]. But Rousseau reversed the truism: society was corrupt and solitude was good. En route for London he had taken refuge for two months on an isolated island – St Pierre on the Bielersee in Canton Berne – leaving behind worldly concerns, bothering to unpack neither cases nor books. He had a trap-door through which he could escape visitors. He later recorded the joy of melting, as it were, into the system of beings, and identifying himself ecstatically with the whole of nature in his *Day-dreams of a Solitary Walker*[6], the first book in French to use the word 'romantic' of landscape:

> Everything on earth is in a continual flux – nothing stays constant or fixed... But there is one state where the soul finds a solid enough seat to rest and gather in all its being, with no need to recall the past or to press on to the future; a state where time is nothing, where the present lasts forever, with no mark of duration or trace of succession.... This is the state in which I often found myself..."

Jane Austen was satirizing Rousseauisms when she made the absurd Mrs Elton in *Emma* plan strawberry-picking while riding on a donkey; or the foppish Tilney in *Northanger Abbey* announce that all he needed to be happy was a modest little cottage seating forty for luncheon; or Lucy Steele in *Sense and Sensibility* employing a rhetoric of the heart to disguise spite and treachery. Though his political legacy is complex, his enemies remember that it was Rousseau's ideas about freedom and equality that Marat was studying while sentencing thousands to death on the guillotine.

By 15 March Rousseau's patience was exhausted. He explained to Price that, tired out by the waiting, he had decided to forgo the invitation to live at Monaughty, and to move to Wootton Hall in Staffordshire instead. Here, in a mood of growing paranoia, he started writing his *Confessions*, spending afternoons botanising in the nearby Derbyshire Peaks. And he was never to visit Wales or celebrate its heroic and 'primitive' virtue.

But the Romantic ideas which Rousseau pioneered arrived in Wales without him, including the cult of solitude, passionate nature-worship and the discovery of the beauty of mountains.

Fifty years before, Daniel Defoe, who commended the wool, hops and cider of the Radnor/Hereford border, went on to bemoan the horrid awfulness of the barren Welsh mountains beyond: even worse, he complained, than the Alps or Andes. Sensitive travellers were advised to draw down the blinds of their carriage, so as not to be discomposed by the barbarity of Welsh scenery.

But now barbarity – renamed as 'sublime' and 'picturesque' – was 'in'. Rousseau helped. He wrote of mountains that there you leave "all terrestrial sentiment behind... finding yourself in a new world... one isolated in the higher realms of the earth... there is a kind of supernatural beauty in these mountain prospects which charms both the senses and the mind into a forgetfulness of oneself and of everything in the world". The history of taste was undergoing the so-called Romantic revolution with whose consequences we still live. Horror and beauty were no longer opposed, and wild country, bog or mountain sought out, solitude and waste the new aesthetic values, ruins and grave-yards more aesthetic than villages. The presence of a solitary farmstead on an abrupt and wild hill, inhabiting, as it were, its own kingdom, is very typical of the mid-March; its capacity to delight us today belongs within this new sensibility.

Such ideas were timely and contagious. There were eighty tours of Wales published between 1770 and 1815, a time when war with France made foreign travel difficult. The best is Thomas Pennant's in 1781 which champions Glyndŵr and records one wild Merionethshire mountain squire eating hung goat and drinking home brew from a dried bull's scrotum while rehearsing his own pedigree back to the Welsh princes. Pennant – an acute observer, naturalist antiquarian, and Welsh patriot – knew well that he was a survivor from an almost vanished past. Few Welsh grandees supported native traditions.

Until 1815 Wales was the nearest place an exotic culture and history could be experienced; and every ruin of a Welsh castle or abbey, each Welsh mountain peak, had tourists "stalking round them"[7]. One English cleric was asked by a Welshwoman whether he did not have rocks and waterfalls in his own country. An 1833 edition of a famous Welsh grammar was augmented by new phrases like "I long to see the Monastery [or water-fall]": Welsh scenery and history were being immortalized in the tours, in the paintings of Richard Wilson and Thomas Jones of Pencerrig, the Radnorshire painter, among the greatest of Welsh artists. And also by English poets, this chapter's main topic.

★

Most Romantic writers made some connection with Wales. Even Scott once took his inspiration from there, writing *The Betrothed* in 1825 against the backdrop of border conflicts between Anglo-Norman and Welsh barons. Earliest was scholarly Thomas Gray (1716-71), famous for his 'Elegy Written in a Country Churchyard', who turned his mind for five years to studying Welsh poetry. This enriched the composition of his ode, 'The Bard', completed in May 1757 and prompted by a wildly successful visit to Cambridge by the blind Welsh John Parry, harpist to Frederick Prince of Wales and friend of Handel, who "set all this learned body a'dancing". (Not long afterwards George IV would employ his own Welsh harpist, Edward Jones, also a great propagandist of Welsh native music and customs; and the future Queen Victoria would attend the great 1832 Eisteddfod with her mother.)

'The Bard' is based on the unfounded story that Edward I burnt at the stake five hundred Welsh bards for refusing to praise him, while the song chosen instead by these martyred poets drives the cruel tyrant-King to madness. 'The Bard' was painted four times – once by Thomas Jones of Pencerrig. In reality only Welsh *books* were burnt in London. 'The Bard' thus melodramatises the role of the poet as defiant martyr and lonely brave truth-teller: roles Romantic poets aped. They too saw the Poet as alienated yet heroic, an essential truth-teller and creator of cultural coherence: the massacre of the Welsh bards was even used in a great patriotic poem in Magyar, János Árány's *A Walesi Bárdok* in 1857. 'The Bard' made Welsh history romantic.

The romanticising of Welsh scenery followed. The cult of the picturesque begins on the Radnorshire/Herefordshire border, where two remarkable neighbours each inherited estates at the age of fourteen, both travelling in Italy and both becoming Whig MPs. Uvedale Price (1747-1829), descendant of a Radnorshire County Registrar, at Credenhill where Traherne lived, and Richard Payne Knight (1751-1824) at nearby Downton created a set of influential working principles for gardeners, architects and travellers.

Price's *Essay on the Picturesque*[8] idealises a landscape neither wild nor tame, like much of Radnorshire, "flourishing, populous, domesticated and need[ing] to be worked". Price condemned the improving landowner who isolated himself from his tenantry, employing gardeners like Capability Brown, who worked in the March but without local roots: Brown re-created an idealised parkland wherever he landed, regardless of local tradition. Price by contrast believed that if the landowners instead maintained their links, socially and economically, with their tenantry, making gardens that expressed this sense of connection, Britain could escape the horrors of the French Revolution. He published such ideas in Hereford in 1797[9], on the occasion of the French landing on the Pembrokeshire coast.

Thomas Love Peacock (1785-1866) in *Headlong Hall* (1816) mocked Welsh squires and their English visitors for romanticising the Welsh landscape and for their schemes of 'improvement': Sir Patrick O'Prism represented Price, and Mr Milestone represented the landscape gardener and ally of Brown, Humphrey Repton, who re-designed three Welsh gardens.

Peacock's own love-affair with Wales began at twenty-five. A devoted solitary, he visited Tremadoc – then a hamlet of seven dwellings – for a short stay in 1810 and was so enchanted he had his books and clothes sent on. He wandered the dense oak-woods that covered the hillsides, watched the clear streams, sought out waterfalls, and soon ventured rock-climbing by moonlight, a foolhardy enterprise endangering the life of his companion and future father-in-law the parson John Gryffydh, with whose daughter Jane he fell in love. He ascended Cader Idris and left a notable account, following this with a night-walk to Machynlleth.

For almost fifteen months he lodged at Tan-y-bwlch in the Vale of Ffestiniog, which he called "a terrestrial paradise", developing a strong attachment to the Welsh landscape and a lasting interest in Welsh traditions[10]. Although Peacock's friend Shelley reported him as a loner, he by other accounts loved to share his enjoyment of life with all around him.

A perceptive commentator on the intellectual life of his time, Peacock's comic fictions stand outside the main traditions of the English novel, like Huxley's later, offering little by way of plot or character development. Three have Welsh settings: *Headlong Hall* (1816) – though it has been claimed for Radnorshire – in the Vale of Llanberis; *Crotchet Castle* (1831) partly in Merioneth. By the time he wrote *The Misfortunes of Elphin* (1829) he had read some ancient Welsh literature, his wife having access to the original Welsh. Arthur and Taliesin accordingly feature. He freely adapted old Welsh songs and is best recalled for his own 'War Song of Dinas Vawr': "The mountain sheep are sweeter/ But the valley sheep are fatter;/ We therefore deem'd it meeter/ To carry off the latter". He married a Welshwoman and hoped to do for Wales what Scott had done for Scotland. Peacock treated friend and foe alike as figures of fun: although Wales and its scenery alone are exempt from mockery, the Welsh backdrop of his novels is rarely more than a stage set.

★

In 1794 Coleridge visited Wales. An odd connection has been mooted between a famous Coleridge poem and Wales. Under the influence of his cousin Richard Payne Knight, Thomas Johnes, sometime MP for Radnorshire, built in 1785 the Gothic mansion of Hafod in Cardiganshire, creating a famous garden according to 'picturesque' principles. This involved a massive programme of renovation of estate cottages and farms, the planting of five million trees, and the encouraging of 'improving' farmers from East Lothian to settle nearby.

The Hafod was a symmetrical classical house with Gothic ornamentation that complemented the romantic qualities of the setting, where Johnes studied medieval French chronicles. Above all there was a celebrated octagonal library by John Nash, with famous Moorish, oriental features.

In July 1794 Coleridge found himself in Cardiganshire on a walking tour of Wales with a friend, a trip during which he wrote 'On Bala Hill'. Geoffrey Grigson has suggested that the natural route Coleridge would have taken between Devil's Bridge and Tregaron would have been across the Hafod parklands, where the outlandish domed library with its Moorish decorations may have started off a train of fancy[11]. The stately pleasure-dome, the gardens bright with sinuous rills, the deep chasm which slanted down the green hill athwart a cedarn cover: the entire enchanted vision might have lodged in his memory and helped inspire the creative trance three years later, brought on by two grains of opium to mitigate a tummy-upset, during which he penned a remarkable poem: 'Kubla Khan'. The house and library, with its irreplaceable collections of Welsh manuscripts, were accidentally destroyed by fire in 1807, then rebuilt in 1810.

Wales fed Wordsworth's imagination, too. In 1791 he had found himself quarrelling about the respective virtues of the Welsh and English languages with a proudly nationalistic Welsh parson. Evidently Wordsworth's ignorance of Welsh – like that of so many English people – did not for a second prevent his pontificating. The Welsh parson, perhaps in his cups – we have only the poet's account – drew a knife, threatening, insulting and alarming him considerably. He described the incident forty years later, smiling condescendingly at the natives, never understanding that he, Wordsworth, was perceived equally as foreign[12]. But Wales mattered to him.

The climax of *The Prelude* is the ascent of Snowdon, in reality – though the poem never says so – accomplished at night.

And the greatest of all his shorter poems is his *Lines Written a Few Miles above Tintern Abbey*, set in the Wye valley and conveying the idea that "all which we behold/ Is full of blessings".

Wordsworth visited the March on eleven occasions. Between 1809 and 1825 his brother-in-law Tom Hutchinson owned the Hindwell Farm near Presteigne after which he moved to Brinsop Court near Hereford. In 1817 Tom also acquired the secluded farm of Gwerndyfnant near Gladestry, where he lodged an elderly aunt, Broadheath near Presteigne and Allt-y-corryn near Glascwm. Wordsworth's first visit to Hindwell in 1809 took four days from Grasmere, He had to shelter in rain atop a stage-coach under an umbrella: his last journeys to Herefordshire were, of course, by train. His 1824 visit lasted a month.

The view from the windows on first arrival was "truly delightful"; he loved the stillness of the pool especially in evenings and by moonlight. His sister also: "You could hardly believe it possible for anything but a lake to be so beautiful as the pool before this house," wrote Dorothy in 1814. "It is perfectly clear and inhabited by multitudes of geese and ducks, and two fair swans keep their silent and solitary state."

The Wordsworths and Hutchinsons were evidently close. When Wordsworth suffered the death of a second child, his Hindwell relatives hoped he might even move to Radnorshire: instead he went to Rydal Mount. And in 1817 Sarah Hutchinson, sister to Wordsworth's wife Mary, but also a member of his household, thought the road to Hindwell from Hereford, with the Welsh mountains behind it, more beautiful than anything on earth: nowhere was so "beautifully wooded as this".

He visited Uvedale Price on three occasions[13]: Price and he collaborated on a quarry garden at Coleorton, Leicestershire. The March stimulated poetry too. 'We are Seven' was written at Goodrich: fifty years later he returned and tried to trace the little girl who inspired that poem but didn't know her name; 'Peter Bell' was inspired by a tinker Wordsworth met between

Builth Wells and Rhaeadr, who beat his donkey to death in frustration and later repented. Wordsworth celebrated many such picturesque unfortunates – a discharged soldier, a blind man, an idiot boy, a leech-gatherer – who taught him about the pathos, dignity and mystery of man and mirrored his own inner solitude too. In 1870 Francis Kilvert learnt that Wordsworth "resembled an old shepherd with rough rugged weather-beaten face and... a perfectly independent mind", that he cared for no one else's opinion and thought the Wye above Hay the greatest scenery in southern Britain.

The young Thomas de Quincey (1785-1859) was deeply impressed by both Coleridge and Wordsworth: their *Lyrical Ballads* had comforted him in depression. Although for many years too shy to press an encounter, he nursed a continuing hope he might one day meet them. On 20 July 1802, not yet quite seventeen, he absconded from Manchester Grammar, a school which was supposed to prepare him for Oxford, but which bored him instead. He started walking and in Chester the following day presented himself at his mother's home, who granted him an allowance to set off on an indefinite walking tour of Wales. He slept often at Welsh-speaking inns and cottages where the harp accompanied traditional songs.

He was to 'drop out' and live a vagabond life, early on visiting Miss Ponsonby and Lady Eleanor Butler, the unconventional 'Ladies of Llangollen', who had eloped from aristocratic homes in Ireland to live together in what amounted to a marriage, in a cottage by a major staging post between England and Ireland. Some assume it was their unorthodox liaison that attracted so many famous visitors. In fact they were passionate Rousseau-lovers, living out exactly the poetic ideal of pastoral retirement he advocated, dutifully wearing Welsh countrywoman's riding habits and beaver hats. Wordsworth, Southey, Mrs Thrale and Sir Walter Scott were among those celebrating them as a paradigm of devoted friendship and romantic Rousseau-istic retirement.

De Quincey was sent one guinea a week to live on. At first

this procured him a bed and "some apology for a supper". You could still find old village inns serving a dinner for sixpence – sometimes good fresh trout – albeit occasionally he shared the dining-room with pigs or poultry and the bed with fleas. But, as he wrote, "under the great revolution of the times.... War prices had arisen in the great markets; a great influx of tourists and artists has begun to set in to the Welsh valleys". Elegant new hotels were now to be found, with matching prices: dinner at Tal-y-llyn went up over eight weeks from sixpence to three shillings.

His money easily exhausted, he took to bivouacking in a tiny portable tent, its pole his walking-cane, fearful of being trampled by mountain cattle. In fine weather the tent could act as a wind-break, while he slept under the stars. No longer writing home, subsisting on blackberries, hips and haws, camping out for weeks in a solitary farmhouse, he was taken in by a kind, intelligent family with seven good-looking children whom he paid for his stay by favours-in-kind. For the son who had served on a man-of-war he wrote a business letter; for two daughters, one very beautiful, he penned delicate love-letters.

Finally, penniless, hungry and fearful of being caught up with by guardians, he broke off communication with his family. He found a Welsh friend who helped him set out for London with a scheme to borrow £200 "against his expectations". At Oswestry he slept in solitary splendour in the ballroom of an inn undergoing repairs, four servants lighting his way there with candles. All these experiences evidently left fond memories. In 1815, he walked right across Wales once more, from Cardiff to Bangor, revisiting scenes of his childhood wanderings. By now he was borrowing Rousseau's famous and scandalous confessional mode to write as a visionary drug-user; and Wordsworth had introduced him to Robert Southey (1774-1843).

Southey had spent ten years writing an epic poem about the civilising mission of the Welsh in the New World. *Madoc* (1805) chronicles the legend that America had been discovered three hundred years before Columbus by a Welsh Prince fleeing English tyranny in 1170, thus planting in the New World a freedom-loving Welsh-speaking tribe. Though admired by Scott, Wordsworth and Landor, *Madoc* has recently been called, not unfairly, both "interminable and intolerable"[14]. Its real interest is Rousseau-istic and cultural: Southey and Coleridge planned a Utopian community on the banks of the Susquehanna – or, failing that, in Wales itself. The legends of *Madoc* fitted such fantasisings precisely. They prompted considerable Welsh emigration[15] and at least one young Welsh enthusiast – John Evans of Waunfawr – lost his life, destitute in New Orleans in 1799 trying to find Madoc's surviving tribe while Southey was composing his epic.

★

Two romances with Wales went awry. Shelley made notable visits. He came on 9 July 1811, aged eighteen, newly sent down from Oxford for atheism and shaken by a break with his father, to recover in a peaceful house and valley belonging to his first cousin, Thomas Grove, and his wife Harriet, Shelley's erstwhile love. Grove, twenty-seven, who owned much land in Wiltshire, also farmed 10,000 acres at Plas Cwm Elan near Rhaeadr. The Shelley connexion went back two generations. Although there is little evidence of him visiting, Shelley's grandfather was high sheriff of Radnorshire and JP[16] in 1784; and Shelley's uncle had bought Cwm Elan from Thomas Johnes of the Hafod in 1792. The Groves made an annual summer visit to Radnorshire of about three months.

Shelley spent four weeks in the elegant, recently rebuilt four-storeyed mansion whose beauty and solitude made a deep impression. "I do not see a soul," he wrote. He was working out his system of radicalism, crudely influenced by Rousseau, and investigating the "conditions of the peasantry". One morning while dressing he overheard a Welsh beggar at the kitchen door pleading for bread. This doubtless reminded Shelley of the noble romantic Solitaries who populate Wordsworth's verse and Shelley pursued the beggar for a mile "asking a thousand questions" until the tired and mistrustful unfortunate begged

Shelley in return to leave him alone. Shelley blamed the church and the aristocratic system alike for the barbarous inequalities of the age.

He was already planning to elope with sixteen-year-old Harriet Westbrook, with whom he duly returned to a neighbouring part of the same valley the following April. There they found Nant-gwyllt, a long handsome eight-bay Georgian house with a plantation of old pines and larches behind it and a front lawn sloping down to the confluence of the Claerwen and Elan rivers. There had been a house here for centuries and its situation, as the *Hereford Times* boasted in 1816, was "as grand and romantic as any in Wales". Shelley loved it. "Give me Nantgwillt: fix me in this spot, so retired, so lovely, so fit for the seclusion of those who think and feel. Fate, I ask no more."

Indeed he dreamed of establishing there an "asylum of distressed virtue, the rendez-vous of the friends of liberty and truth". The house slept seven with ease and the largest room could be fitted out as a library of classical and radical texts. One hundred and thirty acres of arable land and seventy of blue woodland full of spring flowers surrounded them. "We are now embosomed in the solitude of the mountains woods and rivers silent, solitary and old, far from any town," he wrote. Even the ghost haunting the house was friendly, and the neighbourhood boasted witches, fairies and hobgoblins of every description. Shelley delighted in it all. Here was somewhere he and his friends might start the radical commune or little colony of enlightened souls of which they dreamt. They arrived on the 14 April 1812 and within two days started negotiations to take out a lease.

Self-sufficiency and manual labour were part of the plan, income was to be shared, all were to be equal, they would manage their own farm: free-thinking soul-mates in a radical commune. Shelley nonetheless always employed local servants to cook and house-keep. No evidence survives as to whether at Nant-gwyllt he invited his Irish servant Dan to eat at table with him or not. Certainly he all his life ran up extravagant, careless debts with tradespeople, showing an aristocratic contempt for such inferiors that gainsaid democratic pieties.

The annual rent was £98, much of which could be covered if they should opt to sub-let the farmland. But he also needed at least £500 to buy the stock and furniture, and, despite circumspect letters, could not secure it. Moreover, Harriet was ill. Before long, heavy-hearted, they prepared to leave and on Saturday 6 June their melancholy baggage-train crossed the valley the one and a half miles to Cwm Elan House where his Grove cousins offered kindly, if formal, hospitality.

Where to next? A journey back to Sussex would cost the party £30, one to Devon £8. They chose Devon and found at Lynmouth a cottage in scenery that reminded Harriet of Nant-gwyllt. The impression left on him by this interlude was deep. Richard Holmes has argued that the situation of the house acted as an ideal landscape which Shelley, in later travels, kept recreating. In June 1813 he wrote once more to enquire about resuming the Nant-gwyllt lease and soon wrote the 170-line celebratory poem 'The Retrospect; CWM ELAN 1812', among the more accomplished of his early works.

Meanwhile in Devon, because of his radical activities and writings, he was under surveillance by Home Office spies. He escaped once more to live at Tan-yr-allt in Caernarfonshire the following year, greeting Wales again as a land of liberty: "Hail to thee Cambria for the unfettered wind/Which from the wilds even now methinks I feel" and he stumbled on the new would-be model village of Tremadoc. Shelley, ever-Utopian, supported this project, but slowly came into conflict with local interests, culminating in his forced departure in February 1813 after supposedly grappling with a nocturnal assailant who fired three shots at him, an incident that disturbed him intensely. His tone changes. Though Shelley himself was both patrician and, in his own eyes, always right, Welsh society was now very stupid: "all aristocrats and saints". Here villainous lawyers grind the poor – mere serfs fed and lodged worse than pigs – whilst cheating the rich; the gentry have "all the ferocity and despotism of the ancient barons without their dignity".

★

Southey's close friend Walter Savage Landor (1775-1864) also admired Rousseau and in 1808 bought 3,000 acres of a long, dark, romantic valley on the borders of England and Wales including much mountain wilderness, at the centre of which stand the ruined Western aisles of the thirteenth-century abbey of Llanthony and prior's lodgings. His half-sister referred to Landor as the Abbot. Southey, who advised Landor to throw away his Rousseau, hoped the presence of Landor's wife might render "the very Welshmen more endurable". He took his wife there immediately after their honeymoon, and their first guests were Robert and Edith Southey. Landor was building a house, but it was unfinished; he boasted of the nightingales and glow-worms with whom he trysted, always at the same spots.

Landor is best remembered today for Dickens's affectionate portrait of him in *Bleak House* as Lawrence Boythorn, whose exaggerated fierceness of speech conceals a tender heart, given to quarrelling with neighbours and taking them to law. The portrait flatters him. At Llanthony Landor's main occupation was litigation. True, he built a road, a bridge, and a house that later fell down; he planned a forest of 10,000 Cedars of Lebanon; mice ate half the first consignment of 2,000 cones, rain rotted more. War was causing inflation, and rising prices rendered many destitute. "Poor devils, much to be pitied," Landor commented.

This was not his usual tone: his anti-Welsh rhetoric is legendary. If the principal characteristics of Rousseau's 'savage state', Landor mocked, were drunkenness, idleness, mischief and revenge, the Welsh excelled at each. His servants cut down sixty fine trees; his tenants did worse. Moreover they did not pay him. He complained that they treated him as their natural enemy. Not without cause. A famous quatrain of his starts "I strove with none for none was worth my strife". Landor strove with almost everyone, going to Llanthony like a general preparing for war.

His law-suits were unending and often senseless, and his biographer, who records Landor's reckless generosity – he gave one neighbour a Rembrandt – also evokes his reckless vindictiveness. Llanthony lost him the massive sum of £70,000 and, nearly bankrupt, he fled from his creditors first to Swansea, later to Lake Como.

Floods soon swept away the bridge Landor built; his house was demolished not long afterwards, one wall and the carriage-house only remaining. As for both Nant-gwyllt and Cwm Elan, where Shelley dreamt of happiness, they lie under sixty feet of water in the Caban Coch reservoir.

★

The Romantic, colonial habit of the English seeking in Wales an alternative reality, a place to found courts, communities, and principalities – new designs for living – survives today. Clough Williams-Ellis made a fantasy-town of Portmeirion; Richard Booth developed his book-town at Hay-on-Wye; hippies and tepee-dwellers gathered above Llandrindod; the Centre for Alternative Technology was founded near Machynlleth; the Bleddfa Trust two miles from us celebrates the link between spirituality and art.

The landscape, given to so many hidden valleys that stay separate and even secret one from another, favours small autonomous realms; so does the yeoman tradition that often makes Welsh hill-farmers independent of the big landowner. This has long been an area of tiny independent principalities, of Utopian dreamers, of experimental communities, and has continued in a sense to be so. Over recent centuries Wales has absorbed many English enthusiasts for its scenery and history: it can in me find room for one more. Rousseau haunts Wales still.

Autumn 1937 and Summer 1870:
Estrangement and Belonging

O ne Wednesday morning in September 1937, William
Plomer, novelist, poet, friend to Virginia Woolf and E.M.
Forster and gifted, opinionated publisher's reader at Jonathan
Cape, was observed opening his post in his room in Bedford
Square by his colleague Rupert Hart-Davis. Plomer was good at
his job, and beady-eyed about it too. Ladies would ask him
reverentially over dinner about the 'masterpieces' he must
frequently discover. In cold fact he was wearied by the vanity of
authors in general and of the many Great War memoir-writers
in particular. Plomer recognised that that war had often
provided the only intense experience of the writer's life: but that
without talent, such records were valueless. The bound Victorian
diaries he unpacked that day were not typed, their hand-writing
scarcely legible: Hart-Davis watched Plomer groan in mock
dismay that he would have to take the wretched things home.

He returned the following week in a state of excitement: "It's marvellous". He would send for the twenty further diaries and argue – successfully – that Cape should publish. Not the full twenty-two diaries, which amounted to one million words, but a selection he would himself make, and about which historians are likely to continue to argue. Kilvert's diaries appealed to him for various reasons. The Victorian period fascinated him, and Kilvert illuminated it afresh, with his account of bathing nude on a public beach in mixed company, or of rural deans at a conference discussing venereal disease.

Kilvert was a Wiltshireman who had fallen in love with Radnorshire; Plomer a displaced and alienated gay South African who had lived in Japan and experienced England as a foreign country. But he had spent the memorable summer of 1915 visiting a schoolfriend at Cwmbach near Glasbury: they walked the moors, lay in the bracken listening to lark-song, swam naked in the icy pools, and Plomer fell in love with the countryside and felt himself at home.

In Radnorshire Plomer discovered a healing peace of mind. He returned in the winter of 1929, staying in The Royal George Inn at Lingen on the Hereford/Radnor border, paying only £7 a month, exploring the area between Presteigne and Knighton on foot. The roads carried scarcely any traffic and he enjoyed casual encounters out walking where characters emerged both 'in the round' and in variety. He wished that he had been born and bred here "where everybody knew or knew about one another, and felt their roots entwined"[1].

Editing Kilvert's diaries now gave Plomer an excellent pretext for another return visit, and he soon lodged at Crossway Farm outside Clyro. Although many houses had in the intervening years fallen into ruin, here was a world little changed, without cars, telephone, bus, newspaper, wireless, or creature comforts. He showered under a waterfall, feeding on rabbit and eggs with milk or perry to wash them down. His hosts were charming; he wondered in a letter to Hart-Davis "whether this was because they were happy?"

Plomer published his edition in three parts, in 1938, 1939,

and 1940, and they were hugely popular, winning critical acclaim too. Kilvert was the best chronicler ever of life in the Radnorshire hills. But the main appeal was that Kilvert was among the greatest of English diarists, soon compared with Pepys and Evelyn, as with Proust and Hopkins. His diaries also afforded their readers an escape from a terrifying present into a calmer elsewhere, just as sales of Trollope's novels, too, soared during the war. Plomer himself, escaping the Blitz to Worthing in September 1940, described his stay there to Virginia Woolf – he ate mulberries, correcting proofs of the last volume of Kilvert's diary, while his eccentric father, wearing a black skull-cap, did *gros point* tapestry and recited Schiller[2].

Plomer was especially delighted that V.S. Pritchett appreci-ated Kilvert's sincerity, sensibility and dignity, acuity of eye and ear, lack of self-importance or self-consciousness, his art of catching life on the wing and of communicating a tenderness of feeling our more cynical age had forgotten. Pritchett concluded:

> When we contrast the note and rhythm of our lives with those of Kilvert's, we see more than a change of fashions…. We perceive with a shock that it is we who are unnatural, because we do not live within the walls of a long period of civilisation and peace[3].

In July 1948 Plomer helped set up the Kilvert Society in Hereford Town Hall, to foster an interest in Kilvert, his diary, and the countryside that he loved – an area soon known as Kilvert Country.

*

Francis Kilvert (1840-79) is a key player in this story: a tall, bearded priest in Clyro during 1866-72 and then St Harmon and Bredwardine in 1876-77. Collector of Radnorshire folklore; energetic hill-walker; admirer, like his fellow-Oxonian Lewis Carroll (aka Charles Dodgson) of young girls; and, most of all, from 1870, an unparalleled and brilliant diarist.

Kilvert was to die within one month of his marriage, but was also a great lover. Not in the sexual sense, but in the Platonic. He loved children, the Border countryside, Wordsworth, animals (there are wondrous descriptions of shrew and stoat – small animals that when trapped behave as though they conceived themselves fearsomely large); he loved the past and yet was tender towards the present too. Without great artistry his sensibility, so conventional, but also so lacking in self-consciousness and egoism, would never have survived to touch us. But he had communicative talent too. "For some time," Kilvert remarked in 1874, with the pride and the humility of the true artist, "I have been trying to find the right word for the shimmering, glancing, tumbling movement of the poplar leaves in the sun and wind. It was 'dazzle'. The dazzle of the poplars."

Finding the right word to make us see through his eyes is what he excels at. He paints vivid word-pictures and makes us experience the physicality of his world as if we were at his side. As of course, in a sense, we are. Here are some examples:

> The peewits were sweeping, rolling and tumbling in the hot blue air about the tall trees with a strange deep mysterious hustling and quavering sound from their great wings.

> Last night there was a sharp frost, the crescent moon hung cold and keen, and the stars glittered and flashed gloriously. Orion all in a move of brilliance.

> The oat-laden waggon came creaking and swaying and sweeping the hedge along the edge of a brow high above the house and then down a steep rough path into the rick-yard.

> A comely girl in russet brown swept up the hearth with a goose's wing and set on the kettle, and a large black and white sheep dog wandered into the room, and was sent out again.

> A group of people were sitting in the churchyard among the graves, and one woman was dressing a green grave with scarlet and white flowers near one of the vast black yews.

The western sky was in a splendour and every branch and twig stood out clear against the glow and the two twin sister silver birches leaned towards each other and kissed each other in the dusk.

It was a glorious afternoon, unclouded, and the meadows shone dazzling like a golden sea in the glory of the sheets of buttercups. The deep, dark river, still and glassy, seemed to be asleep and motionless except when a leaf or blossom floated slowly by. The cattle by the mill plashed and trampled among the rushes and river flags and water lilies in the shallow places, and the miller Godwin came down with a bucket to draw water from the pool.

As A.L. Rowse noted, Kilvert is always a little apart, watching life itself flowing by, trying to catch it, to ensnare a momentary aspect of its beauty, with what quivering sensibility, with what nostalgia for what is passing, even as it passes, in a paragraph, a sentence, a phrase. His ability to enter into the mystery of things, as if – as King Lear puts this – he were God's spy, is surely connected with virtue.

This "very sleek and glossy and gentle" man, tall, bearded and resembling "a nice Newfoundland dog", had the gift of inspiring affection. He thought this "curious power of attracting" could be a terrible one; but noted too that he might wander all his life in the Radnorshire hills and never want for a kindly welcome, a meal, or a seat by the fireside. This is partly an effect of his own unconscious goodness. We catch him hoeing for an old soldier who had fought Napoleon in the Peninsular wars, carrying a pail for an old woman silently weeping with rheumatic pain, turning a poor paralysed girl in bed – "better than anyone", she avers – and literally going out of his way for hours to show kindness to a newly orphaned bastard boy. One St Stephen's Day he goes to visit a sick child who is in great pain, hoping to read her to sleep: "The light shone through the night from the sick girl's chamber window, the night was still, an owl hooted out of the South and the mighty hunter Orion with his glittering sword silently overstrode the earth."

And yet he was not an 'easy touch': he notes with no smartness or cynicism, but with plenty of good humour, how the second that he pays them money, the groans of two wretched old women unaccountably cease. His taste did not run only towards the morally edifying. He pockets a silver seal from a very rich but mean-spirited aunt who had cut out the family from her will. Virginia Woolf, always attracted by malice, found Kilvert's comic-grotesque evocation of the aunt's Worcester funeral – the servants who knew the will acting superciliously: the bearers nearly losing grip on the coffin – sublimely funny.

Kilvert shared with Dickens and Zola a love of the macabre that belongs to its epoch. Among his best passages are the description of a young boy nearly drowning in human excrement – "like a fly in treacle"; the tale of an impoverished worker, who, hating to lose independence in old age, cut his throat, and then nearly his entire head off; a gruesome suicide by drowning[4]; and the death and belated discovery of the corpse of an arrogant and opinionated Englishman on Cader Idris. Too proud to pay heed to local wisdom about his route, foxes and ravens had eaten his eyes and much of his flesh. Kilvert liked to describe, too, how, when new building works disturbed a graveyard, hedgehogs fed off human body-parts. And he provides details of the atrocities committed by the Indians in the mutiny at Cawnpore, as of revenge-executions by the British, who tied the bodies of the mutineers tightly to the gun-carriages, their chests to the gun-muzzles, before blowing them to pieces.

Kilvert has the tendency of all romantics to be tender toward the past. He celebrates a continuity of recall going back to the Civil War and the jug from which Charles I drank; a story touched upon in an earlier chapter. Kilvert records also an occasion when his son, the future Charles II, in disguise as a lady's servant, asked the butler of a Radnorshire house for a glass of wine; the butler replying in a meaning way, "You are able to command what wine you like". Moreover a few old people could even then still be found who used the seventeenth century valediction 'Your servant sir' as well as others who call him 'Your honour' and 'Your reverence'.

Such usages were survivals that would within a generation or less – Kilvert saw – be heard no longer. Past wars and their veterans interested him. On the sixtieth anniversary of Waterloo he thinks about the "small, sad" annual banquet, and how thin and frail its ranks must be growing. He enjoyed discussing Napoleon with the old soldier, and meeting a Bredwardine parishioner who could reminisce about the coronation of George IV in 1820.

The present he is, like most romantics, more equivocal about: it contains pollution from mines, and destruction of habitat, including the obliteration by axe and saw of a great old green-wood he had loved, and the coming of the railway which, for all its speed and convenience, brings the hated English tourist everywhere. Yet he was also fascinated by improvements in the Hay telegraph office, as by the new laughing-gas used by his dentist. Above all he feels the precious passing beauty of each moment, and makes us experience it with him.

★

There are many mysteries about Kilvert. How did it happen that in 1870, aged thirty, he suddenly started to keep his remarkable diaries, giving each day (it has been reckoned) two hours to the task of writing? What part did his arrival in Radnorshire play in unlocking his formidable gifts? And why, when it is so clear that the Welsh March quickened his imagination to intenser life, did he wait four years after arriving in Clyro to begin recording?

Much is unanswerable, except what is clearest: that Radnorshire suited him, with its wild and empty hills, its hospitable people, its eccentrics and solitaries, and – compared with his native Wiltshire – its apparent social harmony; though there are oblique references to social tension, too. His first year of diarising – 1870 – by common consent is his most brilliant and vivid. And he regarded his sojourn here not as exile but as a form of spiritual homecoming.

Indeed Kilvert announced "I believe I must have Welsh blood": he had that day found himself responding to the good humour, high spirits and natural courtesy of the townspeople of Builth as if they were his kin. No shred of evidence has come to light to support the contention that his ancestry was partly Welsh. Yet this identification, romantic and intuitive as it was, was nonetheless passionately held. Fact had to bow, on occasion, to fancy. Thus, his mother's maiden name being Ashe, on being shown the ancient tomb at Moccas of Sir Reginald de Fresne – *fraxinus* in Latin meaning Ash – he declared, on this slenderest evidence, that this border demesne had once belonged "to his family". On visiting nearby Monnington, moreover, he thought he could identify the grave of Glyndŵr, whose "strong wild heart", as Kilvert puts it, thus rested within hearing of the rushing of the Wye.

If there was such a thing as 'Celtic spirit' Kilvert thought he could identify it: "warm-hearted, excitable, demonstrative, imaginative, eloquent," he wrote, on a visit to Cornwall[5]; and he honoured, too, early British or Celtic Christianity which "came to us directly from the East".

He was of course not alone among Victorians in making quixotic identifications. Augusta Hall (1802-96, later Lady Llanover, after whose MP husband 'Big Ben' was named) invented a Welsh national dress based on local country-wear: striped flannel petticoat worn under a flannel open-fronted bed-gown, with an apron, shawl and kerchief or cap. On her estate near Abergavenny – on which she also closed all pubs – her workers, tenants and guests had all equally to wear something like this 'uniform'; while her maids, whom she encouraged to speak Welsh, were observed when they left the grounds changing quietly at the first opportunity into more fashionable dress.

Guest and Borrow are others. In 1846 Lady Charlotte Guest (1812-95)[6], later campaigner for Turkish refugees and London cabmen, student of Hebrew, Arabic, Persian and Welsh, published a dual-language text of the *Mabinogion*: here were Welsh fairy-tales – some bearing upon Arthurian romance; one, an early version of King Lear; another used by Tennyson in the *Idylls*. Their importance as records of early myth, legend, folklore, culture, and language of Wales is immense; and Guest included tales from the *Book of Taliesin* which, like the *Red Book of Hergest*, with its stories of the Welsh King Arthur, were both discovered in Radnorshire, as we have noted.

George Borrow (1803-1881) is another case. He learned Welsh from a groom in Norwich and published a translation of Ellis Wynne's *The Sleeping Bard* and elsewhere one of Iolo Goch's poems about Sycharth. His *Celtic Bards, Chiefs and Kings*, published posthumously in 1928, mentions the tradition of Glyndŵr retiring to die of a broken heart in his daughter's house at Monnington in Herefordshire: Kilvert's lamentation for Owain Glyndŵr's strong, wild heart echoes Borrow's.

In *George Borrow's Second Tour of Wales* (1910) – following his classic study of Wales and the Welsh, *Wild Wales* (1862) – Borrow tells a famous Radnorshire story. On asking whether Presteigne was in England or Wales, Borrow was surprised to hear her canny answer, "It's in Radnorshire", as if perhaps to say 'And a plague on both your houses'. One century later critic and border-novelist Raymond Williams too saw Border folk like himself as neither Welsh nor English: "I have heard both groups talked about as if they were other than the people here, which is clearly impossible. I suppose it is the kind of thing that happens in a border area, that people can't quite orientate"[8].

There were in the Marches pub-brawls, some fatal, between Welsh and English, especially in Hereford, whose Town Clerk was obliged to speak Welsh until as late as 1850. Pub-brawls, which lasted into the twentieth century, differ, of course for the better, from the anarchic Scottish Border warfare, which also cut treacherously across nationality. If Kilvert is conscious each time he crosses between England and Wales, this is because, though an English outsider, he loved being in Radnorshire, which seemed to him a world apart. He notes that Radnorshire neighbours believe that each time he goes home to Wiltshire he has do this by boat and cross a sea. Wiltshire folk, equally parochial, suffer the same illusion in reverse. He records comical instances both of shakey English and shakey Welsh: this is an in-between place, as Borrow and later Raymond Williams saw.

Kilvert loved the Welsh "because their warmer yet sharper, more percipient, more emotional life" tallied so exactly with his own unfulfilled inner being[9]. So in his imagination he pitted English against Welsh, retelling the story of a Radnorshire house known as the Pant through the middle of whose rooms there happened to pass the border between England and Wales. A parishioner, on giving birth, was prevailed upon in the final period of labour by her midwife – evidently a person of strong and eccentric views – to move to the one corner of the room agreed to be definitively in England: "Stand here, Betsey, in the English corner". There was no room there even to sit, let alone lie down. Around the time in question there had for three hundred years been no legal difference between birth in Wales and in England. And yet emotion around the question of the border-line, and of ethnic identity alike, persisted.

Kilvert called English tourists "vulgar, loathsome, ill-bred, offensive". The English, he charges familiarly, do not feel at home until they have killed. Watching the squire pass by with a shooting party, he reflects, with sadness, " 'What a fine day it is. Let us go out and kill something': the old reproach against the English". And he accordingly chronicles four guns taking 700 rabbits in a single afternoon, and numberless birds. Even though he belonged emphatically to the English Ascendancy in Wales, he did not regard himself as an English tourist.

So far from being Welsh Kilvert was in many ways a conventional member of the Anglican elite: the leisured ruling class that sent its children to England for their education and went in for elaborate picnics, archery and croquet in summer – walks, rides, tours and visits; while winter signified dancing, and skating with blazing torches. He lived a full and enjoyable social life, a welcome guest at many neighbouring country houses, especially at Clyro Court in his own parish, where he was on affectionate terms with the family.

He records watching lights seeming to flash on and off within a big house before realizing that this flashing is caused by serving-maids waiting at table, thus moving constantly between seated guests and windows. Here was the gentry-world to which he primarily belonged, albeit as a poor cousin, characteristically painted from an outsider's perspective. At the same time it was a perspective that did not stop him from sharing the largesse of the wealthier gentry: in a rare passage about food he chronicles a dinner he gave his farmers during his first year at Bredwardine: white soup, roast beef, boiled chickens and ham, curried rabbit, stewed wood-pigeons, beef-steak pie, potatoes and stewed celery, plum pudding, custard, plum tart, mince pies, apricot jam tart.

This was a social stratum later resented for its ignorant condescension towards the Welsh and its support of the iniquities of the tithe-system: the majority of the Welsh attended Baptist or Methodist Chapel, their culture dormant and repressed, and so unfairly obliged to contribute one tenth of their income to the Anglican Church to which they owed no allegiance. Tithe-charges, moreover, were increasing. In the well-written (and now rare) *The Unforgotten Valley: Studies of Life and Character on the Welsh Border* (1926), Joseph Duggan recorded the all-embracingness of Baptist culture not far from Kilvert's Clyro in Hundred House (disguised as 'Llanbadarn'). Recalled with charm and scepticism, the strength and eccentricity of the yeoman culture of Baptists comes over in a series of comical vignettes: Duggan's Baptists live free from dire poverty, but are aware of it.

Kilvert makes occasional references to distress and social unrest: once he meets a boy in search of a crust of bread; young women are dying of consumption, older women driven mad by depression. Autumn 1870 saw a poor harvest and Kilvert, from his room overlooking the Swan Inn, recorded a fight between bitter, drunken and bewildered farmers. Shot with pity, Kilvert asks where on earth the rents are now to come from. In 1873 a miners' strike in south Wales leaves cottagers without fuel and causes starvation among the strikers. After initially blaming the unions, Kilvert came to sympathise with both sides.

In November 1878, moreover, Kilvert went to watch Territorial volunteers drill in Rhaeadr but found the hall deserted: the men had all gone to watch or take part in the Rebecca Riots, a large party of them spearing salmon below Rhaeadr bridge. The original object of the Rebecca Riots, started in 1843 by a secret society of Welshmen whose leaders dressed up as women, is often said to have been the abolition of turnpike charges. In fact they were symptomatic of much wider disaffection caused by agrarian distress, among them the Poor Law Amendment Act of 1834, and an increase in tithe charges. By 1878 salmon poachers had adopted both the name and the cross-dressing disguise of these famous rioters[10].

The inquiry into the causes of the first riots – as of the Poor Law Commission that helped trigger them – was led by Sir Thomas Frankland Lewis of Harpton Court, whose son Sir George is commemorated by New Radnor's remarkable pinnacled seventy-seven feet high monument as 'Radnorshire['s] most distinguished son': MP for Radnor and Hereford; Chancellor of the Exchequer from 1855-8; War Secretary; editor of the *Edinburgh Review* and published author: of whom a little more, later. Here was a family known to Kilvert. Yet on the matters of high politics in which they were involved Kilvert is silent. In fact the rioters were men who could reasonably have taken Kilvert as a class-enemy, as well as a 'treacherous Englishman'.

But such animus is hard to imagine. True, Kilvert was annoyed when one of his Anglican parishioners chose to have her child baptized by a Nonconformist and records an uproar of excitement between Chapel and Church-goers over the election of a parish Guardian, with sectarian feeling running very high and "the dissenters behaving badly". Kilvert did not want the Church of England disestablished and was hostile to dissenters who did.

Yet his own instinctive tolerance also comes over clearly. He went where he was needed and could offer help, and the sectarian divide is mainly forgotten or overlooked. Indeed he was distressed when it was thought he might be angry at learning that a Nonconformist minister had read to one of his flock. His job as a parson uniquely opened all doors. And although Kilvert was sometimes wary of sitting down in a hovel where he observed fleas or lice, he appears instinctively at home in every setting, and, moreover, welcome wherever he goes. Until the coming of the Welfare State, clergy acted as social workers, bringing food, blankets and clothing to the sick and needy. Few clergymen, however, were as golden-hearted or as humble as Kilvert; few loved people and making them happy so well. The unparalleled social range of the diaries that results is a major part of their fascination.

The 'fit' between an individual soul and a landscape is always partly mysterious. Kilvert writes affectingly of how, in the autumn of 1872, he has to give up his first Radnorshire incumbency. The local sawyer weeps. The parish children give him a gold pencil case and beg him not to forget them. Other parishioners present him with a writing desk, an anonymous gift of £5, Wordsworth's complete works, an inkstand, a photograph album. Kilvert weeps twice in church, and recounts "all the dear people" waving as his train departs.

Two centuries earlier Radnorshire folk had been known for unruliness and thieving, especially of cattle[11]. Much had changed, by Kilvert's day: even so, the way his account avoids mawkishness is interesting. This is partly because he records – unsentimentally – how accidental is his Clyro happiness: the Wiltshire squire is stupid, mean, and tyrannical, insisting some of the windows of the new school be kept open even in winter; in Radnorshire, by contrast, kinder counsels prevail. (How much can be generalised from one case? By the strangest of coincidences, Walter Bagehot had in 1861 celebrated

Radnorshire's George Cornewall Lewis as the ideal, responsible country squire and MP in his classic *The English Constitution*.)

Another reason for Kilvert's love of Radnorshire connects with what he terms that county's "beautiful courtesy". In this part of the world people congratulate each other on the spring weather. "Well done; well done" – an expression Kilvert records as local – today is still commonly to be heard. Again and again he will note most "perfect politeness and well-bred courtesy" and "perfect breeding" from ordinary folk. These good manners are somehow essentially class-less, or beyond class, so that he notes the absolute lack of affectation of a woman caught in her working dress and Saturday house-chores taking her place at the head of the table with "all the quiet dignity of a woman in the best society". There may well be something Border Welsh about this classless politeness: much invaded and much conquered peoples – the Poles, Irish, Border Welsh – are rarely noted for lack of charm or wit, qualities which – in situations of danger – pay dividends.

★

Kilvert loved to escape to "the loneliness of the hills" where his greatest moments of religious revelation occur. He delighted in walking from Hay to Clyro without meeting a single person, recording a peculiar liking for a deserted road. He is best remembered for two set-pieces, in each of which he meets another religious Solitary like himself, unaware that these two eccentrics are, in a sense, *alter egos*.

One is Father Ignatius (1837-1908), trying to revive monastic life in the Black Mountains where W.S. Landor had earlier made his retreat. In 1869 Father Ignatius had purchased a property at Capel-y-ffin and built Llanthony Monastery, getting funding through preaching and appeals to benefactors. As Anglican abbot, he adopted monastic customs in an eccentric manner; there were reports of miracles and heavenly visions. (Because of his erratic personality this venture failed. Toward the end of his life he was ordained by a Syrian archbishop, channelling his enthusiasm into the revival of Welsh culture, becoming a Zionist, British Israelite, and believer in flat-earth theory.)

The second Solitary is a wild parson, living in conditions of utmost simplicity and domestic squalor in the hills, perfecting two new systems of shorthand, and greeting all in the Radnorshire way, with "the natural simplicity of the highest breeding". The Solitary's wise recipe for contentment is to be happy with the beauties and blessings that lie around.

Recent scholarship reveals that this Solitary, whose name was Price, extended his hovel by three bathing-machines: respectively his study, bedroom and kitchen. There being few parishioners, he encouraged vagrants into church who duly complained of the cold; he bought oil stoves on which the tramps soon discovered they could conveniently fry bacon during his sermons. When he promised five shillings to every couple willing to marry who had been living in unblessed union, some found it profitable enough to get married to the same partner repeatedly, each time arriving under different names and hats. In 1878 Kilvert recorded that Price fell into the fire and was badly burnt; but he survived until 1895, amazed when he was rescued and his filthy under-clothes cut away, his body washed and cleaned and put to bed, "beaming benedictions and wondering what he had done in life to merit such attention"[12].

★

In 1959 Ffransis Payne met in Glascwm an old man of over ninety years of age who had been baptized by Kilvert on the second Sunday before Lent in 1870 "in ice which was broken and swimming about in the Font". Payne describes Kilvert as a saint, a judgement needing qualification. Kilvert's sexuality is famously immature and his love of young girls well-known. He has a special love of recording glimpses of their bottoms, for example, being afforded "a most interesting view from the rear". And those who assert that all this is nothing but repressed longing for a daughter should recall that Kilvert, whose own father was a strict disciplinarian, has three passages in which he discourses eloquently and without self-consciousness on how apt girls' bottoms are for whipping.

The fact is that we see Kilvert through the prism of Plomer's editing, which he always claimed to have been fair and 'objective'. There is cause for doubt. He claimed to have cut out all repetitions while retaining two identical versions of the story of the same Peninsular War veteran keeping wolves at bay with a "flash in the pan" – putting a charge of gunpowder in his flintlock musket and firing with no bullet to create only a bang. We also know that Plomer kept every surviving passage concerning Kilvert's susceptibility to female beauty while cutting many others concerning Kilvert's passionate devotion to God, his prayers of supplication and thanksgiving and his religious duties.

This has led to as much questioning of Kilvert's sexuality as of his religious orthodoxy. In reality the festivals of the Christian year absorbed him. Christmas Day: "This morning we plainly heard the six beautiful fatal bells of Bremhill ringing a Christmas peal through the frosty air." Childermas Day: "As I came home the sky was black and thick with snow, but through the gloom one great lone star was burning in the East. We have seen His star in the East."

We also know that, although Kilvert loved cats, dogs and horses, Plomer, who did not, cut out references to all of these. So he deliberately left out the extraordinary story – which survives in manuscript – of the death of a poor working horse tormented both by local superstitious quack-remedies and by 'modern' veterinary surgeons, while dying in anguish; and a miraculously beautiful evocation of the dawn chorus that follows.

We are unlikely ever to be able to reach an absolute judgement about Plomer's editing. Firstly Kilvert's widow is believed to have done away with those diaries in which he recorded his courtship of her, and of two others who preceded her. Then, between 1938 and 1956 Francis Kilvert's niece Essex Hope burnt probably a further twenty-two of her uncle's notebooks.

"I've done something naughty," she coyly told Plomer, who himself during the war somehow lost the typescript of the complete journals from which he had made his edited selection, believing the originals were intact and safe.

Why did Essex Hope destroy her uncle's diaries? She claimed Kilvert's sister Dora wanted this although we know Dora loved the diary. Essex Hope claimed too that the diaries were a "trial to the eyes ...exceedingly difficult to read". None of this is persuasive. She also destroyed her uncle's collection of local folklore, after publishing some of it under her own name[13]. And perhaps the fact that in 1940 she set her unregarded novel *I Have Come Home* in a world resembling the one her uncle celebrated, provides another clue. It is possible she acted out of jealousy and resentment of his posthumous fame.

Considering the quality of the journal-material that Plomer helped see to publication, this loss of the chief chronicles of Radnorshire life in the nineteenth century is, at first sight, almost unbearable. There is no guarantee, however, that Kilvert would not have edited his diaries himself, had he survived beyond the age of thirty-nine. Three of the original diaries were saved, and two are kept at the National Library of Wales, one in Durham.

*

One can only imagine how oppressively W.G. Sebald would have written of the grief of this loss of the diaries, in his hypnotically satisfying prose. Sebald would have made a meal, too, of Kilvert's death from peritonitis ten days after returning from his honeymoon in 1879; as Sebald's ghost would surely have had stern things to say of his own heart-attack and resultant car-crash only weeks before the English translation of his stunning novel *Austerlitz* won its well-deserved prizes. And his troubled spirit might well have added some bitter, stoical words on the death of his colleague Lorna Sage, drowning in hospital of emphysema, while her instantly classical chronicle of escape from the Welsh March, *Bad Blood*, won one prize after another.

There is never a shortage of food for the ecstatic gloom at

which Sebald excelled. Yet his is not the only way of seeing into the dark heart of the matter. Francis Kilvert has as much or more to tell us, even today, than Sebald, in the precious few diaries that survive and that he never meant for publication.

Well-born, well-connected yet with no prospect of inherited wealth, there is in Kilvert no trace of contemporary anguish about his 'identity'. Here was an unsentimental man who loved people and making them happy, and loved recording, with unselfconscious skill and passion, the details of existence, because these in turn were his joy. And in Kilvert's gentle, uneventful and exemplary life and his delight in a self-transcending awareness of detail, lie potent clues to answering those questions about the meaning of our existence here – so mysteriously brief and troubled as it is, and (often) so pain-filled and undignified our different leave-takings – questions that will never cease tormenting us, and that merit all our intelligence and curiosity, and all our restless energy and passion.

1905: Sacred Space

Edward Thomas visited the Welsh Borders at the dawning of the twentieth century, in 1905 publishing a book on his sense of the place called – originally – *Beautiful Wales* (re-issued recently simply as *Wales*). He was brought up in London with parental roots in Monmouthshire and cousins in Carmarthenshire. He had not yet discovered himself as a poet – that would happen only in 1914 – 'Adlestrop' was as yet unwritten. He was working as a literary hack on £2 a week, suffering depression and self-doubt, contemplating suicide. Long solitary walking tours in the March helped.

The Oxford Companion to the Literature of Wales is scathing about Thomas's book: cloying, sentimental, unsatisfactory, over-written and lacking in specificity. Robert Macfarlane in his recent *The Wild Places* is kinder, understanding that Thomas's purpose is more poetical than sociological, his book an entranced dream-story or song, written – appropriately enough perhaps – not by pen but with a wild goose feather from the Glamorgan coast, which he cut into an old-fashioned quill.

Beautiful Wales starts with a witty attack on English Celtomaniacs who cross Wales in a state of self-satisfied dejection, seeking there, he implies, compensation for worldly disappointment or failure. (As Auden later quipped, "...when life fails/ What's the good of going to Wales?") If Thomas is secretly among their number – he shares the Celtomaniac penchant for the Arthurian – he never quite acknowledges it. His reluctance to name any place he evokes, he oddly claims, is "to avoid disturbing the dreams of others". He is in pursuit of bigger truths. His book is accordingly one half a collection of portraits of Welshmen listed by profession (bard, preacher, schoolmaster, etc.), one half an evocation of the successive months of the Welsh year, liberally peppered with songs and poems translated into English by Thomas, possibly with the help of his good friend the Welsh poet Gwili.

In his section on 'November' the reader learns why Wales helped cure Thomas's dejection. The Welsh, he earlier noted, are all one family, conversing as such when they meet on trains: even the Welsh word for themselves and fellow countrymen (*Cymry*) carries some implication of shared fellowship. They also extend their kindness to strangers like Thomas himself. He was walking in the November rain as the winter dusk approached with twelve miles still to cover, when invited into a vicarage to stay the night should there be no room at the inn. But room there was, and the inn-keeper's wife gave him a change of clothing before he had requested such a thing. The following day he trekked twenty miles over peat and brindled grass, with only the last wild flowers of the year to keep him company, and was again welcomed into a stranger's kitchen, given dry clothes, and entertained with songs and stories.

So his tale continues. On a twenty-mile hike next day he stops every two miles at the nearest farm to ask the way, always receiving kindnesses. His hosts seat him by their peat fires, give him bread, butter and milk, and often directions, then sometimes cheese, and after that, tea. Thomas finds Welsh kitchens pleasanter, and Welsh drawing-rooms more mysterious, than their English counterparts. At the house of a poor family of sixteen he notes the easy dignity that accompanies their poverty. The following morning the father of this family, who speaks only Welsh, accompanies Thomas for two miles over high boggy ground with no apparent track, until they reach a road. Thomas observes the satisfaction the farmer takes in their hour-long silent companionship; their soundless communing evidently consoles him too. Thomas's celebrations of the English countryside in his writings are always tinged with melancholy and regret. Not so his Welsh journeyings. For him the border divides Welsh good fellowship from the coldness and self-alienation of England. And since this world is old and troubled, "light and warmth and fellowship are good".

★

The pleasure of finding community; the pleasure of finding a track where none is obvious: these are border themes. Both in some sense concern alignment. Alfred Watkins (1855-1935), discoverer of ley-lines, was born in Hereford, and the arena within which he made his famous finding was bounded by the Radnor Forest, the Black Mountains and the Shropshire hills. This huge natural amphitheatre, Watkins said, was "the pleasant land which has been my field of work". He has been compared by his best-known disciple (John Michell) with Vaughan, Traherne and Kilvert.

Watkins's father Charles (1821-88) started as a small farmer who became an inn-keeper, then a notably successful Hereford brewer. As his fortune grew he moved every few years to a larger house, ending in a six-bay eighteenth-century mansion at Bartestree, which he further extended. By the time he died in 1888 his empire included thirty-five hotels, the substantial Hereford brewery and Imperial flour-mill, many pubs and inns in the county, and branches in Birmingham, Swansea and Cardiff.

His son Alfred continued the family business while being also a typical Victorian amateur scientist. Everything interested him. Born in 1855 one year after the railway-line came to Hereford, it was he who introduced the earliest dynamo in Herefordshire into the gloomy family flour-mill. This created the first electrically lighted space in the county: he similarly replaced mill stones with steel rollers and patented complex new baking thermometers to improve the making of bread.

He was broad-shouldered and bearded, a rough diamond. His all-year-round grey flannel Harris tweed suits had no fewer than fourteen pockets, stuffed with letters, pamphlets, tools, rulers and other paraphernalia, his clothing thus affording him a travelling office. He journeyed at first by open, horse-drawn, two-wheeled gig, soon in a succession of steam-cars, gearless, noiseless and fuelled by paraffin, finally in a Jowett motor-car.

Such journeyings often took him to Radnorshire. As a lad travelling for his father's brewery he pulled up his horse one day to wonder at two Radnor sites he intuited were linked, the four standing stones in a field corner near Walton, and Castle Tomen, a motte-and-bailey marked by a clump of trees at Llanfihangel Nant Melan near the summit of the Radnor Forest road. These sights induced in him "unsatisfied wonder".

In 1911 he found himself staying in an inn with a room looking out at the great mass of the Radnor Forest. He had stayed here before in the winter of 1876, on the exact day his landlady had first arrived, taking pictures of the frozen Radnorshire stream with the trees covered in hoar-frost, and carrying in his horse-drawn trap a tent to function as a portable dark-room, and a spirit-lamp to thaw the ice-needles that kept appearing in his many bottles of chemicals.

The wet plate method of photography he then used was cumbersome and erratic. He had first to salt his immaculately cleaned glass plate with collodion solution, immerse it in a silver nitrate bath (3-5 minutes), expose and develop it (using iron-based developer), fix the plate (potassium cyanide) and lastly varnish it (gum sandarac, alcohol and lavender oil). Exposure took anything between less than one second to several minutes, a hit-and-miss calculation, like development. And this entire procedure had to be completed within ten minutes.

Gelatine emulsion on paper film after 1885 changed all this. Watkins helped too. In 1890 he invented a light meter that measured the intensity of ambient light by counting the number of seconds it took for a piece of sensitized paper to darken to a given tint, in that first year of production selling 1,400 meters at a guinea each. Soon a cheaper and hence even more popular version – the famous Bee meter – became standard equipment for photographers, and remained so for the following half century. He also produced a dark-room clock and calculator that helped photographers establish correct development times. On his 1911 trip he boasted an early folding vest-pocket camera, and he experimented with early colour photography.

He was good. His photographs of the building around 1900 of the new dams and reservoirs in west Radnorshire to bring water to the English Midlands are breath-taking in their atmosphere and detail alike. The iconic photographs we have of Scott's 1910 Antarctic expedition were taken with a Watkins meter, just as all the photographs taken by the RAF during the Second World War were processed by Watkins methods. His best-known publication (*The Old Straight Track*, 1925) contains more than one hundred of his own illustrations.

I remember that W.G. Sebald connects photography, spirits and haunting: a photo, he says in his gloomy way, is a device through which the dead can gaze at the living. In other words a photo is a place where past and present intersect. This is a point worth bearing in mind when one moves from photography to what Watkins is now best remembered for. Because Watkins's discovery of ley-lines has been put to strange uses it seems important first to establish him as a careful scientist.

He was president of the Woolhope Club, devoted to the study of Herefordshire and its adjoining areas, writing papers on local dovecotes, old standing crosses, on the seventeenth-century pottery he found at Lingen, on bees and bee-keeping:

the Domesday Book showed Herefordshire tenants paying their dues in honey. In Hereford itself, using childhood memories and inductive reasoning, he helped unearth the first Saxon defences, investigated the sources of a spring, rediscovered an underground passage, and, from the straight lines of whitened grass that appeared in the long drought of summer 1933, deduced the earlier existence there of a Saxon church and tower. Time proved his theory accurate.

A Liberal in politics, he favoured all forms of progress. The picture emerges of a forward-looking empiricist devoted to Enlightenment values. So he backed votes for women and was distressed that the Woolhope Club repeatedly balloted against women members and yet gave lectures and slide-shows to working men. If his book on decimalisation *Must We Trade in Tenths?* (1919) suggests an engagingly nutty side, this does little to undo a general impression of fair-mindedness, realism and common sense.

On Monday 30 June 1921, during a summer of "clear, smoke-free distances", Watkins, by now a 66-year-old magistrate, was on an idle visit to Blackwardine a few miles north of Hereford. His son and biographer Allen described what happened next. Watkins noticed a straight line on his map joining many ancient points of interest, and then, without warning, was struck by the "rush of revelation" that over many years of pre-history all trackways were in straight lines marked out by experts on a sighting system. Watkins told his son that "the whole thing came to me in a flash". Thus were ley-lines born.

He reported these findings to the Woolhope Club at their autumn meeting. After an afternoon excursion that 29 September Watkins gave a lantern-slide lecture in the Club's rooms in Hereford Free Library entitled 'Early British Trackways, Moats, Mounds, Camps and Sites', publishing his thesis in 1922 as the slim, finely produced, well illustrated *Early British Trackways* – priced at 4s 6d and aimed at 'the average reader'. Here he explains how the theory originated in his unusually intimate knowledge of the March, stemming from that very day in Radnorshire half a century before when he had first sighted the Walton standing stones and Castle Tomen. "The note of unsatisfied wonder struck that day has lingered through nearly fifty years... and I know now that my subconscious self had prepared the ground and worked at the problem I now see solved." Watkins accordingly put his photographic collage of the Radnor standing stones and motte-and-bailey on to the front cover. Here ley-lines were direct, expressly commercial routes, surveyed, planned and precision-engineered by a powerful caste of expert Neolithic surveyors, though he thought they might later have turned into objects of superstition and worship.

Ley-lines were 'discovered' at the same time as Tutankhamun's tomb: this was a colourful period for archaeology. A helpful account of Watkins's researches is given by Stephen Daniels, Professor of Cultural Geography at Nottingham, who shows that Watkins articulates a free trade utopia, enabled by an enlightened planning regime, looking back and forward to a liberal landscape without landlordism. He focuses on the way the cultural thinking of Watkins's time shaped his theories. "While Watkins's views are aligned to the pressure for public access to the landscape, one codified by the civilian initiative of the Ordnance Survey to publish its Popular Edition, the military imperatives of reconaissance, for an enthusiastic fundraiser and recruiter for the late war, are evident too... [and] *Early British Trackways* offers a model of ancient Britain as an organised, unified, mobile and expansive society"[1].

In the event Watkins undertook three years further study to allay sceptics. Since his father had insisted he work his way up the firm from being a delivery boy, so that he left school young and never went to college, this research amounted for Watkins, now in his sixties, to self-education. He conducted more map-work and excursions, finding scraps of evidence in a range of related literature, including place name studies, folklore, and literature from Shakespeare to Robert Louis Stevenson.

Sympathetic correspondents are cited, including a girl observed fording a pond and the reports of a local drainage board.

The result was *The Old Straight Track*, published in 1925 when Watkins was seventy years old, and still in print today. While one chapter shows how dense ley-lines are in the Vale of Radnor, and identifies Cascob church as a 'power-spot', the book extends outwards to the rest of Britain and further abroad to Gaza and to Inca ritual sacrifice. There are speculative flights of word association, one tracing a line from the Welsh *twyt*, pronounced 'toot', to the Tut of Tutankhamun and Tooting in south London. At the end of *The Old Straight Track*, he invites his readers poetically to imagine a 'fairy chain' stretched from mountain peak to mountain peak, as far as the eye could reach, and paid out until it touched the 'high places' of the earth at a number of ridges, banks, and knolls. Then the reader was to visualize a mound, circular earthwork, or clump of trees, planted on these high points, and in low points in the valley other mounds ringed round with water to be seen from a distance. Then great standing stones brought to mark the way at intervals, and on a bank leading up to a mountain ridge or down to a ford the track cut deep so as to form a guiding notch on the skyline as you come up. Thus was the scene set for lighting up the ley:

> Here and there, at two ends of the way, a beacon fire used to lay out the track. With ponds dug on the line, or streams banked up into 'flashes' to form reflecting points on the beacon track so that it might be checked when at least once a year the beacon was fired on the traditional day.

Watkins never demonstrated that such alignments, if they existed, or the markers along their lengths were genuinely ancient. While some markers, such as standing stones, were prehistoric, the majority were not. Instead, he speculated that just as most medieval churches were built on sites that had been sacred in prehistory, so lanes in the countryside have run on the same course for millennia; and that straight lengths of Roman road adapted these earlier tracks. This did not convince professional archaeologists.

The Church Times was approving – Watkins after all appearing to under-write the ancient sacredness of church-sites – but the *TLS* complained that the book lacked direction, and the editor of the archeological journal *Antiquity*, who had a rival theory, refused to advertise or review it. But there was a groundswell of popular approval, sixty-seven admirers forming a Straight Track Club for whom, in 1927, Watkins issued a portable field guide called *The Ley Hunter's Manual*.

Watkins's theory of leys received a more hospitable reception from followers interested in Earth Mysteries in the 1960s, a time when the New Age took an affectionate view of the Stone Age. During this recovery of the sacred, his observations were re-invented in cultish grammar. Leys were now the geomantic veins or magical fields of occult earth-energy and force explored in Chinese Feng-Shui or geomancy. Accordingly John Michell in *The View over Atlantis* (1969) tied Watkins's leys to the Druids, UFOs, flying saucers, the New Atlantis, the New Jerusalem, the Great Pyramid, fringe science, ESP and the supernatural. Small wonder, perhaps, that the title of the website devoted to debunking much of this is 'bad archaeology'[2].

Another website, written by the editor of the periodical *The Ley Hunter*, appears at first to offer common sense[3]. There is, he argues briskly, no evidence whatsoever that leys were ever created by peaceful ancient tribes or by survivors of any lost civilisation. As for leys being lines of power in a global energy matrix, the pendulum swingers, channellers and pagan mystics: all of these loonies too are peremptorily dismissed. This sounds promising. So what, in fact, are leys? The website suggests they are vestiges of medieval corpse ways and coffin paths. This accounts for the occurrence on leys of non-prehistoric features such as medieval churches and burial grounds.

If this last – corpse way – theory is anything to go by, ley-lines seem likely to remain a non-proven and wacky hypothesis.

But what they point to – a recovery of the sacred – will not go away. And in this context, as in others, Wales really does differ profoundly from England. Wales must be the only country in Europe where cathedrals (St David's, St Asaph's) were deliberately built in villages, rather than in cities. If in England churches were likewise built within settlements where people lived, in Wales they were created in places chosen for reclusive prayer or sacred power. Even the word *Llan*, so commonly found in Welsh village and church-names, has the connotation of sacred enclosure. Here in Wales the sacred really did have a generative role[4], and churches have been called merely the most recent markers of sacred space. And so Watkins's thesis that medieval churches were built on sites that had been sacred in prehistory works also best in Wales, where the adoption of pagan sacred sites does appear to have happened.

From this perspective the local legend that the last Welsh Dragon lies asleep deep in Radnor Forest has interest. Four churches encircling the Forest, Cefnllys, Rhydithon, Nant Melan and Cascob, are dedicated to St Michael, associated with high ground and dragon-slaying alike, thus creating a magic circle to ensure the sleeping dragon does not escape: the legend states that if any one of these churches is destroyed the dragon will awaken and ravage the countryside once more. It is a magic circle repeated in miniature in Cascob churchyard, round and once encircled by ancient yews, something unique to Wales. Of course Christian heroes had to slay the old powers: the Dragon is the Devil in the story of St Michael and his Angels vs. the Dragon in *Revelations* (Rev. 12: 7-9). Pendragon, literally 'head of, or chief dragon', is a term used in Welsh poetry metaphorically for a brave battle-leader or soldier[5]. But dragons also signify the power of the earth in certain ancient sites of worship. It feels appropriate that a red dragon is the heraldic symbol of Wales.

The word 'magical', so often used to describe our landscape, and of Wales in general, is worth pondering. What, when you strip the word of its Disney connotations, does the word 'magical' mean? Its Disney meaning is something like getting something for nothing in a way that is counter-natural. One truer meaning seems to be something like 'in harmony with the energetic nature of things'.

Having tried to resist some of his more mystically-minded followers, Watkins reckoned that ley-lines required more than a straight functional explanation. The year before his death he confessed to his son that his original 1921 revelation followed a near death experience from a heart attack, and the receipt at that time of an 'unusual gift' like second sight: "I have been psychic all my life, but I have kept it under and never told anyone about it". Small wonder, perhaps, that at one point Watkins tries to recruit the scientist and magician John Dee to his cause; or that the writer of superb horror stories M.R. James, who clearly knew about Watkins, set his 1925 short story 'A View from a Hill' in Herefordshire. This story explores the nightmare consequences of sealing the liquid produced by boiling the bones of executed criminals into a pair of paranormal binoculars. Thus misplaced curiosity and overzealous archaeological research are punished.

Radnorshire, whatever you choose to make of this, lies at the epicentre of leys. It is suggestive that these lines of connexions were discovered in the Marches, that area of debatable boundaries. The full records of Watkins's touring club rest dusty and unvisited for seventy or so years, in a county library. Meanwhile his quest to understand landscape and history resembles the quest behind all narrative: to seek secret connexions, to make links visible, to find coherences – *to tell a persuasive story*. And the recovery of the sacred, to which he made his unwitting and strange contribution, no longer seems, in a world threatened by eco-catastrophe, foolish or quixotic.

★

The search for the sacred in the March in the 1920s continued at Capel-y-ffin. "Goodness and quietness and even holiness... [have] gone forever from England" wrote the artist Eric Gill in

1923. These precious qualities had accordingly to be looked for, or so he believed, outside England, in places such as Wales and France. Gill hated industrial society: mechanization had degraded and deformed modern life. It enslaved the workers, the Many, reducing them to a state of zombie-like irresponsibility; and it entailed worship of profit at all costs, to be enjoyed only by the Few. While Gill contributed to the Arts and Crafts Movement he was dismayed that its products were so exclusive – so highly priced as to be available only to the rich.

An ideal life would be one of Holy Poverty. Gill accordingly worked to time like an artisan, costing his labours by the hour, and humbly, at a lowly rate. He side-stepped Modernism, excelling as a stone-cutter, with the elegant clear line apparent in his invention of simple and fresh typefaces (Perpetua, Gill Sans-serif, Solus) still in use today. He thought much about the place of art in the modern world, and wrote pamphlets on the topic. He believed in the sacredness of the everyday.

Gill at forty-two in a smock and rough black cassock gathered in at the waist, cross-gartered black stockings and sandals, resembled Tolstoy. He wore at work a stone-mason's paper-hat; walking abroad, a biretta. He seemed a combination of priest, monk and artisan. Gill was accompanied by, among others, the painter and writer David Jones, who had stayed after the war in a Sussex cottage of Gill's nick-named the Sorrowful Mysteries, an allusion both to the rosary and also to the fact that its war-veteran residents were prone to gloom and introspection. Jones wished to convert to Catholicism, and Gill was already a Catholic. They shared other sympathies too.

For four important years Capel-y-Ffin offered both refuge. Gill's life at Ditchling in Sussex had become too public for his taste: he preferred to live where he could be master of all he surveyed, unquestioned by anyone. The isolated Ewyas valley with its two thousand foot cliffs offered a fastness from which the wicked modern world could be denounced, and then, on frequent forays and sallies, enjoyed. Giraldus Cambrensis in 1188 noted how suited this valley was to the life of contemplation, and how many human wants it was able to satisfy, though Giraldus observed too how given the valley was to rain and wind, how often cloud-capped in winter. Here Gill could pursue his art, exploring a bohemian life-style that included occasional incestuous relations with his daughters, as well as unconventional ties with others. There were further attractions. Letters were delivered once a day only, by a postman on horseback. The Doctor, also on horseback, came up the valley from Hay once a week. Above all there was an abundance of stone, both for building and for carving, at no extra charge, lying about on the mountainside.

Gill knew that the seclusion he enjoyed at Llanthony was purchased at a price. The valley population was but a quarter of what it had been fifty years earlier: young men had escaped to work in the mines in the Rhondda, where many now drifted about in poverty, unemployed. Their fathers could not call them home since, as he wrote, "the city of London found it more profitable to foster Australian Capitalist sheep farming than to preserve the thousand year traditions of the South Wales mountains". The countryside had the air as a result of "a dying land – unspoiled but dying". Such a quiet if moribund unspoiledness nonetheless appealed greatly to him.

Father Ignatius, whom Kilvert had visited with such interest, had built his monastery in his vain attempt to revive Benedictine monastic life within the Church of England, but he quarrelled with Church authorities and lacked staying power. When he died in 1908, three only of his original community remained. The monastery, built in local sandstone and once painted white, offered until 1916 a daily Mass and Sacrament, but by 1924 had stood empty and dilapidated for two years.

Now the small central courtyard had a broken fountain and a decaying wooden cross to mark the pitiful grave of a nun from a neighbouring convent. The rooms surrounding this courtyard were dark, depressing, inconvenient, and covered by a film of muddy dust. A profusion of ivy had pushed in the diamond panes of glass in the windows, and trees overhung the roof, in which holes gaped. An outside staircase sagged alarmingly, while a mess of metal fittings rusted, entangled in nettles and brambles with fallen masonry. The sewers blocked easily and the fire-places smoked. To cap all, the monastery had been built on the side of the valley enjoying the least sun. At least in its present state it was not, or so they hoped, a place to encourage casual trippers.

The arrival in a downpour in mid-August 1924 of the Gills and their friends was a scene of happy confusion, with a large lorry disgorging its cargo of adults (six), children (seven), pony (one), cats, dogs, goats, ducks, geese, two magpies and much luggage. A tree had to be felled to allow them passage on the narrow route from Pandy station[6]. The house was swept and dusted and friends brought into the house great masses of late foxgloves. There was a pervasive and disgusting smell of goat.

Unlike Father Ignatius, Gill and his family were Catholic. Gill, a natural egoist who required to be at the centre of the drama, under-played the connexion with Ignatius and dismantled his reredos when he found it in the church, which he also decided to abandon. Worship happened in a small chapel within the house. Visitors still flocked to see Father Ignatius's grave and had to be warned off by bold letter-forms on notice-boards. On occasion such trippers were found wandering in and out of the bedrooms and, when asked what they thought they were doing, would retort "Can we please see a monk?"

"It is beautiful here in the Welsh mountains," wrote Mary Gill. "We love the Monastery – and it is extraordinary how little the outside world seems to matter"; while Eric celebrated the fact that its "heavenly" geography compelled them all to live in a way that would have seemed "fantastically heroic and unnatural and pedantic in any place less remote from industrial civilization".

Gill thought everyone in the valley "most kind and friendly" but probably did not engage at any deep level with his surroundings. He wanted a convenient stage-setting for the creation of his art and for his designs for living alike. He made, during his four years at Capel-y-ffin, no fewer than two hundred and eighty blocks and plates. His close friend and Capel-dweller, the writer and painter David Jones, was by contrast more genuinely reclusive than Gill. Jones did little or no housework. He found the local people strange and frightening and talked to few. *In Parenthesis* shows how acute an observer Jones nevertheless was of tensions between English and Welsh, and for Jones this was a return home, to a pony-filled landscape that would continue to haunt his painting, with all its latent sense of mystery, for the next forty years. The terrain, affecting him profoundly, helped to mature him as a painter.

David Jones and Edward Thomas – the poet with whom this chapter began – were both, though differently, casualties of modernity in general, and of the Great War in particular. Thomas's depressions preceded the war; Jones's major breakdowns followed afterwards. Both applied in 1915 to join the Artists' Rifles, composed of painters, sculptors, musicians, architects, actors and members of other artistic occupations. Edward Thomas's enlistment was, he said, the "natural culmination of [his] moods and thoughts" and he was posted two years later to the Western Front. For him the Great War was simply a continuation by other means of the terrible dislocations of modernity. He thought often while in France of his walking days in Wales and elsewhere; and just after dawn, during the first hour of the battle of Arras on 9 April 1917, he was killed by shell-blast. He did not live to see any of his poems published.

Unlike Thomas's, David Jones's attempt to join the Artists' Rifles failed, and he enlisted instead in the Welch Fusiliers on 2 January 1915, serving as a private soldier until December 1918, in a London unit of Lloyd George's 'Welsh army'. He was wounded in the leg on the night of 11 July 1916 in the attack on Mametz Wood on the Somme. He returned to action in October but by happy chance avoided the Passchendaele offensive and left France with severe trench fever in February 1918, which probably saved his life. On demobilization he wished at first to rejoin, but accepted a grant and some parental help to work (1919-21) at Westminster School of Art: his first job to paint the lettering of the war memorial at New College, Oxford.

The Great War made of Jones both an emotional casualty and – arguably – a Catholic convert. He had been brought up at home on Bunyan and Milton, but with strong touches of inherited Catholic feelings. Just behind the front line he had been deeply moved by a Mass glimpsed through a barn wall: he liked its business-like atmosphere in the midst of Armageddon. War-trauma left him a great procrastinator, indecision-prone, and the prospect of marriage to Gill's daughter Petra, to whom he was engaged, put the wind up him horribly, like an impending doom. In the end she married another war-veteran, Denis Tegetmeier, while Jones would end his life with many lonely years in a residential hotel, his love-affairs conducted on the telephone. Meanwhile he tried through writing and painting to come to terms with his wartime experiences, the camaraderie and the horror alike.

Mary wrote, "Capel is a most glorious place… we never want to leave it – but it is a very strenuous life." Their last winter at Capel they were snowed-in and fog-bound, the roads dangerous with ice. The combination of this harshness of the Welsh winter and a felt lack of Catholic neighbours induced the Gills to decamp to bases in south-western France, and also in the Chilterns, in autumn 1928, trailing the family of children, cats, dogs, goats, ducks and geese. Gill's quest to establish a holy life would now continue closer to London itself.

As for Capel, Gill wrote that it would remain always untouched by "the industrial-capitalist disease", and its green valleys would always "lead nowhere". He meant to praise the Black Mountains, but came unwittingly close to disclosing what many city-dwellers want of the country, and what English visitors selfishly hope for from Wales: unchangingness, or, since that is nowhere to be found on this earth, the illusion of it.

Solitude and Community

Not long after its first publication in 1969, I found Elizabeth Clarke's *The Valley*. I admired its striking blue, black and white Charles Tunnicliffe-designed jacket, depicting sheep caught within a ruined doorway overlooking Elan. This recalled his design for Henry Williamson's *Salar the Salmon*.

I devoured this book at a sitting with the intense pleasure that makes one read fast and miss things. It evoked a vivid picture of life on the Radnorshire hill-farms up to the Second World War. I remembered over intervening years Clarke's account of the laughter caused when, in 1939, farmers were invited by Whitehall bureaucrats to give up the use of all tractors for farm-work and return to hill-ponies. Since there were in 1939 only two tractors in the neighbourhood, little sacrifice resulted: hay, for example, still being largely turned by hand. Then there was the description, as I believed, of west Radnorshire shepherds between the wars being sewn for the winter into fleeces, unstitched only in the following spring: an outlandish notion given thrust by London friends who, when told of this awe-inducing and unhygienic custom, nodded sagely as if to imply that they always knew as much.

The Valley seemed one of those memoirs that contrive to be valuable social history. True, she misses interwar dependence on rabbits for sustenance and sale – though salmon and trout poaching are memorably described. Nor does she discuss the last of the colourful drovers, who now took their stock much shorter distances than Hampshire or the London markets, but who are remembered nonetheless and who feature, albeit fleetingly, later in this narrative.

There is a kind of book that combines elegy for the lost innocence of childhood with evocation of a vanished social order in the countryside: Laurie Lee's *Cider with Rosie* and Flora Thompson's *Lark Rise to Candleford* spring to mind. *The Valley*, published by Faber, which under T.S. Eliot's directorship favoured the genre, added notably to a tradition that belongs to the time before agri-business, when farmers could still appear as brave culture heroes, rather than as short-sighted or mercenary. Perhaps the coming economic pressure towards a return to self-sufficiency makes such histories of topical interest, more than just exercises in simple nostalgia, or mythology.

To compound its pleasures, *The Valley* documents the ancient dream-life of upland Radnorshire, the Calan Mai and summer-cottages or *hafodai*, where life was still lived through mid-summer among the high pastures. Here was a detailed account of those who, as R.S. Thomas translated that beautiful Welsh folk stanza, lived "At the bright hem of God/ In the heather, in the heather [where] time stands still … and it is easy to forget the contemporary world". Nonetheless the fiercely independent-minded Geoffrey Grigson accurately noted that Clarke's book was neither nostalgic, falsely exhilarating, nor falsely bleak: it was, he thought, "life as it comes".

Returning to *The Valley* now, nearly forty years later, I learn better. Firstly it contains no mention whatsoever of winter-fleeces. Its shepherds instead are saturated with the tallowy smell of sheep-wool, mutton and peat and, as a result of all this, are charged by the maid-of-all-work Siân – who puts them through their paces – with "stinking of sheep". Then, like many reviewers in 1969, including those of the *TLS* and *Economist*, I had also carelessly taken it as autobiography, rather than a mix of documentary fact and fiction. Elizabeth Clarke had pioneered in her 1964 book *The Darkening Green* exactly this unique genre of pretend-memoir. Also published by Faber, *The Darkening Green* tells the story of Clarke's real-life husband's incipient blindness as if it were her own or, rather, that of her fictional surrogate, Lucy. That book was set near Dartmoor and celebrated the folk ways of Devon.

Such a narrative strategy suggests a writer with an extraordinary gift for close observation and a love of losing herself within the lives of others. The first-person narrator in *The Valley* is called not Elizabeth Clarke, but Kate Jonas. Sure, both Clarke and Kate were born in 1910, and both take husbands with a sense-impairment – blindness in the case of Clarke's husband, deafness in Kate's. Yet *The Valley* is not autobiography.

Clarke was an Englishwoman, the child of estranged parents living beyond their means. Her father was tried for embezzlement. She probably never learnt that he might also have been abusing Elizabeth's elder brother. In any case this was far from a happy childhood, and may help account for her interest in idyll within her writing. When she was five years old her father killed himself.

She went to the Godolphin School in Salisbury, trained as a physiotherapist, made an unhappy first marriage to Peter Taylor. Her second marriage to a naval commander, Shene Clarke, was happy and they lived in Dorset and came to settle (as opposed to merely holidaying) at Pentreceithon, her secluded house in the Elan Valley in Radnorshire, only in 1963. She was short, wiry, twinkling, spry, searching, warm and reserved. Today her bachelor son by her unhappy first marriage survives in the same house. Over seventy and in the aftermath of a stroke, his intelligence is wholly unimpaired but his communicative skills are cruelly reduced to answering questions only in the Russian he acquired in the army, and, later, living in the USSR: *Da/Nyet, Bozhe moie* (my God) *Kharakhov* (great!).

Through Ted I learnt how hard Clarke researched *The Valley*. She was interested in everything, with that gift of making the talker feel special that loosens tongues. A list of eleven neighbours who provided information survives in her estate, and though she acknowledged only one portrait as being 'from the life' – that of 'Mr Meredith' who sang with Dame Clara Butt, based on the grandfather of Donald Jones – it is thought that her closest neighbours 'sat' for *The Valley*'s two sisters. *The Valley* is packed with the bright detail and intense life that might attract the notice of an outsider. If she has no native claim on the traditions of the Welsh heartland and therefore no entitlement to act as chief mourner at their passing, no more had R.S. Thomas who, for all his anti-English chauvinism, came, like Clarke, from somewhere different (as the next chapter explores). Perhaps we are all impoverished by the loss of such ways of life, and may without apology lament their disappearance.

The mapping of this loss is Clarke's burden, and there is little that she misses. Language interests her. Kate's grandmother was the last in the family to speak Welsh and older people still sometimes speak in exact translation, Welsh usage haunting English expression: 'The hens are sorry to lay now' and 'There's not on you a need to talk about everything you see!' Now the beautiful, mobile, West Saxon-descended dialect of the county replaces Welsh, where 'tidy' is an all-purpose compliment and 'piert' can mean lively. Verbs that are intransitive in standard English are still active in dialect: you 'loose' livestock into a field, 'rise' potatoes and 'fall' trees.

(Where is the Ffransis Payne who might mourn the passing of this dialect, so characteristic for two centuries of the March, now more threatened than Welsh itself? W.H. Howse gave a good account of it, though not of the famous apocryphal gravestone inscription: "Him that's dead be gone from we / Us'm left will soon join he" or the once common acknowledgement of blood relationship, 'Him be a cousin for I'. Few under sixty speak broad dialect today.)

All speech is used obliquely, direct inquiry then as now being thought highly impolite: and so Kate's father, known as 'The Boss', evades ignorant and ill-bred questionings about how many sheep he has with the answer 'several'. It is not done to 'rush at the subject in view'.

The golden time Clarke evokes is the last gasp of an ancient way of life whose perennial hardship now, in its final years, is especially intense. Farming is compared at one moment to the nose-diving of a stunt-flyer glimpsed in Brecon: prices are plunging too. Eggs, which sold in 1921 for five shillings the dozen, by 1933 sink to six pence (in today's currency, from 25p to 2.5p). Trussed fowl over the same twelve years drop from 2s 2d to 10d: (12p to 5p). And Welsh ewes sell in 1932 for only 15s (75p) with fat lambs going for 2s 6d (25p).

Public demand for cheap food was one hazard; another the succession of ruined harvests of the 1920s. For want of winter-keep, farmers were reduced to selling young stock at rock-bottom prices. Many farmers went bankrupt, their cottages abandoned and falling rapidly into weed-infested ruin, "eyeless husks, like the skulls of birds". And life in the towns and cities, to which some escape, is in some ways worse: so poor that they cannot even afford to buy shoes, the children of miners have to miss school....

Clarke is good on economic privation, yet never depicts a depressed or demoralised world. On the contrary, it is as if hardship – Blitz-like – gives rise to a greater solidarity. Doubtless her picture is idealised. She refers to greed, but only in passing. There is mention of grumbling and fraying of tempers but no vivid representation of either. And likewise friction between Kate and her sister Jenny, a tomboy educated in Presteigne, is never shown. She sees that quarrels could divide a family for a generation or two but is more interested in the way that the wishes of the dead are nonetheless strictly respected. And she describes the death of Jenny, who becomes a nurse and is killed in the Blitz, in a single sentence. Kate's grief is evoked only obliquely through her country wanderings to places both cherished.

Then there is continuous comic warfare between Siân and the two shepherds that may be inspired by Laurie Lee's wonderful evocation of the literally life-sustaining hatred between his two grannies – when one dies, the other swiftly follows. This cat-and-dog scrapping comes to life with the shepherds calling attention gleefully to Siân's mortality, and their last word on her after her death was, as always, "strict as a judge".

None of this is at the centre of Clarke's vision or concern, however, which is to paint a believable yet carefree Radnorshire pastoral, a scene of simple happiness and tranquillity in beautiful surroundings. She wants to capture the traditions and lore of an old continuous culture that resembles the Australian aboriginal Dreamtime, that sacred 'once-upon-a-time' belonging to a vast spiritual cycle in some ways more real than reality itself. So that when she refers at one point to the "enchanted days of old" she is also referring to a still extant, albeit vanishing, present.

This note is struck throughout. Kate is brought up by a peat fire that practically never goes out, and fed stories "from before the time we could remember", often about moleskin-waistcoated ancestors who seem so much larger than life that it is as though, as she puts it, they had originated the world. Here is a time-beyond-time when religion matters, prayer meetings migrating every week from farm to farm, where everyone sings hymns, and when nostalgia for the Promised Land "carried heaven to our very doors".

Small wonder that the old people, guarding a culture valued above easy affluence, deplore the tidal wave of innovations offered by the new century. Their world is indeed intensely conservative. Kate's grandmother's fondness for old-fashioned style is shared by many. Centuries of tedious handwork underpin this culture: "We clung to the past," she observes mordantly. Hereditary implements for peat-lifting include a sickle-knife sharpened on its outer edge, ace-shaped spade, four-tined fork and turf-irons; while for harvesting there is a horse-drawn mower, a swath-turner, and a self-releasing rake. The shepherds' shears have such individuality that they work well only for their owner. Not the smallest item that could be made or improvised at home is bought or paid for. So there are also wonder-filled accounts of the details of candle-making, poultry-dressing, bacon-curing, the making of rush-lights for the winter months, the weaving of wool and its dyeing with lichens: stockings are home-knitted. While both the livestock market and the farmyard are places for the exchange of witticisms, even the jokes that circulate there are often 'evergreen'.

Frugality and hard work are chief virtues: an hour spent with nothing to show for it is a cause for shame. And yet, if there is one value that counts for more even than hard work, it is a sociability that over-rides sectarianism: chapel and church people mingle at prayer meetings and at one another's festivals; they also share some pagan superstitions. Sociability counts among the highest virtues. A hired boy who can add to the family's sociability may be forgiven minor shortcomings as a worker; while another hireling who saves every penny of his earnings is by contrast given the reference "a good worker" together with the damning qualification "but poor company". Thus, too, shopping is expected to be time-consuming as you meet a steady procession of friends, with each of whom news and gossip must be exchanged. On Mayday Fair to walk two hundred yards takes one hour.

Much work is communal, and so is much play. Neighbours help each other: teamwork. Shearing is famously a time when womenfolk rise for one week at five to bake bread and pies and boil puddings, to roast both beef and mutton, to make Welsh cakes and tea. Then they feed the men in great successive batches of twenty at a sitting, and even the dogs are joyous.

Given how back-breaking much of this labour was, Clarke conveys throughout a remarkable sense of carnival. This is partly because visits to the Hafod where the action happens take place in summer, when the young Kate and her sister are on holiday, children playing their way over the hills; and even when not on holiday, kids are still let out of school for high days in the farming calendar. She wonders at the sunny weather prevailing in memory. Such a memoir tends necessarily to revolve around seasonal festivity, from the summer fairs through to Christmas, greatest feast of the year, when some of the geese that have been memorably brooding young inside two of three kitchen cupboards (the third being a shoe-store) are finally killed and lovingly dressed.

This is a world both tough and vulnerable. Its toughness shows on those occasions when it deals with the casualties of modernity. A soldier from the Crimean war in 1854-56 would call at the Hafod and tell stories of old battles in exchange for bread and cheese. He is followed by a master-scaffolder who remembers the horrors of the agricultural depression of the 1870s, when holdings first fell in value by three-quarters, wool being stored for years in the vain hope of its return to a saleable price. He too tells tales and meets with instinctive and generous hospitality, the hill-folk non-judgemental about their accurate suspicion that he is a Great War deserter.

Clarke knows that war estranges, maddens and is out of nature. So she tells in one late chapter the tale of Minky (a.k.a. Domenica), a lonely evacuee from Liverpool, happy at last in the hills, able to confide her troubles to the sheepdog, Sweep, who proudly carries her gas-mask. When Minky's selfish mother arrives to reclaim her so she can avoid being called up for ATS war-work, Minky's tears on being forced to leave for Merseyside stand in for those of all war-victims.

Clarke depicts an old tension between the values of the hill-farms and those of the modern world that threaten it. Outsiders wander into the hills and into the narrative, full of wonder at the beauty and seclusion of a place whose inhabitants are quietly content to be left to themselves. Two visitors are famous. The sexton Mr Meredith finds himself in duet one day with a lovely-voiced lady, who turns out to be Dame Clara Butt; while at the Electric Theatre in Brecon in 1921, Mary Pickford plays.

The coming of the Second World War is decisive. The international chaos and disastrous slump of 1938 both contribute to upsetting the 'usage of centuries'. After Munich late that year a programme called *Farming Today* (still broadcasting seventy years later) starts on the wireless, a film called *Speed the Plough* shows in cinemas, and trespass is punishable by up to £50 fines. With the coming war, sheep-farming – most individualistic of trades – will both come into its own and be subject to new restrictions. Even farmers going uphill soon need police permits.

Clarke interestingly sees the last war as a period of what we today are starting to call 're-wilding': one of those periodic returns to primitive conditions men are forced to make for their survival, "and possibly need for their own regeneration". Happily, Radnorshire hill-farmers started closer to the ground and so in some sense were able more easily to 'come into their own': broadcasting seed by hand continued until these farmers were boys and constituted no shock. The war-time return to pony traps enchants officers' wives, soldiers on the spree and civilians escaping from the bombing. War also means a further depopulation of the hills: many soldiers, having tasted a wider world, will not wish to come back afterwards to farming. Drastic changes are coming. Opinion "stirs in its sleep".

Such critical change was first heralded by the coming from the 1890s on of the dams and reservoirs near Elan to water the west Midlands. The farmers' landlord is now Birmingham Corporation. Francis Brett Young appears in *The Valley* collecting material for his novel based on Shelley's tenure, *The House Under the Water* (1932): neighbours preserve folk-reminiscences of mad Shelley hurtling down river on a plank, or setting light to paper boats with five-pound notes for sails. The houses he loved are now under reservoirs famously used during the war for trying out the bouncing bombs to burst the Ruhr dams and flood nearby cities, later recorded in *The Dam Busters*. At the time Radnorshire folk felt a horrified fellow-feeling for the Rhinelanders. What if *that* happened *here*?

Elizabeth Clarke movingly ends in March 1892, imagining three hill-farmers dressed in their best chapel clothes – breeches, leggings, boots – deposing evidence to puzzled MPs and civil servants in Whitehall. For this section she was indebted to the House of Commons Select Committee on the Birmingham Corporation Water Bill, which had eye-witness transcripts. The farmers, bewildered yet immensely polite, proud and self-conscious, try to explain to the city-folk the value of a way of life that the new dams threaten, reaching out across a deep mutual ignorance. They struggle to communicate what it is like to farm three sheep to every two acres, and what their endangered chapel and school mean to them. They repeat a simple mantra without sense to Londoners: "I would like to keep it all as it is". "You would rather things are left as they are?" ask the Committee. To which one farmer, at last abandoning polite indirectness, answers in the book's final word quite simply: "Yes".

Clarke never repeated this success. She published in 1972 a children's novel called *The Secret*, published in translation also in Germany, but *A Few Kindred Spirits*, another children's book, was rejected, and she died, on her own and at home, in July 1978, of an asthma attack. *A Winter Place*, on which she was working at the time of her death, has never been published. Faber found what they had read thus far "fascinating... beautifully written". And as I write, *The Valley* is out of print.

★

The most famous post-war novel about Wales, Bruce Chatwin's best-selling *On The Black Hill* (1982), is also set in a fictionalised Radnorshire. I can't discover whether Chatwin had read Clarke's *The Valley*, and neither of his biographers make this connection, but he was known as a 'demon researcher' and one scene, as we shall see, suggests on Chatwin's part a deliberate echo.

The success of the novel generally is famous: it was swiftly an A level set text and first a play, then a film. But in the Borders which it depicts, its success has also been remarkable. "And 'ow's you?" "Middling". "And the wife?" "Poor". That is one early exchange. Radnorshire felt listened to, seen and captured in fine writing.[1] Richard Booth, who helped make Hay a successful centre for second-hand bookselling, feared that Chatwin patronized local speech-patterns; nobody in Radnorshire agreed. Many local stories Chatwin ingested and recycled were recognizable. So was the flattering fact that a good writer had at last tried to understand and map the area. And the novel had epic ambitions: most Radnorshire farmers preferred the Old Testament, Chatwin reminds us, because the Old had more about sheep-farming than the New. So Chatwin gives his sheep-farmers a quasi-Biblical dignity, the Israelites being "essentially wandering sheep-thieves".

His attachment to the Welsh March was long-standing. He had been conceived in Wales, his father drove him to Rhaeadr when he was seven, his school, Marlbororough College, had a farm at Capel-y-ffin where he stayed, and Llanthony was where he courted his wife. "This is the place I love," he wrote: partly for its physical beauty, partly for its immunity to twentieth-century fashion. The area had scarcely changed since his grandparents had visited: you could still buy the same double-fronted striped shirts in Hay-on-Wye.

The novel deliberately mixes up Radnorshire, Breconshire and Monmouthshire, making of these a single mythical landscape. The action could, Chatwin asserted, be thought of as taking place anywhere from South Shropshire to the Black Mountains, the whole of which, in his view, had "the same character". Thus early on Sam the drover teaches his twin grandsons Lewis and Benjamin both how to identify the high peaks of the Radnor Forest – Whimble, Black Mixen, and Bach and the Smatcher near to which he was born – and 'Father Ambrosius's monastery' nestling in the valley below, a clear reference to Father Ignatius at Llanthony. Chatwin invents a county town nearby called Rhulen which shares only a name with one of the tiniest, most remote, peaceful and picturesque churches in Radnorshire, possibly in all Wales. Chatwin said in interview that his fictional and busy Rhulen could be thought of as Hay-on-Wye, Knighton, Kington or as Clun.

Chatwin, an outsider, felt at home here. He certainly made himself at home, in at least seven houses. He stayed with the Wilkinson family near Clunton and in two winters washed up not one single plate, while similar tales were told by George and Diana Melly, Lady Penelope Betjeman and Tom Maschler, all on or near the Black Mountains. They variously noted that "like a child, he took everything", that he was solipsistic and "heroically selfish". If he paid his hosts at all it was in anecdotes and with his considerable charm. He was a born guest, restless, hungry, poetically intense and, perhaps, inwardly vulnerable.

Here he researched his new book hard, reading and talking to locals. Some of the characters he invented had real-life originals but were invariably sea-changed in composition; he found it hard to distinguish fact and fiction. He was introduced to and then made friends with shy and gentle Jean-the-Barn, who lived in domestic squalor with Joe, who treated her as both wife and daughter, and who would never cause harm to any animal. On Jean he modelled Meg-the-Rock. He also met the Howells brothers who had never been inside a bus or a train, had never visited either London or the sea, but were obsessed with airplanes and made one trip in a plane at the age of seventy-five. These brothers had a year's difference in their ages and slept in single beds in their shared bedroom.

The Howells brothers were one set of real-life originals for Benjamin and Lewis Jones in the novel, who, by contrast, are twins besotted with one another and who for forty-two years share their parents' bed. Their lives, starting in 1900, span much of the century. Their parents Amos and Mary meet in church and fall in love, their marriage compounding a difference in class: unlike the Howells' mother, an ex-maid, Mary is a clergyman's daughter and a lady. The agent with whom she deals charges her with "joining the peasants" through marrying Amos and a solicitor holds her a class-traitor. Sometimes Mary has to strain to follow Amos's dialect; and she twice to his disgust "pulls rank" through knowing the right people to secure the occupancy of their house – first its rental, later its freehold.

This farm, with one hundred and twenty acres, is poetically called the Vision since a local girl in 1737 saw the Virgin Mary hovering there over the rhubarb; the border between Hereford and Radnor runs through its staircase. "The house had rough-cast walls and a roof of mossy stone tiles and stood at the far end of a farmyard in the shade of an old Scots Pine. Below the cowshed there was an orchard of wind-stunted apple trees, and then the field slanted down to the dingle, and there were birches and alders along the stream." It is a very recognisably Radnorshire scene, and holding. The house gives onto two walks, a 'Welsh' one up the mountain, an 'English' one downhill; and a minor theme of Welsh-English antagonism runs through the book.

The marriage between Mary and Amos is passionate and stormy, the truces that follow its frequent battles sometimes preludes to tenderness. Amos's mother sets the tone by sneering at Mary as 'Your Ladyship' and attacking the extravagance with which she cooks with butter, a note picked up by Amos when he is enraged by her wish to grow asparagus, or cook a curry. A limited and in some ways oafish man, he is both stirred and also threatened by the breadth and scope she represents.

Frustration at the constriction of life leads to violence. His boys Lewis and Benjamin have a pet pig they dote upon called Hoggage, which – on the grounds that it is a runt and therefore un-economic – he soon butchers. Education is another battle-field. Mary takes the boys to school and even teaches them herself a little Latin, Shakespeare and Dickens while Amos fears that all such schooling will cause them to despise and later desert their roots. But a brutal neighbourly feud leads Amos and the boys to many hours of chapel religiosity, while their schooling meanwhile gets left behind and forgotten. If a battle is going on for their souls, this round is won by Amos.

One of the charms of the novel is the relationship between

the boys. Chatwin energetically researched twinship. Although they are identical twins born from a single egg – monozygotic, as they learn to call their condition – they differ none the less. Benjamin is a physical coward who once drenched himself in his mother's perfume and dressed up in her clothes, who likes to bake and is distinctly his Mother's 'pet'. "He did not like girls" and, it is clear, is gay. He wants to live in a perpetual stasis with Lewis, eat the same food, wear the same clothes, and share a bed. Lewis is more 'manly' but in some ways less emotionally tough. Dependence on his brother and mother costs Lewis the sexual happiness he might otherwise have enjoyed with women: they collude to keep Lewis celibate.

Such differences feed an essential sameness. When his twin sons are threatened by conscription during the Great War, Amos confides that they are not two persons but one. This paradox exercises Chatwin's imagination and leads to flights of fancy. We learn that, as children, Lewis not merely knows when Benjamin is stung by a wasp, but has the ability to "draw the pain into himself". They split their sandwiches in two, exchange halves, give identical answers and make the same mistakes in school, snore in perfect time, soap each others's backs, and even quarrel telepathetically.

Each mistakes his own mirror reflection for the other, and they sometimes exchange names. Each also knows when the other is in trouble, and often where. In 1918 Lewis knows when Benjamin is lost in a blizzard and in danger, and where he is to be found, and when he is soon afterwards detained by the Army and punished Lewis knows from the pains that wander around his own body, exactly what indignity or hurt Benjamin is being subjected to. And sixty years later Benjamin knows instantly when Lewis is killed by a falling tractor.

Chatwin has a private investment in the themes of solitude and one-ness. While enjoying hob-nobbing in New York with such as Jackie Onassis, Robert Mapplethorpe and Nureyev, his marriage was falling apart. There were the double strains of his homosexual affairs, and of his restless love of movement and nomadism, and he was perhaps experiencing his own necessary aloneness with a new vividness. He would commune with himself out loud while writing, partly debating, partly trying out all the different voices. Writing itself was a form of escape.

So, arguably, were his flimsy theorisings about the necessity of nomadism, whose spokesman in *On The Black Hill* is Theo the Tent, living with few possessions in a yurt (this theme would flower in his next book, *Songlines*, set among Australian aboriginals). Here the final sermon asserts that we are all nomads in the sense of being visitors to the planet: "our life is a bubble. We are born. We float upwards... we glitter in the sunshine... then all of a sudden &tc". The critic Karl Miller commented: "the country is better than the town..., but the country is terrible. Where, if not in heaven, are we to live?" He thought the novel "a tour-de-force of door-step exoticism that fails". Certainly, such religious rhetoric apart, the novel has little of interest to say about nomadism.

Reclusiveness is the book's true theme, which (more than nomadism) is used to criticise conventional life. Chatwin must have known, as did Clarke, that real mid-Welsh farm-life before the war was often communal, with team-harvesting and team-shearing. The novel ignores this, abounding instead in eccentric solitaries inhabiting a bleak, denuded scene. When conscription starts during the Great War Amos plans to hide both sons high up in a secret place in the Radnor Forest, while after the war the twins do not merely stay in the Vision but "turn away from the modern age" itself, making the house into a museum to the past, changing nothing.

The themes of stopping time and escaping from modernity recur. Thus also Meg, who feeds the wild birds from her own hand, and, like her father Jim, preaches non-violence towards most animals – "Let 'em live" – does not in thirty years so much as leave her house. And Rosie Fifield moves with her illegitimate son into a house where a reclusive defrocked priest recently died, "shut[s] herself off from the world", her family dead, living in squalor and unknowingly on charity handouts. There she too stays for thirty years.

All the characters Chatwin admires share this willingness to be alone, including Nancy's courageous niece Philippa, who spends months each year riding alone round India on a bike and is clearly based on Penelope Betjeman. He misses few chances to underline his theme. The Vision itself belonged to an old umarried sister who lived there alone before being taken into a madhouse, while a trip to Bacton and the tomb of Elizabeth I's maid Blanche Parry reveals that Parry too lived and died in retirement. Thus Chatwin celebrates the reclusiveness and individualism alike of the March.

It is an individualism that leads to a serious feud between Amos and Tom Watkins at a neighbouring farm called the Rock. While Amos threatens to burn her novels, Mary reads *Wuthering Heights*: but it is Amos who unwittingly lives out himself the drama that that novel describes.

It starts as a boundary dispute, with some thieving to spice Amos's rancour. Soon a vendetta develops, during which Tom sets fire to Amos's ricks, and the flaying of a lamb, the killing of a calf and a gander lead up to Aggie setting her dog on Mary. Tom then murders Amos's dog while Amos disembowels Tom's mule. (Cruelty to mules is a weird sub-theme: Tom later hammers a nail into the skull of a mule belonging to his foster-son Jim, who had invented war-time gas-masks for mules; while at the end of the book Theo lives alone with a mule called Max that loves him.) Small wonder that Mary, who later turns into a good farmer herself, is depressed by hill-farm life, and contemplates escape.

Chatwin is anxious not to sentimentalise the lives he celebrates. So the worst sins in his eyes are committed not by feuding farmers, with whom he keeps faith, but by townspeople leading settled lives. Of these he presents a veritable rogue's gallery. A snobbish, lazy and venal land-agent nearly loses Mary occupancy of the Vision. Bickerton, who employs that agent, is a man capable carefully of exempting two of his hunt servants and his valet from conscription, while his son Reggie is a villain who seduces, impregnates and then abandons Rosie. A shifty antiques dealer with rotten teeth from Ross-on-Wye cheats the twins out of their mother's Sheraton desk. The worst – exemplifying all the rest – is the solicitor Mr Arkwright, obsequious to the rich, bullying to the poor, who publicly accuses Benjamin of cowardice, has black market dealings, and is finally exposed as having poisoned a rival solicitor after killing his wife with arsenic. His case is clearly based on that of Major H.R. Armstrong, hanged in 1922 for poisoning his wife, as well as for attempting to poison a rival solicitor, a case that rocked Hay society. To no-one's chagrin, Arkwright too is duly hanged. He embodies all the depravity of town-life.

In the long, long passage describing the post-World War One peace celebrations, Arkwright accordingly figures as Benjamin's chief tormentor. Here, unusually, the narrative pace slows, and the many satirical pages of tired jingoism that ensue are wearisome to read. Generally Chatwin provides a cinematic succession of small scenes, where inattention would cause us to miss new twists of plot. But the Great War occupies one sixth of his text.

After these war-time humiliations the twins make no investment in modern farm machinery, telling their father not to waste his money. This is symptomatic of a larger refusal: "Deliberately, as if reaching back to the innocence of early childhood, they turned away from the modern age". The Second World War, accordingly, almost passes them by. Its ending is memorably signalled when the local newspaper runs a defiant headline: 51lb salmon "grassed at Coleman's Pool – brigadier tells of three hour struggle with titanic fish", followed by a shorter column mentioning the death of Hitler and the entry of Allied troops into Berlin. This is finely and humorously done. It is clear that Chatwin thinks this Radnorshire-centred perspective carries a truth to which we might attend.

The apotheosis of this vision comes near the end, when the twins' newly-found great-nephew Kevin, who will inherit the Vision, arranges for their eightieth birthday a surprise flight in a Cessna. Lewis takes the controls and experiences a joy dependent on the fact that their souls, though outwardly so circumscribed, are free: in a similar spirit Elizabeth Clarke had also rewarded her shepherd Emrys with a flight up the valley, and it may perhaps be that Chatwin is paying Clarke a quiet homage. Soon Lewis is killed and a bewildered Benjamin, now rendered marginal by his nephew's family in his own home, finds daily solace in communing with Lewis in the churchyard.

This is a moving ending to a fine book. Paul Bailey nonetheless wrote a notably spiteful review: to some the rural poor with their archaic dialect were somehow absurd, only the lives of the urban poor apparently being fashionable or deserving notation. Despite this, the novel was generally well-received, winning the Whitbread and James Tate Black Memorial prizes and, as we have seen, by 1988, one year before Chatwin's death from AIDS, becoming an A level set text and memorably a film. It was small surprise to lovers of the Welsh March that Bruce Chatwin found Radnorshire exotic, little-known and mysterious. He is a romantic writer, in love with elsewhere.

Seers and Remembrancers

Among the poets who have celebrated mid-Wales are three that make a triptych. Ruth Bidgood celebrates life in the sparsely populated hills of northern Breconshire and is without question *the* pre-eminent poet and historian of upland mid-Wales. Roland Mathias was born in Talybont-on-Usk in Breconshire and lived in Brecon for many years. R.S. Thomas was a bird of passage. He and Mathias left a number of Radnorshire poems, six of which have overlapping subject-matter.

Bidgood was born in Glamorgan in 1922, went up to Oxford to read English, and served during the war in Alexandria. The daughter of a Welsh-speaking vicar, she returned from working in London to settle in Abergwesyn in the 1970s and it was there that she found herself as a poet. "All the steps of my life have brought me home" ('Roads').

She wrote between 1974 and 1980 a series of seven scholarly

articles on the families of Llanddewi Hall, the 'big house' at Abergwesyn, published in the *Transactions of the Radnorshire Society*, using letters, land deeds, wills, ledgers and tombstone inscriptions to recreate the life of the district over many generations. Her interest in local history – "the more local the better" she once said – was further developed in her *Parishes of the Buzzard* (2000), a study of the twin upland parishes of Abergwesyn in northern Breconshire, among the most isolated in all Wales.

Through much painstaking research, Bidgood recreated eloquently the religious, social and agricultural life of a little-known community. Her book celebrated ways of being typical of rural mid-Wales: individualistic to the point of eccentricity, in which, to take one random example, one Congregationalist minister, nick-named 'the dog-deacon', admitted into chapel on Sundays only "well-conducted, *seriously-disposed* dogs". Any dog showing signs of frivolity was duly hit on the nose with a shepherd's staff. Another Independent minister, the patriarchal radical Kilsby, scandalised his hearers by musing about whether, on the Day of Judgement, God would bother to judge Kilsby's neighbours one-by-one, or whether He might simplify matters and to avoid "losing time" over such fools judge them instead in lots like sheep at an auction!

Her book is not an exercise in nostalgia. As she said of Abergwesyn, "I have never wanted to escape from the world by coming here – this is the world". It was a world following the old hill-pattern of isolated farmsteads linked by narrow tracks, many of these now lost or, in local parlance, 'gone down'. Churches, schools and inns had also gone, the small valleys of Irfon and Gwesyn dotted alike with ruined houses and disused fields. Her poetry is interested in absence.

What is evanescent evokes in Bidgood a tender curiosity, and her poetry and historical interests are part of one project: she is a poet of place with a sense of the sacred. "What is forgotten cannot be healed," she wrote ('Unhealed'). So the writer becomes a necessary remembrancer, an objective chronicler of the pains of change and loss, and thus also – perhaps – a priest-like healer. One pleasure of reading her is how self-effacing she is – cheerfully free from what one of her poems terms the "draggled old bitch-hound" of Self.

This subtraction liberates her to imagine the lives and loves of others. One poem is entitled 'Letter' and imagines a woman addressing her sister on the subject of "the Great Harshness of the Winter/amid these Rough Welsh Hills/and the long Hours of Darkness... these things weigh heavy on me". This persona fears that spring might never return, but loses her fear within the need to minister to her sick husband. The poem is an artful mini-novel. In a similar spirit she also writes sequences of 'found poems': centuries-old letters tellingly set out as verse.

All is transient. She knows this intimately: in 'Leasehold' she comments mordantly that the only lie is any promise of permanence. Such unshowy perceptions – constancy is an untruth, mutability the law of existence – work to bring her poems mysteriously alive. If the present is, as one early poem notes, haunted ('The Given Time'), it is haunted not just by the shadow of the past but equally by its own shadowed future, such instability rendering it mysterious too.

Thus in another early poem – 'Little of Distinction' – the poet records being surprised by joy at a visit to a place that quite unexpectedly offered much, including views of "the miles on hazy miles/Of Radnorshire and Breconshire below,/Uncertain in the heat – the mystery/That complements precision". Objectivity and numinousness go hand in hand.

Such mystery has its under-side. Not only that it makes present time itself into "A boundary zone/between known and known;/a place of blurred identity" ('Question'). But also darkness, night and desolation invade the poems. As in the sequence 'Valley-before-Night', where poetry itself is all that helps hold these alarming forces at bay. So the poet is herself an agent of light, each poem resembling the open fire that acts as "a charm against death-wish darkness" ('Log Fire'). Winter is an active force, too, with the "high white silence" of 'Blizzard';

the memory of two brothers who "lived, in their solitude,/a present that was most men's past" but now, thirty years after they died, are fading "into ultimate snows" ('Shapes in Ice').

She elegises an old lead-mine ('Carreg-y-Fran') as also the sexual loneliness of the men who worked it; recreates in words the Old Pump House at Llanwrtyd. And the deadening arrival of conifer forests with the felling-machines that accompany them, and the arrival on the coast of an oil-slick exercise her too. Everywhere she hears the tick-tock of time.

Above all, there is the dereliction of houses, together with the loss of all the noisy life they once contained. For example, 'The Hermitage' evoking a visit to find the ruin of an ancient house. Or the final day of human habitation at Cefn Cendu – where "One beauty died/ when the last owner, leaving, shut the door/ and heard for the last time an echo/ follow him from empty rooms". Here the poem itself arguably constitutes another version of the echo that the last owner was listening out for. Or 'Hennant', where a tree grows out of each corner of what was once the house.

How well she writes of such farms, the disappearance of which can numb the onlooker and excite wonder too at all that supervenes: silence, rank grass, trees.... Or religious houses like the Abbey at Strata Florida where, instead of the vault of the Cistercian roof, "we look up and find/only our own late August sky".

Bidgood is interested in legends such as King Arthur's, in angels, and in Edward Thomas. She can capture, as could D.H. Lawrence or for that matter Kilvert writing his lucid diary-prose, the mysterious otherness of animals: the stupid panic of a sheep caught in a hedge, making life hard for those wishing to free it, a bantam wonderfully stalking "in miniature grandeur", and then a pig, a ferret, a squashed hedgehog, a coquettish mare. Then there is a scattering of poems to ancient peoples other than the mid-Welsh: Mayans, Aran Islanders, Romano-British, for the last of whom she writes epitaphs.

The poems I love best chronicle little domestic scenes.

'Snow' evokes the poet falling asleep at a film on telly, while a short winter day's devil-dance of tumbling snow outlasts and dwarfs the indoor entertainment. "Here, outside,/ night, a blind and silent valley,/ and snow falling, snow falling". Repetition here is no cheap device, but enacts the unceasing patience with which snow brings its deathly changes into a world which it makes into its own.

'New Telephone' observes the laying on a hot and airless day of a new phone cable up which "Back and fore,/ words will dance and stumble,/ check and flow". The welcome arrival of a breeze, for which onlookers have long waited, is at last compared to "an enigmatic hint,/ like ambivalent words/ waiting in the wires". Both breeze and telephone are welcome harbingers of change.

She is no simple Luddite, but an objective observer of mid-Welsh life, and a celebrant of all that nourishes and sustains it – telephones included. In a recent poem called 'Yard in Winter' Bidgood asks us and herself the question what it is that an accurate perspective might confer on the human and natural scene on which she gazes? And finds the moving answer: "a sort of gratitude; a sort of love".

*

Houses fall into ruin and die. So do poets. The landscape of good poetry itself recalls mid-Wales, each time depopulated when the old voices 'go down' like houses. Later new talents invade and colonise. And meanwhile across the unpeopled spaces poets hail one other and their readers: poetry, after all, having always functioned among other things as a species of long-distance conversation. So the death of R.S. Thomas in 2000 prompts Ruth Bidgood to address his spirit, starting "Now is the time/ of the dark house,/ the empty shore", measuring how much he and his work meant to all his readers and thus how big a gap Thomas left behind him ('Bereft').

Bidgood was not alone. Under the heading 'Death of Welsh poet' the *Mid-Wales Journal* reported on 29 September 2000:

R.S. Thomas, the foremost Welsh poet writing in the English language, who died this week, was no stranger to the Presteigne area, for he lived in a cottage close to the town for some time, a few years ago. He later married Betty Vernon, the widow of his close friend Major Richard Vernon of Titley, who survives him, and with whom he lived near Criccieth in North Wales.

The Rev Ronald Stuart Thomas... was 87 and a former priest of the Church in Wales, and he had been ill for some time. His friendship with the Vernons goes back many years, at least as far as the days when they were neighbours in North Wales and he pursued his hobby of bird watching, which he shared with Major Vernon. Mr Thomas was greatly attached to Alice, Mrs Vernon's daughter by a previous marriage, who later lived at Norton, near Presteigne, and following her untimely death a few years ago, he read a poem which he had specially written for her funeral service...

We do not at once associate R.S. Thomas, greatest of all twentieth-century Welsh poets in English, with mid-Wales: rather with the mountain fastnesses of the West and North in which he passed his last years. And yet he had twelve notably productive and contented years as vicar of Manafon in Montgomeryshire, from 1942 to 1954, the one place and time his only child Gwydion remembered as being happy. And after the death of his first wife Elsi on March 10 1991, his future second wife Betty Vernon with her husband took him in during the winter of 1994, at Burcher Cottage, Titley, outside Presteigne. This period is missing from both biographies of him thus far published. The marriage of R.S. Thomas and Betty happened one month after Betty's first husband Richard died at Titley in July 1996.

Betty's daughter Alice Maitland, who had a husband, a son of eleven, and a daughter of fifteen, was gravely ill when Thomas published the moving poem 'To a Lady' in his 1995 volume, *No Truce with the Furies*:

> I don't know
> who I write to,

the frocked girl,
pretty but pert,
or the grown-up
mother, doll-less
but dolled. Nor
does death either
who, liquidating
her lungs, applying
irons to her heart,
discovers, astonished,
a being somewhere
between both, perter
than a child, prettier
than a parent, and
wiser than each
of them in the way
she treats his fumbling
familiarity with contempt.

Alice died, aged 40, in March 1997, and Thomas attended her burial in Norton, outside Presteigne, reading his remarkable farewell poem, 'For Alice', which pays tribute to her stoical courage and her showing of an "affirming flame". In the first stanza Alice pretends to be immortal purely to reassure family and friends. In the second Alice soothes the poet's terror too:

Seeing those small bones,
her breath a butterfly
endeavouring to escape her;
her eyes wounded
by failures of taste
never to be mentioned,
I gave my breath rein
only to see how
it was brought up short,
trembling and then becoming
quiet again under
the stroking of her infirm smile.[1]

Thomas is remembered hereabouts dressed in tweed jackets

and cavalry twills like that retired Brigadier class of Englishmen for whom, despite all his passionate anti-Englishness, he reserved such strange respect, sharing after all both their reserve and their cold formality. Here, as his son Gwydion recorded, he was able to indulge his hankering to be an English country gentleman. Indeed his second wife Betty Vernon hunted.

And Thomas had earlier written four other Radnorshire poems. One, published in 1975, is 'Llananno', and pictures the poet stopping by the small church with its fabulous rood-screen on the river Ithon, waters that convey a "quiet insistence on a time/ older than man". He stops in order to declare his independence from the speed and aggression of modern life; inside the church he finds a serene presence "that waits for me till I come next". Like the hills in the Psalms, Llannano is a place that offers spiritual sustenance.

His other three Radnorshire poems by a strange coincidence share topics with his near-contemporary and fellow-pacifist Roland Mathias, founding father of post-war Anglo-Welsh literary studies, who lived for many of his latter years in Brecon. Mathias admired Thomas but also differed from and debated with him. While Thomas was an Anglican, Mathias, born in Talybont-on-Usk, son of a Welsh-speaking Congregational army chaplain, had a strongly Nonconformist conscience. He returned to Wales in 1948 as headmaster of Pembroke Dock Grammar School. It was there, during his ten-year appointment, that he took a leading role in founding *Dock Leaves*, a magazine which, as *The Anglo-Welsh Review* from 1957, took as its principal aim the healing of the breach between writers in Welsh and their counterparts writing in English; as editor from 1961 to 1976, Mathias insisted that English-speakers had a part to play in the cultural life of Wales. This, together with Nonconformism, puts him at odds with Thomas.

Their shared Radnorshire subject matter begins in the 1940s with two lyric poems about Maes-yr-onnen (field-of-ash). This most beautifully preserved of all early chapels in Wales has been well described by T.J. Hughes in his recent, admirable *Wales's Best One Hundred Churches*. Standing alone among the hills above Glasbury, Maes-yr-onnen began life as a barn "long, low and earth-brown" adjoining a sixteenth-century farmhouse with a sundial on one of its gables and a small minister's or keeper's cottage. Although it was not formally registered as a Congregational chapel until 1697, the names of ministers painted on the pulpit go back to 1645: the Toleration Act in 1689 finally allowed Dissenters, though still excluded from universities and public office, freely to worship in licensed meeting houses. Maes-yr-onnen, with its early furniture and tie-beamed roof alike wonderfully intact, is the closest we can get today to the first chapels of three hundred years ago. The essence of all later chapel design and positioning, Hughes points out, is here: two joined communal tables dated 1728 dominate, at the heart of the congregation, not railed off at an altar as in the established Anglican churches, together with a big seat – *sedd fawr* – for Deacons.

Here is a setting deliberately echoing the earliest Celtic churches: simple, communal, conveying the sense of a small like-minded gathering pressed up close; and a survey of 1715 shows attendance at 250. Cromwell is said to have visited and the early Methodist George Whitefield to have preached. Bruce Chatwin in *On The Black Hill* unmistakably used Maes-yr-onnen as the original for the similarly-named Maes-y-felin: here he stages the long final sermon that presages Lewis's death, which explains how Chatwin wishes us to understand all the life that has preceded it.

One August day just after the war R.S. Thomas visited only to find the doors locked, and so started to imagine the life within. He wrote his fine sonnet, 'Maes-yr-onnen', that opposes what he calls "the stale piety, mouldering within" to an ecstatic vision "You cannot hear as I, incredulous, heard/Up in the rafters, where the bells should ring,/The wild, sweet singing of Rhiannon's birds". His first biographer explains that Rhiannon, a figure from the *Mabinogion*, typifies for Thomas the highest seal of Welshness, her birds with the gift of quickening the dead and entrancing the living. Thomas later recorded that there at Maes-yr-onnen he had a visionary realisation whose essence was that: "there is no such thing as time, no beginning and no end but that everything is a fountain welling up endlessly from immortal God". This understanding his sonnet struggles to convey.

In an essay in Welsh entitled 'Two Chapels' written soon after, he nonetheless compares Maes-yr-onnen unfavourably with Soar-y-mynydd, perhaps the most remote and astonishing chapel in the whole of Wales. It stands near the banks of the river Camddwr on the road from Tregaron to Llyn Brianne. Here, among the bog-cotton, pilgrims still make their way to hear preachers – under a wall-painting announcing that '*Duw Cariad yw*' – God is Love – discourse in the old and fervent Welsh style which centuries ago was said to have caused a so-called *tân grug* – a fire in the heather or wildly spreading enthusiasm. Soar-y-mynydd belongs to the third generation of Welsh Calvinistic Methodist chapels and evoked in Thomas a sense of something he approvingly calls the Welsh soul, rather than the Welsh spirit – evidently the lesser of two goods.

By chance Roland Mathias also came to Maesyronnen, which he chooses to spell without hyphens, around the same time in the 1940s, and wrote a longer poem with the same title. Mathias's poem is full of the living detail that marks him as a poet, as well as the mandarin obscurity that frustrates some of his admirers – 'tenebrate' here for shadowy, for example. He was for much of his life a schoolmaster, and his poetry explores history with care and pedantry alike.

Mathias's Maesyronnen chapel, long and white, leans "beyond the lordly hedge". Within, he sees the "dusty hymn-books only ten years old" that indicate that the chapel has come down in the world "to indicate the poor and present few" to oppose to its braver past. He sees, too, the "stiff-necked family pew" where worshippers attended to passionate sermons against the sinfulness of the Established Church as well as casti-gating their own sins.

While Mathias denied looking over his shoulder at his older contemporary, he nonetheless wrote a long 1972 essay in which he objected to Thomas' "needless sectarian asides" and occasional confusions[2]. And he took issue with Thomas very directly in another poem called 'Sir Gelli to R.S.', where Thomas is the 'R.S.' referred to in Mathias's very title.

Sir Gelli Meurig or Meyrick was an Anglesey-born squire who rose to be Lieutenant-General and, through marriage to Elizabeth (Margaret) Lewis of Radnor, came into Radnorshire lands. Thus Sir Gelli inherited the late medieval court at Gladestry and an estate at Llanelwedd on the Wye, both in Radnorshire; he also owned Wigmore Castle. The Earl of Essex memorably rebelled against Queen Elizabeth, inciting her anger by his failures in Ireland against its 'rebels'. Sir Gelli duly sought financial backing for Essex among Herefordshire squires with Catholic sympathies, and was consequently caught and executed with Essex on 13 March 1601. His estates were confiscated but later restored in part to his son Roland and daughter Margaret at Lucton and Eyton in Herefordshire.

Thomas in the late 1960s had written 'Sir Gelli Meurig (Elizabethan)', in which Sir Gelli becomes the very type and figure of Welsh quisling or traitor, his crime not at all that of conspiring against Queen Elizabeth, but entirely that of turning his back upon his native Wales, toadying to the English. Thomas's Sir Gelli is typical of Welsh turncoats over the centuries who deserted their homeland for "the town/ And its baubles" – for fine clothes and power. "Helplessly they dance/ to a mad tune, who at home/ In the bracken could have remained/ Humble but free'. His beheading, by implication, is apt punishment for such greedy opportunism. As Thomas memorably puts the matter, Sir Gelli is no more interesting than a mere "Welsh fly/ Caught in a web spun/ For a hornet". "Betray Wales and deserve to die" is the moral.

In 'Sir Gelli to R.S.', written a few years later[3], Roland Mathias awards Gelli right of reply. Indeed Gelli challenges Thomas across the centuries to a duel (!) his poem ending "I'll blood you sharply an [= if] you'll not declare/Which of us left an innocence in Wales". Mathias's Sir Gelli – by contrast – always kept faith with his country and his cause alike, never dazzled by baubles, fine clothes or by London, which is after all only "a place/To pass through for a Welshman, always was": London in this poem is the port from which Sir Gelli reached Cadiz on the Queen's business – he was knighted for his part in the capture of that city – as well as the place he meets his come-uppance. The poem showcases much picturesque detail about life and language in sixteenth-century Britain; and it champions a more tolerant vision of the complex, necessary compromises of Welsh history than the extreme and simplified picture advocated by Thomas.

Mathias and Thomas shared one further Radnorshire topic, this last overlap an accident. Between 1955 and 1957 Mathias composed 'Cascob', about a place he had visited one summer holiday afternoon. It runs

> Just here's the middle of a silence that
> Has already sung the centuries like a gnat:
> The valley's middle too, by the hill sound
> Topping the trees. Perhaps the full circle, for the bound
> Of the churchyard circles and the black yews
> Are markers. Each on the circuit ropes and screws
> Giddily, wind having caught it widdershins
> At the clock's three. No true arrest. For two pins
> I'd leave in a hurry, were it not absurd...
>
> Blank wall facing west, belfry of weather-board
> Raised on a druid's mound, none of it
> Reassuring. Within, a brass of familiars, habit
> Of clergy, pater, pater, pater, noster, noster, noster
> Three times for Saturn. O save our sister
> Elizabeth Lloyd from spirits, amen. Behind
> My back is a thin medieval tongue, the wind
> Carrying it woodward, tang and tone.
> Service at three. Who is it coming? Afternoon, afternoon.
> The thin hymn wavers to the circuit hedge.

The yews grimace at my ear, there, at the edge
Of being. Sister, sister, night follows day
Out of these bounds, loping beyond the yews, away
Giddily over wall and number and ken.
Quiet these centuries. Who is it going now? Amen, amen.[4]

It was the difficulties of this 'strange' poem that led Mathias's best critic, Sam Adams, to edit and explicate his collected poetry, with footnotes to gloss difficult allusions. Adams drove up the two and a half mile single track road hidden in an eastern fold of the Radnor Forest to Cascob thirty years ago, noting that the place was not even mentioned on certain maps, though it appears in the Domesday Book. He was in pursuit of the writer T.J. Llewelyn Prichard (1790-1862), who collected and published tales and adventures of the so-called Welsh Robin Hood Twm Shon Catti and on this quest knocked on my front door.[5]

Pritchard had stayed at the old Rectory – to which I re-directed Adams – at various times during the second quarter of the nineteenth-century, finding there at the rectory, home of his loyal friend, the Revd William Jenkins Rees, rest and succour, and access to a library to assist his own historical studies. Rees was Rector of Cascob for some fifty years and notable among the *Hen bersoniaid llengar*, that group of Church of England clergymen who fostered Welsh culture in the first half of the nineteenth century, often in the face of apathy or opposition from the bishops of the Established Church. Jenkins's rectory must have featured as a kind of Welsh Abbotsford. Adams found the house – now a farmhouse – a rather imposing, if altered, whitewashed building in the midst of its fields.

The church drew him back. Here Adams quickly found the memorial tablet to the Revd William Jenkins Rees, "Priest, Author, Antiquary, Litterateur", whose grave he had sought outside in vain. As though in preparation for visitors, a few sheep had been turned loose in the graveyard to trim the long grass but, while leaving ample droppings, had hardly begun to get to grips with the task. On a dank day with scudding clouds, he thought it an eerie place, or perhaps recollection of Mathias's poem made it seem so.

Mathias misses the fact that the north side of the church is virtually unbroken wall since it was the traditional side of the devil; as also the related fact that parishioners huddled to be buried exclusively on the sheltered south side. Mathias neglects the myth that the last Welsh dragon is sleeping in the Radnor Forest and that if any of the five churches on the Forest edge dedicated to the Archangel Michael should fall, the dragon will escape and terrorise the neighbourhood once more.

Yet the tension between pagan and Christian absorbs the poet. Apart from the objectivity of "service at three" – half a century later this is still the time of the monthly services – many uncanny aspects of the place are singled out by Mathias, starting with the fact that it is one of Wales's circular churchyards. Then there are its black yews, one of which fell victim to the hurricane of October 1987, thought to be between one and two thousand years old. Both the yews and the circle keep out those timeless evil spirits that invade our world through corners, just as the gnostic Abracadra Charm from 1700 hung inside the church protects one Elizabeth Lloyd from "hardness of heart".

He mentions the five-foot-high "druid's mound" on which the church tower sits, though recent excavation declares this little more than the remains of an earlier collapsed tower. He even makes the wind blow 'widdershins': counter-clockwise and so counter-natural. Finally he singles out the Abracadabra Charm, a protective incantation dating from 1700 to preserve "Elizabeth Lloyd from all witchcraft and all evil... the witches compassed her abought [sic] but in the name of the Lord I will destroy them Amen ****** pater pater pater Noster Noster Noster". Mathias believed that the father of Queen Elizabeth I's sometime astrologer John Dee, the possible model for Shakespeare's white magician Prospero in *The Tempest*, and conjuror of the souls of the dead, was born two miles away at Nant-y-groes.

Elizabeth Clarke too noted Radnorshire folk who visited a

so-called 'conjuror' in the early twentieth century, and there is plenty of evidence of the survival of magical belief in Radnorshire into the present age. And yet, impressive as Mathias's poem is, it evokes somewhere different from the place where I have slept better than anywhere else on the planet for more than a third of a century. Not to be a little superstitious, it has been said, is to lack generosity of spirit. Despite this, and living so close to this churchyard that I can watch its bluebells, wild daffodils and quiet gravestones from my bedroom window, I have never experienced it as threatening, only as a place of magical peace.

Perhaps Adams is right that the poem's subjects are the terrors of mortality and the mixing of Christian present and pagan past. T.J. Hughes too argues that at Cascob more than anywhere else can still be felt the "deeply wooded world of dark-age Wales".

By coincidence R.S. Thomas also published a poem – using a Welsh spelling – on the same place. It comes in a 1978 collection and is called 'The Sign-post':

> Casgob, it said, 2
> miles. But I never went
> there; left it like an ornament
> on the mind's shelf, covered
>
> with the dust of
> its summers: a place on a diet
> of the echoes of stopped
> bells and children's
>
> voices; white the architecture
> of its clouds, stationary
> its sunlight. It was best
> so. I need a museum
>
> for storing the dream's
> brittler particles in. Time
> is a main road, eternity
> the turning that we don't take.

Few Welsh hamlets can boast of having been celebrated by both R.S. Thomas and Roland Mathias, the two greatest Welsh poets recently writing in English. Time and silence feature in both. That Cascob sits towards the end of a cul-de-sac, impassable, leading nowhere, strongly contributes to its sense of mysterious isolation, somehow pocketed in a space-time of its own, a magical kingdom. Both Thomas and Mathias associate Cascob with the idea of being lost in time; but while Mathias's is sinister, menacing and particular, Thomas's place is innocent, dream-like and general.

Both poets explore the idea of escape. Mathias wishes to leave Cascob behind, Thomas to get there; and Thomas makes a conceit of never having visited. His "stopped bells" – the school closed in the 1940s – and "stationary sunlight" symbolise that timeless world which, he teaches us, is "the turning we don't take", a place of ambiguous longing. Cascob here is, in other words, another version of Abercuawg, a perfect place of lost delight, subject of an important essay of his, and never-never land of his imagination to which he aspired.

★

The glory of west Wales, Thomas wrote in his *Autobiographies*, is its changeable weather. It blows in off the Atlantic accompanied by rapidly passing effects of light and shade that hold the attention and compel poetic awe. 'The Small Window', written in the 1960s, starts:

> In Wales there are jewels
> To gather, but with the eye
> Only. A hill lights up
> Suddenly: a field trembles
> With colour and goes out
> In its turn...

That is marvellously accurate; recognisable in mid-Wales too. The poet goes on to take a side-swipe at the incomers who crowd and dirty the view with their breathing. This sequence is of a wonderfully-caught natural effect followed by nationalist sentiment and the reader will decide which part of the poem works best. Justifiable hatred can make for good art, but not often for great art, and Thomas's oeuvre also contains some malevolent attacks on neighbours and family.

He returned to this theme of miraculous momentary illumination in another short lyric written ten years later, called 'The Bright Field':

> I have seen the sun break through
> To illuminate a small field
> For a while, and gone my way
> And forgotten it

In 'The Bright Field' en-lightenment (literally) is related not to anglophobia, but rather to Moses's burning bush, a transiently bright taken-for-granted beauty that could connect us to eternity itself. This time the aesthetic leads on not towards the political, but the spiritual.

Byron Rogers's prize-winning biography, *The Man Who Went Into the West,* skilfully presents a sacred monster who first inspires in us incredulity and laughter, but gradually later compassion and awe. Here is both an unmistakably great poet and a pitifully frail human being. He starts by impersonating an upper-class Englishman, and ends play-acting a member of the Welsh *gwerin* who has to be rebuked by the then Plaid Cymru leader Dafydd Elis Thomas for echoing the French extremist right-wing leader Jean-Marie Le Pen. This followed Thomas's proclamation that the death of an English incomer in an arson-attack on his holiday cottage would scarcely weigh in comparison with the jeopardy threatening Welsh culture.

Stephen Spender once pointed out how naturally hatred and nostalgia cohabit, a truth Thomas demonstrates. He 'hates' the English, he hates the English-speaking Welsh for abandoning their language, and despises many of the Welsh-speaking Welsh for not defending it. He hates the industrial revolution, the twentieth century and the modern age in general. Like Kilvert he hates London, where he swears he can smell evil on stepping off the train. He is scarcely a lover of his fellow man, preferring bird-watching, and has a tortured relationship to his God. He conjures Welshness into existence through the power of *hiraeth*, his passionate sense of loss and the intensity of his love and longing.

Poets are allowed to be contradictory: Thomas fits the bill. He declined to teach his only child Welsh or even speak it with him, sending him off to a posh English boarding-school instead. Although sometimes capable of acts of quiet kindness, he is remembered – to put it mildly – as an eccentric minister of the Church, hiding behind hedgerows to avoid his flock and answering one parishioner's "What a lovely day" with the riposte "We can see that", vaulting a churchyard wall to avoid having to talk to mourners at a funeral he had just conducted, bursting out laughing and unable to continue reading in church when the week's notices sank to the banality of a Mothers' Union meeting. He became notorious for his offensiveness to callers at the door and on the phone. His son Gwydion believes that they had few or no friends; no-one stayed the night, and few visitors were not 'rubbished' afterwards. Gwydion cannot be a wholly dispassionate witness. But few dispute that Thomas was distant even with friends, impatient and disdainful of activities other than Art and its accomplishment.

Gwydion remembered Manafon, where the family was happiest, as a place where his stoical and admirable mother Elsi, a richly gifted painter, made purses out of moleskins, and rabbitskin berets and waistcoats he had to wear. Elsi also painted dead animals and the house featured an assortment of owls, moles, rabbits, and squirrels gathered from road-kill and awaiting resurrection in her paintings, strung up in the orchard to see off the worst of the rotting and allow the skulls and skeletons to be revealed. Elsi used to draw them, stuffing them with cotton wool and formaldehyde, and hope for the best.

His parents' final years at their tiny cottage Sarn on the Llŷn peninsula after 1978 were yet stranger. Elsi, finding the central heating radiators unaesthetic, had them ripped out; she recorded in her diary a temperature indoors even with the fire lit of only one degree above zero. Water oozed down the walls and Gwydion saw mould growing on his father's shoulders. Elsi painted with her feet in a cardboard box containing a two-bar Belling Electric stove, burning herself severely on several occasions. She would sometimes climb a six-foot ladder into the loft, where you could not stand up, the roof being only about four and a half feet high, and work and sleep up there, the mice scurrying around her.

Ruth Bidgood points out in *Parishes of the Buzzard* how deeply English such Rousseauism is: no Welsh person in their senses embraces domestic hardships they have spent bitter centuries trying to escape. It is always incomers who find living at subsistence level without mod cons attractive, and read into such austerity a spiritual significance. The picture emerges of an austere aesthetic-bohemian couple heroically unfitted for modern life. And yet it may well be exactly this heroic estrangement that helps make of him a great international, as well as so great a Welsh poet. Thomas – the lonely priest tormented by unbelief – is a figure out of Ingmar Bergman.

Although Thomas in his introduction to his selection of George Herbert's poetry for Faber championed Anglicanism and was hostile to dissenting "misery and mortification", Thomas himself abounds in the sense of sin without great hope of redemption. His invention of Iago Prytherch, the peasant hill farmer living in solitude who haunts many poems, is an alter ego. Real hill-farmers with their quick wit, wry humour, and careful love of gossip are a different species from Thomas's desolate personification. He finds redemption chiefly within poetry, which offered the only miraculous cure for despair that can move and speak to us all, regardless of denomination or nationality.

In 1968 Thomas wrote the text for *The Mountains*, a limited edition illustrated book now out of print and changing hands for over £500. A passage from which this present essay draws its title and epigraph runs:

> But the hill remains, keeping its perennial freshness. Life with its money and its honours, its pride and its power, seems of little worth if we are to lose this. This it is that haunts men, that epitomises Wales in a phrase – the bright hill under the black cloud.

> I'r estron, os myn,
> Boed hawl tros y glyn;
> I ninnau boed byw
> Yn ymyl gwisg Duw
> Yn y grug, yn y grug

> I don't know who wrote those words, but they translate like this:

> Let the stranger, if he will,
> Have his way with the glen;
> But give us to live
> At the bright hem of God
> In the heather, in the heather.

We have met these lines before. Thomas himself translated them – freely – from the Welsh and he quotes them three times over forty years: from 'A Welsh View of the Scottish Renaissance' and 'The Depopulation of the Welsh Hill Country' to *The Mountains*. The lines "Give us to live/At the bright hem of God/In the heather, in the heather" evidently spoke intimately to him[6]. His translation is beautiful, moving and memorable. Here are lines that wring an aesthetic and moral victory out of historical defeat. The English may have won the prosperous valleys and glens: but the Welsh secretly took the real prize – to live in the uplands, on the bright hill under the black cloud, their proximity to God and to heaven alike guaranteed henceforth by nothing less than the landscape itself.

The passage continues:

It is to this that men return, in thought, in reality, seeking for something unnameable, a lost Eden, a lost childhood; for fulfilment, for escape, for refuge, for conquest of themselves, for peace, for adventure. The list is endless. The hills have all this to give and more: to the broken mind, peace; to the artist, colour; to the poet, music; to the brave man, consciousness that he has looked into the eyes of death and has not flinched, hanging upon the rock face with the wind clawing at him.

It is in the Welsh hills that R.S. Thomas, like Ruth Bidgood and Roland Mathias, finds the solitude, time and silence that provide the soil from which inwardness grows; inwardness that encourages the writing of poetry. England may have won many of the battles, but in some sense, if Thomas is right, Wales secretly won the war.

PART THREE
NOW

Now

Not so many years ago a snaggle-toothed neighbour asked whether we were planning to "watch the Indian eunuchs dancing on a neighbouring hill" (a stubborn indifference to costly modern dentistry still marks valley inhabitants, as if not to be a little gap-toothed signalled want of local pride). The cost of viewing these dancing eunuchs was, I think he said, a few pounds.

In their brilliantly coloured, swirling silken saris these twenty or so Indian eunuchs duly danced, through the poignantly beautiful twilight of a late summer evening, to a sizeable, respectful audience; and then promised to return from their warmer South, like swallows, the following year.

I asked my neighbour, astonished, why on earth would eunuchs fly all the way from South India thus to dance on a mid-Welsh hillside? He sounded as puzzled by my question as I had felt by the need to pose it. "I reckon," he replied, "they couldn't find anywhere better". And with this simplicity I had to rest content.

In a recent *Guardian* Hywel Williams, historian and polemical journalist, noted sceptically that British geographers had identified Powys residents as top of a UK league for happiness.[1] Williams is rightly dubious about how objective or reliable any index of happiness can be. He also disbelieves in the social cohesion and "good interpersonal relationships" claimed by the geographers for the county. Powys, he says, is mainly empty wilderness, a "Welsh Alaska", marked by depopulation and rural poverty. One respondent based in Breconshire wrote to agree with Williams: poor locals were squeezed here both by rich English incomers and by corruption in the local planning scene. Nineteen other bloggers disagreed, and thought Powys a fine place to live[2].

If Powys people count themselves happy, Williams maintained, then they are simple-minded and ought not to. Politics offers him a clue to their self-deception. He scorns the March for having early anglicised its laws, ignoring the fact that it stayed independent of the Crown three hundred years after west and north Wales succumbed in 1282. And, having traced a royal nanny living near Hay (a worrying sign), he believes anglicised Powys to be, against much evidence, a "gentry society" with large estates and a tenantry marked by apathy, myopia and deference[3]. Noting that Powys currently returns two Lib Dem MPs, he claims that Liberalism here is unchanged since Gladstone in 1868, and therefore neo-feudal.

Williams carelessly overlooks the difference between southern Powys, where in the seventy-three years between 1924 and 1997 the constituency of Brecon-and-Radnorshire, a mainly Labour stronghold, elected only one Liberal MP, and Montgomeryshire in the north. The latter, by contrast, does indeed have the longest Liberal parliamentary tradition of any constituency in England or Wales. Although Williams does not spell this out, its Liberalism also remains largely untouched by the two dominant forces of Socialism and Nationalism.

To this perception one is tempted to riposte that there may

be other considerations equally urgent now that global eco-crisis threatens our planetary future: perhaps rural self-sufficiency and simple-lifery alike represent not just the past, but the future too? *Du chong chok shi* advised the Lord Buddha in Tibetan: 'Few Needs, Great Contentment'. Even the metropolitan habit of patronising rural literature as backward - looking, nostalgic, and irrelevant might possibly be due for a change.

Williams is censoring Powys for not being up-to-date: the old sneer that has been used to justify meddling in Wales ever since Giraldus eight centuries ago. Alwyn D. Rees in his seminal work in Welsh community studies – *Life in a Welsh Countryside* – famously praised Powys on identical grounds: that here precious continuities survived.

On a summer Saturday in 2008 we paid homage to Rees by visiting Llanfihangel-yng-Ngwynfa in Montgomeryshire. We rose early and chose a slow route, travelling via two places that enshrine the past glory of Powys, and then its subsequent eclipse. In the steep, conifer-wooded valley of Cwm-hir, once stood an Abbey with the longest nave in Wales (242 feet). You can still just discern its shape and size from remaining founda-tions. Here in 1282 Cistercian monks smuggled the body of Llywelyn the last Prince of Wales for secret burial, his head having been cut off for display in London. No sign-posting on the road guides you to the unenclosed grave; over which, once you have found it, with its carved sword and simple inscription in Welsh, cattle are to be found peacefully grazing.

Glyndŵr's beloved Sycharth, where we travelled next, feels almost as secretive, equally remote and unsignposted from the tiny winding single-traffic lane overlooking a branch of the Tanat river. Once you find your way to the twin mounds that are all that is left, guided by a local farmer, it is in its way impressive. You proceed up the hill by an adjoining farm near the yard of which Cadw – the Welsh government body with the mission to protect, conserve, and promote the built heritage of Wales – have put up a placard informing you that the original motte-and-bailey castle dated from around 1100, that the future Henry V burnt it down in 1403, and that much evidence of the sheer scale of the burning was uncovered by archaeologists only in the 1960s. There are lines from Iolo Goch's poem praising the scope and generosity of the manor in Glyndŵr's day, and an artist's impression showing a tiny fairy-tale hamlet within its moated enclosure, a trifle Disneyfied.

We finally reached the scattered hamlet of Llanfihangel in the noon-day sun, swallows hawking over the trees and a cuckoo calling somewhere not far off. A worrying bilingual sign on the main road one mile away pleaded 'Save our School. Save our Language. Save our Community'.

The village tea-rooms advertised a two-course lunch for £7, and 3 courses for £9.50, suggesting both how low agricultural wages are and also, perhaps, how many pensioners live locally. These tea-rooms were closed. During half-an-hour's walking around, and after admiring the monument to the great visionary Christian poet Ann Griffiths, we saw no living person. The Goat Inn at the centre of the hamlet, moreover, appeared closed for business long past mid-day. We consoled ourselves with a wander in the enchanted Coed Pendugwm Wildlife Refuge nearby with multiple nesting-boxes on its ancient sessile oaks for the local dormice, which appeared to be attracting as much care and investment as their human neighbours.

Members of the Llanfihangel-yng-Ngwynfa local history evening class recently decided to bring Rees's great study up-to-date for the millennium: and like Rees in 1940, they started with a questionnaire to each house. This new book has many contributors, none a professional social anthropologist, and so the book lacks uniformity of style. But it is largely upbeat and always informative. We had been dismayed to find the Goat apparently closed on a summer Saturday but this new study suggests that you should enter through the front door of the adjoining house and through what resembles a living room. Typical of the March to have a renegade village pub.

Many of the social changes notated over the past half

century are true of all villages at this period. For example: most tenants did well during the war, buying their holdings from the estate afterwards. The arrival of mains electricity around 1960 costing £25 per household is eloquently evoked. It produced the first generations ever to have lived their entire lives not in interiors made dark and smoky by wood fires and oil light, but brilliantly and artificially lit. Suburban bungalows are now built right on the road either for the farmer or for his newly-married son, in stark contrast to the dignified older farm-houses set back from the road. The smithy closes. Rectory, disused schoolhouse and one shop are now converted into private dwellings, probably for incomers. Decayed cottages are similarly done up. Indoor WCs, bathrooms and new freedoms follow. Couples openly set up house before marriage, to find out whether they get on. The motor car, too, brings independence: youths leave for the excitements of city life and the younger generation of wives have jobs away from home. There is an increase in population of the elderly and retired. Payment in kind is giving way to money. Farmers' wives today no longer (as in 1940) consider tinned foods superior to fresh food, and are often good cooks.

Other changes – such as pregnancy scanning, indoor wintering and lambing, quad-bikes – have made farming much easier nowadays but also more intensive and so dangerous to the environment. Fewer field-mice mean fewer barn-owls, corncrake and red squirrel have gone and the draining of wetlands hurts skylarks, curlew, snipe, lapwing. Such drainage also means increasingly the flooding of English cities such as Shrewsbury nearby: the marshes that once acted as a sponge to hold the waters in check have disappeared. On the other hand buzzard, kingfisher and otter return – and the hated, predatory mink arrive.

Nothing thus far reported is unique to Llanfihangel: it describes village life everywhere. Alwyn D. Rees valued the Welshness of Llanfihangel because it gave its citizens the sense of unique value, belonging and significance. There were in 1940 only twelve English monoglots in the parish. He understood the conformism of this world, which tended to infantilise young men, kept psychologically and emotionally dependent by their parents long into adult life: something the novelist Alice Thomas Ellis – who lived partly in Montgomeryshire and before marriage wanted to be a nun at the Carmelite convent in Presteigne but was prevented by back trouble – diagnosed in *Unexplained Laughter* in 1985[4]. Ellis found life in the March black and repressive for native Welsh sons with powerful mothers. But Rees took a larger view, seeing the social traditions of the village in 1940 in terms of what he called "deep time", showing cultural continuities going back centuries, even millennia.

And Llanfihangel is today still a distinctively Welsh village, where the coming of television has not yet killed off a rich and various community life. The conduct of public meetings is more relaxed and less agenda-driven among the Welsh; farmers are still reluctant to admit the size of their farm or number of their stock; an unstated protocol governs how conversations are conducted. You start with the weather, move to family news and then local gossip, only at the very end bringing the conversation around to a desired topic and disclosing any business-in-view.

All of this, moreover, happens in Welsh: the loss of the Welsh language has been slower than elsewhere in Montgomeryshire, where the speaking of Welsh (as in Wales in general) fell from 40% to 23% between 1931 and 1991. Welsh is, by contrast, even today still Llanfihangel's main language of everyday life: in 1997 there were (out of 415 living in the parish) 269 fluent Welsh speakers; 77 who spoke 'some' Welsh; and 69 monoglot English speakers.

Exactly this sense of community makes Llanfihangel attractive to outsiders, who of course risk by their presence diluting what they treasure; parishioners now include company directors, a ship's purser, bird breeders, and a diamond mounter. The foreword notes the tension between those escaping the congestion, crime and pollution of cities – where life is dominated by materialism and stress – and the indigenous way of life. And one major interest of *A Welsh Countryside Revisited* lies in what it hints at of this contrast.

Many incomers try to learn, not only Welsh, but also the traditional art of conducting conversations: weather/family/village before business. Victoria Morgan, who inspired the writing of this book, and who fell in love with a Welsh farmer and moved to Llanfihangel forty-five years ago, recounts soon after her arrival helping at harvest festival. Her suggestion that buying sliced bread for the supper might be fast and practical fell into an astonished silence. She slowly came to see and then to understand how the unhurried home-baking of loaves that then required slicing, buttering, filling, trimming and setting out on plates was a companionable community task enjoyed exactly because for one afternoon it brought the womenfolk together.

Rees described the tradition of the *Plygain*, the annual festival of carols held on the second Sunday in January in which each family jealously guarded its own traditional songs. Even Rees did not then understand how old the tradition was: 1960s research suggested that some carols are pre-Reformation. The tradition survives and is now widely imitated elsewhere in Wales.

Meic Stephens adds a wry postscript. He notes that the carols are very beautifully sung, in something half-resembling a chant, and that some English newcomers felt moved to play their part in the service by offering "Jingle bells, jingle bells, jingle all the way". "People do not cross national boundaries without bringing a lot of baggage with them," Stephens comments[5].

What act of public contrition could atone for that American carol? In December 1970 West Germany's Chancellor Willi Brandt fell to his knees – in unforgettable, spontaneous expiation – at the Warsaw Ghetto memorial, his *Warschauer Kniefall* provoking worldwide comment. There are in the history of relations between the English and Welsh scenes that invite public acknowledgement if not sorrow. Perhaps it was for such reasons that Horatio Clare in his recent memoir *Running for the*

Hills noted good-humouredly how delighted his new Monmouthshire neighbours were in the 1970s when he and his young brother arrived from London with their parents to farm. They had been looking in vain for someone to play Judas in the school Nativity play each year…: the Clare boys' posh English voices were *just right*.

Alwyn D. Rees's dream that a place still, by some miracle, retaining many ancient ways might help yet to heal the sickness of the age seems more urgent today. And part of the perennial interest of Rees's elegant study comes from the way – as his nephew Professor M. Wynn Thomas argues in an afterword to *A Welsh Countryside Revisited* – he shows the hamlet always to have been a 'mixed' society, a site of cultural exchange and a confluence of different cultures. That makes Llanfihangel typical of the March, but it also makes the March typical of everywhere. Since Rees published his *Life in a Welsh Countryside*, a Roman road has been discovered nearby, linking a fort at Caersws to another at Caer Gai near Llyn Tegid, and both, by implication, with Rome itself. Two thousand years ago the parish was already part of a bigger Empire, and of a more global scene.

*

The lives of many writers associated with the March show how hospitable and tolerant an environment it is. Roland Mathias lived for 55 of his 93 years outside Wales before returning to his roots in Breconshire, much as Ruth Bidgood came back at around the age of fifty. Geraint Goodwin in the 1920s was encouraged to return and write in and about Newtown, Margiad Evans came from Uxbridge in Middlesex, and Elizabeth Clarke was made at the age of fifty to feel welcome.

Hilda Vaughan, who married the then famous writer Charles Morgan, was born in Builth in 1892, her father a well-to-do country solicitor holding many Radnorshire offices including Clerk of the Peace and Clerk of the County Council. Most people, she comments wisely, lack the courage to be publicly out-of-date: this is not a courage that she is short of. In the 1930s she wrote two fine essays about her childhood[6].

There were in her childhood house known as the Castle, she recounts, twenty-two clocks, each keeping a different time. The maids quarrelled in Welsh, a language young Vaughan preferred to the French and German her governesses spoke, because it sounded more dramatic; her mother warned her against acquiring a Welsh accent in English. The roads were untarred and her family, loving its Welsh cob Taffy, long resisted the urge to change to a motor-car. They preferred the dog-cart, which her father drove adventurously. There were also expeditions by wagonette to show off to visitors the scenery she loved and was proud of, with a driver blaspheming and cursing the horses in Welsh; he would drive them splashily through fords that afterwards necessitated everyone's changing their clothes. There were visits to a Pembrokeshire house in which everything was a relic of the past, including its owner, who never threw anything out, and in every one of whose bedrooms some relative or other was said to have died; and then visits also to church, delayed by Miss B's august and inordinate fussing over details of her dress, and ending in her grandly leading her spaniel up the aisle of the church to the family pew.

Most of Hilda Vaughan's novels, dealing often with the stuff of passion, are, like so much Radnorshire-related literature, currently out of print. It would be good to have back in print Kilvert's *Diaries*, Clarke's *The Valley*, and Vaughan's much admired *A Thing of Nought* (1934), a novella telling a tale of star-crossed love in the hills of Radnorshire. She lived much of her life in London but is buried in the picturesque church on the river Ithon at Disserth, with its ancient box-pews.

*

Vaughan, who died in 1985, saw much change. The grievous poverty of the 1930s, when rabbits featured so importantly in the diet and the rural economy alike, has long gone. Vaughan remembered red squirrels. The greys that now replace them are verminous, ring-barking young trees and robbing birds' nests. It says something for social change that BBC Radio 4's *Today* programme featured a local, smart Shropshire butcher selling grey squirrel meat, who broadcast to the nation a recipe for roasting squirrel in a clay-pot: one might as well eat this vermin, which purportedly tasted not unlike rabbit, ran his argument.

This might seem a frivolous example of change. How radically and profoundly the area has altered is remembered best by living witnesses. Ethel Gosling came to Cascob from Birmingham in 1930 with her mother, the new schoolmistress, whose first act was publicly to break and burn the canes her predecessor had too often wielded. Much shocked Ethel and her mother: for example, 'clodding' (the hurling of mud, not always for fun) and the vandalising of her bicycle-tyre. While the children of foresters were better-clad, those of farmers had hobnailed boots and poor clothing.

Much pleased them too. The dialect took time to learn. Ethel liked 'big-sorted' for proud or big-headed, and 'him' and 'her' for 'he' and 'she'. There was considerable suspicion of townfolk and a degree of shock that Ethel, who was ten, wore shorts in summer, though some copied her. Her mother was addressed always as 'Madam' and she as 'Miss'. The school cleaner bobbed a curtsey on arrival and brought water up from the brook in two buckets on a yoke. Shopkeepers delivered, except in the frequent winter snows, so everyone kept masses of tinned food, and flour for making bread. There were whinberries, wild strawberries and cranberries to pick in season. Shire horses did the farm work, not tractors, and visits to the town were by pony and trap. The arrival of the pig-sticker generated excitement in the children, terrible squealing in the pigs, and presents of meat thereafter. Hunts also interrupted schoolwork, as did busy times in the farming year.

In one cottage with only two bedrooms, into which fourteen children were born before the first war, seven, who were buried close together with nothing to mark the spot, died in infancy, some doubtless from TB. One daughter of this cottage poisoned herself for shame at being caught petty thieving, while no more was heard of her brother after he purportedly left, after happy home leave with the family in the summer of 1918, back for the Great War. His story has disturbed me ever since I first heard it. Shortly before the Armistice, beaters working the sessile oak woods that October found his hanging body. He had been dead for some time, preferring to end his life rather than leave home again and return to the trenches. If ignorance and dire poverty did not kill you early (the seven infants), then fear of your Calvinist God might later (the sister). Finally the state was given its chance (the soldier).

A much more ancient March was still just in view at this time, with a few remaining drovers taking stock to market or the train station: Archie-the-drover on his way with his cattle and dog to Knighton market to some degree dressed as a tramp, yet was popular, given free meals by many. The decoration by the children of the church at Easter, using wild violets, anemones and primroses, had not changed since Kilvert's time.

The arrival of the telephone to service the new schoolmistress's household was a major drama. Her husband was killed in a road accident in Ireland, whither some able-bodied English and Welsh sought work during the Depression. She lived alone with her daughters in the schoolhouse in primitive conditions – no running water or electricity, not even an inside lavatory. They felt especially this latter lack as a source of shame. The telephone, with its black speaking-tube, upright dial, separate ear-piece, and the number Whitton 212, was the only one in the valley for decades and contentious, objected to on grounds that – like the wireless, which ran on an accumulator sold by the local garage – it interfered with the weather, which duly worsened soon after its arrival. Still, farmers and their wives would also queue up for use of it.

This school she taught in was itself the creation of the Whig government of 1857 – the Church Schools Act for Wales. The infamous 1847 Blue Books had reported that the common Welsh people were "dirty, lazy, ignorant, superstitious, deceitful, promiscuous and immoral", and blamed the Welsh language and Nonconformity. It was accordingly thought progressive to teach the Welsh to think in English and open up the professions to them. Thus begins the latest stage in the thousand-year self-imposed English task of 'civilising the Welsh'. The arrival during the Blitz of numerous evacuees from Merseyside kept the school in use during the war, but it closed soon afterwards, being converted first into a working men's club, and later sold to us.

The schoolroom is 34 by 17 feet with a 20 foot high cross-beam roof, big handsome double lancet and quatrefoil windows at each end, and further large sets of windows on the side-walls, out of each of which you see the majesty of the hills, and the weather; all of us who visit this beautiful room, featured in the 2002 BBC *Omnibus* on Iris Murdoch, feel our good fortune. Ethel, now living in the South, remembers her years here fondly and likes to visit. She loves its wildness.

*

'Wildness' speaks to a need deep in all of us. Was the first 'wild' title George Borrow's *Wild Wales* in 1862? At any rate recently within a very few years Robert Macfarlane published his *The Wild Places*, Simon Barnes *How to be Wild*, and Roger Deakin *Wildwood*. Wildness is a key theme, too, in Ffransis Payne's *Exploring Radnorshire*, which celebrates the way that wild and fertile landscapes co-exist here. His book ends by pointing out that this closeness of tame and wild constitutes "the special magic ...of this enchanting county from one end to the other".

In 1984 we made a 'wild' islanded lake with the help – in this order – of two civil servants, one wielding a long-handled augur, a government grant, the good luck of finding blue clay six feet down with its own spring, and a kindly farmer-neighbour with a caterpillar-wheeled JCB digger. He opened up a new long canal or leat down which brook-water rushed and along which three big, silver, leopard-spotted trout were at once thrillingly seen to be swimming. Later he got stuck in the muddy lake-cavity so that he had to spend two hours trying to drive the JCB up and out, while it opted instead to teeter stubbornly and slide dangerously backwards and sideways into the large hole up the sides of which the new waters could be seen steadily rising. "Heck," he exclaimed stoically, later, having finally won this battle, "I'd no idea it'd be so greasy". A water-vole arrived soon afterwards.

This new lake-water now attracts many kinds of dragon-fly, and an otter who spraints visibly and is sometimes on show, especially around late winter when she whelps and needs extra food to produce her milk. She will break the ice to dive for fish, and our gamekeeper neighbour has shown us how to recognise the spoor her long, heavy tail leaves in the snow. He explained that the dog otter leads a mainly solitary life, only 'sociable' when the bitch is on heat, and otherwise jealous and hostile to his whelps.

It is therefore unusual, we learned, to sight a family: Henry Williamson, after his post-Great War walks through the wilds of Devon, describes Tarka the Otter as very fearful of his father, even though his mother is able to defend him. Two years ago in May, to our astonished delight, three otter arrived busily down the leat and for ten minutes swam and played around the island, pouring themselves in and out of the water and catching and sharing the eating of a trout.

Kingfisher visit. Their tropical colours are heart-stopping to sight against mid-winter ice and snow: they are of course still feeding in the bleak and cold months. Thought to be shy, they in fact announce their arrival with a characteristic cry before flying brilliantly, sometimes almost hovering, like pieces of costume jewellery bewitched.

And then heron, playing grandmother's steps with their quarry, swallows, hawking low for flies, and light-flotillas processing across the surface. Trout, which we feed but do not catch, move in the water like glass within glass. When thrown fish-meal they thrash competitively as if to make the pool boil, and snap it up, and are so used to this routine that on hearing your approach they will eel swiftly up to the side, sometimes breaking the surface with their tails, to win your notice and reward.

They don't seem to mind our swimming with them. In 1997 and 1998 Iris Murdoch, whose *Life* I was writing, and her husband John Bayley stayed with us for an aggregate of eight months and swam when it was hot enough.[7] John stripped down to an astonishing vest that had so many loops, strands and holes you could no longer tell which were the arm-openings. His index finger to his lips, he whispered owlishly, "Mustn't let the moths think they're winning!" After swimming, Iris sat regally in a white chair by the water's edge, dragon-fly darting and hovering around her head, while my partner Jim carefully cut her hair; John thought Radnorshire made him feel exactly like the Chinese nature poet Li Po.

The first time I had a one-to-one conversation with Iris was in Edinburgh in 1982, when, telling her about Radnorshire, she at once quoted the old doggerel: "O Radnorshire, Radnorshire,/ With never a park nor never a deer/ Nor never a squire with five hundred a year/ Excepting Squire Fowler of Abbeycwmhir". Dating from the seventeenth century and sometimes cited to demonstrate Radnorshire poverty, it more properly evidences the small but prosperous yeoman tradition that – *contra* Hywel Williams in his *Guardian* piece – often has mid-Welsh hill-farmers independent of any big landowner.

★

Ronald Blythe has written of the life of the sheep-farmer as necessarily "lonely and contemplative". It is partly sociable too. Watching neighbours, once lambing is over, chatting for an hour is instructive. The scene is unremarkable; it must be replayed every day, among the sheep-farmers of Dartmoor or the Yorkshire Dales, in the Scottish fells and the Cheviot Hills. Neighbours exchanging news and gossip about sheep and dogs, the sale of land, other neighbours, talking of births and marriages and deaths. You cannot claim it specially for Wales, let alone for the Border.

But this is the only place I know well, and for me it speaks of a frontier to modernity, with its painfully impatient speed, its empty knowingness, its social isolation and its catastrophic loss of the sense of place. There is nothing subversive or consciously rebellious about two neighbours talking; yet it suggests a quiet and unconscious limit to all of this, a world elsewhere, the survival of a kindly slowness worth cherishing. What Dylan Thomas once called the countryman's sane disregard for haste has not yet disappeared. Such disregard is equally on view in the tale of an Elan valley shepherd, living in one of the remotest farms in Wales, who has been forced on occasions to leave his land and home at weekends. He is apparently driven away by the noise of tens of unruly motorcyclists rampaging on and off the unpaved, beautiful wilderness Monks Trod trackway that runs between Ystrad Fflur and Elan.

And earlier this year a painting believed to be by Bernardino Luini of Christ Teaching was lifted off the wall in daylight and stolen from St Peter's church in Evencoyd near Presteigne, where it had lived unremarked for a century. It seems somehow typical of the precious backwardness of the March that this work ascribed to a leading disciple of Leonardo da Vinci had never been valued, and was hanging un-secured[8]. A blogger reports that another painting ascribed to Luini, works by whom hang in the Uffizi, Prado, National Gallery and Louvre, sold in 1999 for just under three million. Bitter comfort.

The recent careful restoration of Cascob church included that of its fine bronze bell, and I was there in May 2008 when the specialist firm from Malvern returned the restored bell and explained their craft. During the eighteenth century change-ringing became fashionable and for this purpose many old bells were melted down and re-cast. Happily Radnorshire was too remote and poor for the new fashion to catch on, and so a greater proportion of ancient bells survive here than in any other Welsh county. The Cascob bell weighs half a ton and is three foot high, and the words "Jesus be our speed: 1633" are engraved on it in fine lettering together with initials indicating that it was made by a Richard Dawkes of Worcester.

Bells have their own lore and language and I struggled to follow all that was explained. This one has elegant side-loops called canons. Then there was an oaken headstock with nailed sheerbands and an axle called a driving gudgeon within a stock-hoop: so I think I was told. Originally it had certainly swung on a half-wheel, later made up into a full wheel; the U bolt from which the clapper hung had been iron, which rusted and, as it expanded, threatened the bronze shell. So this had been replaced.

The re-hanging of the bronze bell entailed a complex system of pulleys and chains. It was moving to witness its relatively swift ascent – considering its huge weight – into the newly roofed tower, proofed at last against the jackdaws that had left a few centuries worth of droppings around it, and hidden above a new oaken floor with only its rope on show. Nearly four hundred momentous years elapsed between the first ascent of our bell and its most recent.

Our church is newly locked against vandals. If those who try to rob the church now are drug-addicts from the towns and cities, the thieves stealing livestock and farm-equipment were for a spell professionals from the North or Midlands. Livestock would get rounded up at night into huge lorries with chimneys where they were at once butchered and flayed, their fleeces rapidly burnt in a working furnace to render identification, and so proof of crime, impossible.

Civil servants came in 1990 slapping conservation orders on the old farmhouses, one reported as elated at an unchanged eighteenth-century interior. Application is made for planning permission on every ancient barn, and almost all the derelict cottages have been or are being renovated. Not all the big money needed for 'buying and doing up' the barns comes from the City, and nor are all their owners unsociable or drivers of SUVs. Given recent abandonment, such renovation cannot be cause only for complaint.

The red grouse have, for now, gone. We never saw the ring

ousel on Radnor Forest that William Condry wrote of in the 1970s, and have yet to see the nightjar that are said to have recently returned. Pheasant – part gypsy, part dowager – strut about with their odd air of quizzical determination; and you can recognise woodcock by their evasive swivelling flight. Our piped water, which used to come from a spring at Cwm-y-gerwyn, and was so sweet and soft, now comes smelling of chlorine via a town.

Some time after we came, population scarcity made our county attractive to the Ministry of Defence, which sent RAF jets to practise low-level flying over the hills, shattering the peace, portending new wars, terrifying people and live-stock alike: the volume of complaint is no doubt lower where there are fewer to complain of shivered greenhouse glass, or ewes miscarrying from shock at the eerie cacophony. The jets scream overhead less frequently nowadays.

The uninhabited and roofless summer *hafod* nearby, where, house-hunting, we spent our first night in a blizzard in December 1974, now has a roof, but no modern amenities. Its vegan owner will not have it connected to the grid in case a percentage of nuclear-generated electricity enters his house. His small windmill powers a few low-voltage lamps and human waste is re-cycled to help the kitchen garden. In a similar spirit he spent a year not washing, having read that the activity is not natural. A barn owl still roosts in his out-house and, a great white ghost, flies out at your approach. He still walks two miles from any made-up road to get home, but his house is no longer a ruin.

Our valley had in the 1970s many ruined cottages. The farmer in one drowned himself around 1970 in fear of a lawsuit; that in another, becoming confused in old age, and entirely cottage-bound, would shout each morning from his upstairs window commands appropriate to the season and the time of day to the long-since dead horses he had in earlier life worked with and loved, until, one morning, he announced himself through the window finally too tired to continue further with this exhausting 'labour', shouting out, "This is hard work, I think I should retire". And died that afternoon. The farmer in another cottage died after being gored and eviscerated by his own bull.

On Litton Hill there is today still one ruined upland cottage in its own lost demesne, last inhabited, without modern amenities, comforts or road apart from a stony track, in 1950, whose bohemian and bespectacled inhabitants lived a quiet, orderly, parsimonious life, walking the ten miles twice a week that took them to the nearest shop and back. They died. Nobody else was willing then to brave such a life, and the Victorian iron nails in the roof rusted and gave up their task in the winter storms so that the tiles lifted in the gales, frost and rain cracked and flaked the poor shale-stone walls, the doors rotted and during blizzards black-faced Clun and Radnor sheep were soon wandering in to shelter from the weather and add to the mess and hasten the decay.

Rupert Brooke has a line about "the falling house that never falls". But this one will, and soon. You can still see where the garden once was, where gnarled, wind-tormented and untended fruit trees stand, and give the place an unsettling sense of being poised between existence and non-existence, at the furthest border-line of an imaginable world.

There were for many decades wild ponies running around the moorland periphery of this demesne. Mostly bay or chestnut, rarely grey or white, never black, their shared family resemblances included an unmistakable white blaze down their muzzle, and some said they were related to sturdy Welsh mountain ponies, an ancient race even before the Romans came, with fewer now than a thousand left.

Each had a handsome mane, with that sweet shyness that the French word *sauvage* has as a possible subsidiary meaning, but the English word 'wild' wholly lacks. You could watch the races the foals ran with their elders, cantering for joy in wide circles in their first spring, so long as you sat still in the bracken and did not seek to get too close. They would never approach you, standing. But lying patiently on the ground within their purview, they would slowly advance and scent you on the air, and snuffle for more news of you, then view you with as much – or more – inquisitiveness than you felt about them, as if you came – as of course in a way you did – from a different world.

These were descendants of the pit-ponies that had worked the south Welsh coal-mines before the war, where, neighbours say, pigeon-Welsh was the *lingua franca*, duly learnt by the Cornish and Basque immigrant coal-workers as much as by the otherwise often anglophone mid-Welsh. Wild now, the ponies were neither shod nor broken in. And in times of blizzard when food was non-existent a local farmer drove up on his tractor and left them a bale or two of hay.

This tale of the ponies, in its way, reflects upon globalisation as much as the unexpected invasion of Indian eunuchs. Conflicts between local farmers and incomers can be bitter, especially where profit is concerned, as, for example, when a county plan proposes that a hamlet be 'developed' for new housing. Since planning permission increases field-value by many factors, landowners may well approve 'development'; while escapees from city life, who are sometimes both knowledgeable about how to be heard and vocal, will go to lengths to ensure that their peace is undisturbed.

A bossy 'incomer', one of the summer-folk, rang the County Council to make an anonymous, fearful, wrong-headed enquiry about the possible lack of winter-fodder for the ponies. The farmer who had been feeding them for decades caught wind of the complaint and greatly feared bureaucratic interference. All the ponies went to be butchered in the knacker's yard. The hill is lonelier without their gentle company, and not in a way that is welcome.

Bureaucracy has won other battles, and bridleways and tracks are now marked by wooden sign-posts as if we were in Surrey. That aside, the hill now is left to the rare walker, and commoner sheep, animals and birds. Pine-marten are back. There are fewer curlew and snipe, but during winter teal that rise suddenly from a lake and flock and turn together like some gaseous cloud, closely observed on occasion by those who like to shoot them; while in March the many skylarks all tune up together, a distant air-borne orchestra, pendant in the sometimes cloudless skies which, like a child learning to write its own name, tentatively bespeak the coming days of spring.

Proceeding eastwards from the Pales in 1975 and again later, we walked over the top of the Radnor Forest, getting lost until it became obvious that you must aim for the radio mast, since every other route across the moorland is precipitous, not just the alarmingly steep Harley Dingle. The Forest is only seven miles from one end to the other but seems further. There are generally few other walkers and the tracks, when you find them, are close to two thousand feet high. With cotton-grass for company you can lose your bearings not only in space but also in time, and at some point find yourself "at the bright hem of God/ In the heather, in the heather". Home is precious when you get to it.

The pursuit of solitude continues. The present Archbishop of Canterbury has participated in west Radnorshire in a number of Christian-Buddhist small group retreats. A Buddhist centre has opened ten miles off; our house is used for retreats, a practice we love; a Buddhist nun in a three-year retreat elsewhere is allowed one letter a month; while an Anglican nun has locked herself for life, quite improbably, in a garage, from where she takes telephone calls for one hour every evening from the distressed and needy.

Sceptics term this pursuit of quiet a higher form of egoism, and perhaps they are right. R.S. Thomas's life-story concerns someone who loved the company of birds more than that of people. Maybe the quest for peace of mind within a small place in the country itself, with all the neurotic agrarianism this implies, is unvirtuous. A selfish pride of ownership, for most of us, 'goes with the territory'.

Yet whatever the strict morality of it, many writers – like contemplatives – feel the need to experience the self-imposed solitude within which creative thought can gather and take shape, the necessary re-charging of batteries, as well as escape from the push, aggression and knowingness of the world and the dissipation of the city. Some creative folk have favoured the Marches and, like all of us who move in a globalising age, savour what our presence dilutes.

A space centre opened recently two miles south of Knighton, since Radnorshire has the lowest levels of light pollution of anywhere in England or Wales – so star-gazing here is memorable – to gather information on near-Earth objects such as asteroids and comets and monitor their threat to Earth. Many threats to life, however, now seem to come from somewhere closer than outer space.

In a time when nobody any longer belongs anywhere or (the same thing) everyone is at home everywhere, the valley even now stays stubbornly different. My neighbour David, not at all a fool, but wholly indifferent to metropolitan matters, once told me proudly that he thought he had visited London for the day on a school-trip. He then added, after a ruminative pause, "Although I suppose it might equally have been Birmingham".

And another neighbour, a painter who also farms, took his young sheep-farming partner for his first and only weekend in London, and was at first confounded when this hill-farmer elected to sit completely still in a window embrasure for three long days. He gently declined offers to go sight-seeing and implied that he had enough to do as it was. He seemed to his hosts to be watching in a rapt and wondering silence the unceasing flow of the North London traffic that elicited in him a sort of contemplative trance. It was as if he had been given a complicated mathematical problem to work out and knew, given time, that he might arrive at a solution. He never communicated what this was. He would only vouchsafe mysteriously, yet with the most obvious sincerity, as he prepared to return home to his farm in deepest Radnorshire, that he now felt entirely satisfied.

Acknowledgements

My thanks are due to Simon Davison and the Poetry Group at the Bleddfa Centre for the Creative Spirit, on whom some of these ideas were first tried out; and to the Welsh Academi for assisting these Bleddfa seminars. Professor Meic Stephens, of Radnorshire descent, gave ceaselessly kind and generous tutelage, and made gifts of books; Dr Marged Haycock taught me about Radnorshire's Ancient Books and fifteenth-century poets; Dai Hawkins kindly allowed me to quote from his English translations of Ffransis Payne; Mick Felton at Seren provided encouragement, Dr Jason Walford Davies, Byron Rogers, David Hiam and Justin Wintle helped me research R.S. Thomas; Professor M. Wynn Thomas shared memories of his uncle Alwyn D. Rees; Adam Fenn guided me patiently around volumes of the *Transactions of the Radnorshire Society*; Sam Adams helped introduce me to Roland Mathias; Julia Smith, author of *Thomas Traherne* (forthcoming) answered queries about Traherne; Simon Edwards helped explain Rousseau; David Elvins of the Kilvert Society answered queries about Kilvert; Ethel Dickens (nee Gosling) wrote out her memories of Cascob in 1930; Professor Patrick Simms-Wilcox shared his work on Celtomania; Anne Roberts and Jane Jantet eased very many research tasks; Nancy Palmer-Jones, Sue Best and Ted Taylor helped me access Elizabeth Clarke's estate; Annette Kobak alerted me to the tale of Rousseau in Radnorshire; the late Richard Dynevor gave me Emyr Humphreys' *The Taliesin Tradition* which he originally published; and the librarians of Llandrindod Wells and the London Library gave unstinting help.

Draft chapters were read and commented upon by Dr Marged Haycock, Richard Holmes, Mary Fahrenfort, Norbert Hasenoehrl, Rose Tremain and Meino Zeillemaker. Professor Meic Stephens read and corrected a draft of the whole; he, my partner Jim O'Neill and Daphne Turner alike made many very helpful suggestions. For all errors I'm solely responsible.

Select Bibliography

General

The Transactions of the Radnorshire Society [TRS] 1930-2006
The Oxford Dictionary of National Biography [ODNB] (2004)
Condry, W.: *Exploring Wales* (1970)
Davies, J.: *A History of Wales* (1990)
Davies, L.: *Radnorshire* (Cambridge County Geographies) (1912)
Duggan J.J.: *The Unforgotten Valley: studies of Life and Character on the Welsh Border* (1926)
Edwards, T.: *The Face of Wales* (1950)
Ellis, A.T.: *Wales, an Anthology* (1989)
Emmett, I.: *A North Wales Village* (1964)
Fletcher, H.L.V.: *Forest Inn* (1946)
Frankenburg, R.: *Village on the Border* (1957)
Fraser, M.: *Welsh Border Country* (1972)
Gibbings, R.: *Coming Down the Wye* (1942)
Godwin, F. & Toulson, S.: *The Drovers' Roads of Wales* (1977)
Green, J.: *The Morning of Her Day* (1987)
Gregory, D.: *Radnorshire: A Historical Guide* (1994)
Grice, F.: *Water Break Its Neck* (1986)
Hanmer, W. B.: *Radnorshire: History, Topography, Romance* (1914)
Haslam, R.: *The Buildings of Wales: Powys* (1979)
Leitch, D. and S. (eds.): *A Radnorshire Farm Diary 1879-1883* (1999)
Lewis, G.F.: *Haber Nant Llan Nerch Freit – an upbringing on a Radnorshire Hill farm* (1998)
Lewis, G.F.: *Henfryn – Radnorshire Farming life in the 1930s & 40s* (2002)
Massingham, H.J.: *The Southern Marches* (1952)
Morgan, L.: *A Plough on the Mountain* (1955)
Morris, J.: *The Matter of Wales* (1984)
Morris, J.: *Wales, epic views of a small country* (2000)
Morris, J.: *Wales: small Oxford books* (1982)
Palmer, R.: *The Folklore of Radnorshire* (2001)
Parry-Jones, D.: *Welsh Country Characters* (1952)
Simpson, J.: *Folklore of the Welsh Border* (2003)
Suggett, R.: *Houses & History in the March of Wales: Radnorshire, 1400-1800* (2005)
Stephens, M. (ed.): *The New Companion to the Literature of Wales (1998)*
Thorseby-Jones, P.: *Welsh Border Country* (1938)

Toulson, S. & Forbes, C.: *The Drovers Roads II, Pembrokeshire & the South* (1992)
Williams, G.A.: *When Was Wales?* (1985)

Chapter One: 1965
Davies, J.: *History of Wales* (1990)
Davies, R.R.: *The Age of Conquest, 1063-1415* (2000).
Howse, W.H.: *Radnorshire* (1973)
Terry Jones' Great Map Mystery, BBC2 (Wales) Tuesday 18 May, 2008
Lieberman, M.: *The March of Wales 1067-1300* (2008)
Morgan, M.: *Growing up in Kilvert Country* (1990)
Rogers, B.: *The Bank Manager and the Holy Grail* (2003)
Nelson, L.: *The Normans in South Wales* (1966)
Stephens, M.: *A Semester in Zion* (2003)
Suggett, R.: *Houses & History in the March of Wales, Radnorshire 1400-1800* (2005)
Williams, J.: *The History of Radnorshire* (1859)

Chapter Two: 'Psychogeography'
Howells, E.: *Good Men and True: lives & tales of shepherds of mid Wales* (2005)
Rees, A.D.: *Life in a Welsh Countryside*, (1950)
Rogers, B.: *The Bank Manager and the Holy Grail* (2003)

Chapter Three: 1176: Summer
Bartlett, R.: *Gerald of Wales* (2006)
Bartlett, R. & Mackay, A.: *Medieval Frontier Societies* (1989)
Breeze, A: *Ancrene Wisse Introduction*, originally Pub. in *Ancrene Wisse* Kalamazoo, Michigan: Medieval Institute Publications, 2000 ed by Robert Hasenfratz to be found at <http://www.lib.rochester.edu/camelot/teams/aw intro.htm>
Davies, R.R.: *The Age of Conquest: Wales 1063-1415* (1987)
Dobson, E.J.: *The Origins of Ancrene Wisse* (1976)
Gerald of Wales, *The Journey through Wales and the Description of Wales* (1978)
Lieberman, M.: *The March of Wales 1067-1300* (2008)
Remfry, P.M.: *TRS* 1995, 'Cadwallon ap Madog 1140-1179'
Thomas, P.: *Celtic Earth, Celtic Heaven* (2003)
Williams, G.: *The Welsh Church from Conquest to Reformation* (1976)
Stefan Zimmer, 'A Medieval Linguist: Gerald de Barri', in *Études Celtiques*, 35 (2003)

Chapter Four: The Great Century
Clancy, J.: *Medieval Welsh Poems* (2003)
Davies, R.R.: *The Age of Conquest: Wales 1063-1415* (1987)
Davies, R.R.: *The Revolt of Owain Glyndŵr* (1995)
Gregory, D.: *Radnorshire: A Historical Guide* (1994)
Haycock, M.: (ed.): *Legendary Poems from the Book of Taliesin,* (2007)
Haycock, M.: 'Scholarship and Creativity in the work of Ffransis G. Payne', *TRS* (2005)
Henken, E.R.: *National Redeemer, Owain Glyndŵr in Welsh Tradition* (1996)
Humphries, E.: *The Taliesin Tradition* (1983)
Lloyd, Sir J.E.: *Owen Glendower* (1992)
Payne, F.: *Exploring Radnorshire and other writings* (as yet unpublished), tr Dai Hawkins
Payne, F.: *TRS* 1938, 'Welsh Bards & their patrons'
Suggett, R.: *Houses & History in the March of Wales: Radnorshire,1400-1800* (2005)
Wheeler, R.: *The Medieval Roodscreens of the Southern Marches* (2006)
Williams, G.: *Owain Glyndŵr* (1993)
Williams, G.: *Renewal and Reformation in Wales c.1415-1642* (1987)

Chapter Five: The Paradise Within
BBC Radio 4 *Great Lives: Henry VII* Sep 2 2008
Bartley, J.: *Teague, Shenkin and Sawney* (1954)
Bloch, C.: *Spelling the Word: George Herbert and the Bible* (1985)
Blythe, R.: *Divine Landscapes* (1986)
Charles, A.: *A Life of George Herbert* (1977)
Davies, S.: *Henry Vaughan* (1995)
Hutchinson, F.E.: *Henry Vaughan: A Life and Interpretation* (1947)
Malcolmson, C.: *George Herbert* (2004)
Marchette, G.: *Two Gentle Men: the Lives of George Herbert and Robert Herrick* (1960)
Parker, K.: *Radnorshire from Civil War to Restoration* (2000)
Salter, Keith W.: *Thomas Traherne: Mystic and Poet* (1964)
Singleton, M.: *God's Courtier: Configuring a Different Grace in George Herbert's Temple* (1987).
TLS Sep 14 1984; *TLS* (7 Nov 1997); *TLS* (2 June 2000)

Chapter Six: Rousseau and Radnorshire
Archeologica Cambrensis 1873, series 4, p.410
Bentley-Taylor, D.: *Wordsworth in the Wye Valley* (2001)
Blanshard,F.: *Portraits of Wordsworth* (1959)

Blunden, E.: *Shelley: a life story* (1946)
Carruthers, G. & Raws, A. (eds): *English Romanticism and the Celtic World*, (2003)
Darnton, R.: *The Great Cat Massacre* (1984)
de Beer, G.: *J-J Rousseau and his World* (1970)
de Beer, G.: 'Six Lettres inédités de J-J Rousseau' in *Bulletin de la Société et 'archéologie de Genève* XIII, pp.297-307, 1966
Edmonds, D. & Eidenow, J.: *Rousseau's Dog* (2006)
Field, J.: *Landor* (2000)
Forster, J.: *Walter Savage Landor: a biography*, 2 vols. (1869)
Gill, S.: *William Wordsworth: a life* (1989)
Gittings, R. & Manton, J.: *Dorothy Wordsworth* (1985)
Gray, C.: 'Wordsworth's First Visit to Tintern Abbey' in *PMLA*, Vol 4
Hogg, T.: 'The Life of Shelley', in T.J. Hogg and others, *The Life of Percy Bysshe Shelley*, 2 vols. (1933)
Holmes, R.: *Coleridge: early visions* (1989)
Holmes, R.: *Shelley: The Pursuit* (1974)
Inglis-Jones, E.: *Peacocks in Paradise* (1960)
Johnston, K.: *The Hidden Wordsworth* (1998)
McNulty, J.: 'Wordsworth's Tour of the Wye' in *Modern Language Notes* vol 60, May 1945
Moorman, M.: *William Wordsworth: The Early Years, 1770-1803* (1957)
Moorman, M.: *William Wordsworth: The Later Years, 1803-1850* (1965)
Morgan, P.: *The Eighteenth Century Renaissance* (1981)
Morgan, P.: 'The Hunt for the Welsh Past in the Romantic Period' in Hobsbawm & Ranger (eds.) *The Invention of Tradition* (1983)
Reed, M.: *Wordsworth: the Chronology of the Early Years, 1770-1799* (1967)
Reed, M.: *Wordsworth: The Middle Years, 1800-1815* (1975)
Reiman, D. & Fischer, D. (eds.): *Shelley and his Circle, 1773-1822*, 10 vols. (1961–2002)
Roe, N.: *Wordsworth and Coleridge: the Radical Years* (1988)
Stuart, D.: *Anecdotes of the poet Coleridge*, (1838)
Super, R.: *Walter Savage Landor: a biography* (1954)
Williams, G.A. in 'Romanticism in Wales' from Porter & Teich, *Romanticism in National Context* (1988)
Wordsworth, C.: *Memoirs of William Wordsworth* (1851)
Wright, H.: 'The Associations of TL Peacock and Wales' *Essays & Studies* Vol XII (1926)

Chapter Seven: Estrangement and Belonging

Alexander, P.: *William Plomer, A biography* (1990)
Borrow, G.: *Wild Wales* (1862)

Borrow, G.: *George Borrow's Second Tour of Wales*, eds T.C. Cantrill & J. Pringle Y Cymmrodor, vol. XXII, 1910.
Collie, M.: *George Borrow*, Eccentric (1982)
Colloms, B.: *Victorian Country Parsons* (1977)
Grice, F.: *Francis Kilvert and his world* (1982)
Hughes, K. & Ifans, D. (eds): *The Diary of Francis Kilvert: April-June 1870* (1982)
Ifans D. (ed): *The Diary of Francis Kilvert, June-July 1870* (1989)
Le Quesne, A.: *After Kilvert* (1978)
Lockwood, D.: *Francis Kilvert* (1990)
Lockwood, D.: *Kilvert the Victorian – a new selection from Kilvert's diaries* (1992)
Maber, R. & Tregoning, A. (eds): *Kilvert's Cornish Diary, 1870* (1989)
Plumer, W. (ed): *Kilvert's Diary 1870-79, a selection* (1977)
Toman, J.: *Kilvert: the Homeless Heart* (2001)

Chapter Eight: Sacred Space

MacCarthy, F.: *Eric Gill* (1989)
Michell, J.: *The View over Atlantis* (1969)
Miles, J.: *Eric Gill and David Jones at Capel-y-Ffin* (1992)
Savile, J.: *Rural Depopulation in England and Wales, 1851-1951* (1957)
Shoesmith, R.: *Alfred Watkins: A Herefordshire Man* (1990)
Spears, M.: 'Shapes and Surfaces: David Jones, with a Glance at Charles Tomlinson' *Contemporary Literature*, January 1971
Thomas, E.: *Wales* (1983)
Watkins, A.: *Early British Trackways* (2005)
Watkins, A.: *The Ley Hunter's Manual* (1989)
Watkins, A.: *The Old Straight Track* (1974)

Chapter Nine: Solitude and Community

Chatwin, B.: *On The Black Hill* (1982)
Clarke, E.: *The Darkening Green* (1964)
Clarke, E.: *The Valley* (1969)
Miller, K.: *Doubles* (1987)
Morgan, K.O.: *Rebirth of a Nation: A History of Modern Wales* (2002)
Murray, N.: *Bruce Chatwin* (1993)
Murray, N.: *TRS*, 1992, 'Bruce Chatwin's Radnorshire'
Shakespeare, N.: *Bruce Chatwin* (1999)

Chapter Ten: Seers and Remembrancers

Adams, S., in *Moment of Earth, Poems & Essays in Honour of Jeremy Hooker*, ed. C. Meredith (2007)

Bidgood, R.: *Parishes of the Buzzard* (2000)
Bidgood, R.: *New & Selected Poems* (2004)
Brown, T.: *R.S. Thomas* (2006)
Hughes, T.J.: *Wales's Best One Hundred Churches* (2006)
Mathias, R.: *Collected Poems* ed. S Adams (2002)
Rogers, B.: *The Man who went into the West* (2006)
Stephens, M. (ed) *Poetry Wales*, R.S. Thomas Number, Spring 1972
Thomas, G., in interview with J.W. Davies: 'Quietly as Snow' *New Welsh Review* 64, summer 2004
Thomas, R.S.: *Mountains* (1968); *Collected Poems 1945-1990* (1993); *No Truce with the Furies* (1995); *Six Poems* (1997); *Autobiographies* (1997)
Wintle, J.: *Furious Interiors* (1996)

Chapter Eleven: Now

http://news.bbc.co.uk/1/hi/wales/mid/7423835.stm
Llanfihangel Social History Group, *A Welsh Countryside Revisited* (2003)
Vaughan, H.: 'A Country Childhood' and 'Far Away: Not Long Ago', *TRS* 1982, vol 52.
Williams, H.: 'An Abstract Sort of Joy' *Guardian*, 11 September 2008

Notes

1965

1. *La Nouvelle Heloise,* quoted in Sara Maitland's *The Book of Silence* (2008) p.66 – my emphasis.
2. One of many points I owe to Dai Hawkins's translation of Ffransis Payne's *Crwydro Sir Faesyfed.* See *TRS* 2008
3. This paragraph is indebted to Hawkins's translation of Payne – ibid.
4. See Meic Stephens' entry on Jenkins in *ODNB.*
5. The modern view would by contrast be that many Britons in the east were absorbed rather than retreated to the west, as is the way of these things, and that there were always Britons in the west, too.
6. One minor recent example. During the considerable time that the historically important Radnorshire sessions rolls were at the National Library of Wales, no conservation work was carried out on them – unlike the session rolls for Montgomeryshire and for Breconshire (many of which were cleaned and guarded). See Anna Page forthcoming *TRS* article.
7. A point I owe to Meic Stephens.
8. Knucklas is also claimed as a site for the betrothal of King Arthur and Guinevere: see http://news.bbc.co.uk/go/em/fr/-/1/hi/wales/7704048.stm
9. Until the Restoration many Quakers – such as James Naylor – served in Cromwell's New Model Army and defended their cause robustly.

'Psycho-geography'

1. Thoreau lived at Walden, Concord, Mass., July 1845-Sep 1847: "I went to the woods because I wished to live deliberately, to front only the essential facts of life, and not discover when I came to die that I had not lived."
2. See ch.3 for further exploration of this theme.
3. *Royal Commission on the Employment of Children, Young Persons, and Women in Agriculture* (1867), Report on Monmouthshire and Radnorshire, cited in Richard Suggett *Houses & History in the March of Wales, Radnorshire 1400-1800* (2005).
4. See Meic Stephens, *A Semester in Zion* (2003), p.232.
5. Thomas cites these lines in three separate prose works: 'A Welsh View of the Scottish Renaissance', 'The Depopulation of the Welsh Hill Country' and *The Mountains.*
6. Liverpool was of course a large industrial city and major port. But our Anglo-Dutch cousin belonged to a network that played a part in making

Liverpool a target: around 1850 his ancestor in Os, Brabant, together with two friends, claimed to have helped discover margarine, thus contributing to the making of a large company in Port Sunlight, where the cousin went to work.

7. Cited Tony Brown, *R.S. Thomas*, p.31.
8. See Glanmor Williams, *Welsh Church* pp.524-5.
9. A point I gratefully owe to Meic Stephens.
10. See Byron Rogers: *The Bank Manager and the Holy Grail* (2003) p.xv

1176: Summer

1. Ffransis Payne, see *Crwydro Sir Faesyfed* passim.
2. *TRS*, 1995, Cadwallon ap Madog, 1140-1179, P.M. Remfry, pp.11-32.
3. Stefan Zimmer, 'A Medieval Linguist: Gerald de Barri', in *Études Celtiques*, 35 (2003), 313-50.
4. Described in *Itinerarium Cambriae* 1191 (Journey through Wales).
5. Patrick Thomas, *Celtic Earth, Celtic Heaven* (2003) p.64.
6. R.R. Davies p.175.
7. R.R. Davies p.176.
8. Bartlett p.145, a propos Gerald's *Topographia Hiberniae* (Topography of Ireland, 1188).
9. See essay by Ffransis Payne, 'The Old Welsh Garden' *Yr Hen Ardd Gymreig*.
10. The evidence of a dream or vision he had during the 1190s in which he was indeed offered St David's suggests that this was only partly true: his friends in the dream were dispirited, having "hoped for better things for him". This suggests he at first wanted, like most of his peers, to gain a rich English bishopric, and settled on St David's only when this was not forthcoming. Indeed in 1184 King John had offered Gerald the bishopric of Wexford, then that of Leighlin, both in Ireland; six years later Bangor and Llandaff were offered. All of these he refused, because they were, in his own words, "poor and barbarous".
11. More probably Henry II, who had just suffered from conflict with and then the murder six years before of one turbulent priest – no less than Thomas à Becket – was too shrewd to want to repeat this experience. Gerald's admiration for St Thomas is well documented.
12. Gerald of Wales, *The Journey through Wales* and *The Description of Wales* (1978) p.23.
13. See John Davies p.203, c1436 'Libel of english Policye'.
14. As one Welsh writer – Byron Rogers – has observed.
15. R.R. Davies p.178.
16. Lieberman p.50.
17. "In an ingenious argument centring on a possible anagram, E.J.

Dobson speculated that the author might have been Brian of Lingen, thought to have been an Augustinian canon of Wigmore Abbey, and furthermore that he might have been the brother of the original three readers. While attractive, this contention remains unproven, ...Bella Millett... suggests Dominican authorship" *Ancrene Wisse* website.

18. For *Book of the Anchorite of Llandewibrefi*, see R.R. Davies p.209.
19. Peter Brown, *Body and Society*, p.222, cited AW website.
20. Andrew Breeze, in *Ancrene Wisse* introduction, originally published in *Ancrene Wisse* Kalamazoo, Michigan: Medieval Institute Publications, 2000 Ed by Robert Hasenfratz to be found at <http://www.lib. rochester.edu/camelot/teams/awintro.htm>.

22 June 1402: The Great Century

1. Thus called by Saunders Lewis, writer, scholar, nationalist.
2. See Richard Wheeler: *The Medieval Roodscreens of the Southern Marches* (2006).
3. Compare the 126 years of the partition of Poland by its neighbours, and the disappearance of the Polish nation-state off the map, when its great poets, Norwid, Mickiewicz, Slowacki helped keep Polishness alive.
4. See e.g. Glanmor Williams pp.76-7: "Guto'r Glyn drove sheep".
5. See *The Taliesin Tradition* p.51.
6. See Ffransis Payne, 'Welsh Bards & their patrons' *TRS* 1938.
7. It recalls, perhaps, the blind court-poet Demodokos whom Odysseus listens to in disguise, while visiting the court of the super-civilised and effeminate Phaicians, observed weeping when hearing Demodokos recite his own – i.e. Odysseus's – story.
8. I owe Dai Hawkins a huge debt for allowing me to read and quote from his English translations of FfransisPayne.
9. In Richard Parry's old book about the history of Kington.
10. By Dai Hawkins. As I write the editors of the *TRS* hope to bring out this translation as *TRS* 2008.
11. In Evan Evans's famous phrase.
12. Payne lists these bards as: Llawdden, Ieuan Swrdwal, Lewis Glyn Cothi, Llywelyn ap y Moel, Gwilym ab Ieuan Hen, Morgan Elfael and Lewis Dwnn.
13. *Black Book of Caermarthen, The Red Book of Hergest, The Book of Taliesin* and *The Book of Aneirin*.
14. Thus Emyr Humphreys p 40. Gerald of Wales writes of Henry II doing the same.
15. Jonathan Williams in 1800, by contrast, declares that "no Welsh was to be heard within fifteen miles of us".
16. In the notorious 1847 report on Education in Wales, J.C. Symons

found by contrast that, with the exception of two parishes, Radnorshire was then English-speaking, estimating that 23,000 out of its total population of 23,356 spoke English. Symons was assisted by two Welsh-speaking Commissioners, neither from Radnorshire [*TRS* 1993 Colin Hughes, pp 45-53].

17. e.g. Howell Harris.

1593-1695: The Paradise Within

1. Glanmor Williams, *Welsh Church*, p 545.
2. Jonathan Williams in his *History of Radnorshire* (1859 ed.) p.164 claims that Dee was born in the parish of Beguildy, but provides no evidence for this. His birth-place is usually given as London. Possibly Williams was using a local tradition. The claim by W.H. Howse that Dee owned Nant-y-Groes is probably based upon the second of two articles by Sir Joseph Bradney: 'Dr John Dee', *TRS*, 3 (1933); and 'Pilleth, Nant-y-Groes and Monaughty', *TRS*, 21 (1951). See also Ffransis Payne, 'A poem by John Dee and Jenkyn Gwynn', *TRS*, 31 (1961); F Noble, 'A letter from Dr John Dee to a Radnorshire Cousin in 1577', *TRS*, 25 (1955); F Noble, 'The identification of Dr. John Dee as the author of Harleian MS 473 based on its Radnorshire references', *TRS*, 26 (1956); and N de Bar Baskerville, 'A matter of pedigree: the family and arms of Dr John Dee baptised in wine', *TRS*, 68 (1998). But see Roy Palmer, *Folklore of Radnorshire* p.106 – which is unequivocal.
3. *Henry IV Pt 1*, III sc I.
4. See Prys Morgan p.81.
5. The seat was held by his step-father in 1614, and by a brother in 1626.
6. His mother married in 1608, and he in 1629.
7. For example Cristina Malcolmson in her *George Herbert* (2004).
8. John Milton in *Areopagitica* (1644), defending the liberty of the press, famously attacked the desire to escape the world – the impulse towards retreat or retirement – as selfish and un-fruitful. "I cannot praise a fugitive and cloister'd virtue unexercised and unbreathed, that never sallies out and sees her adversary, but slinks out of the race, where that immortal garland is to be run for, not without dust and heat".
9. See Vaughan's ODNB entry, to which I owe this argument.
10. This and the previous paragraph are indebted to F.E. Hutchinson's fine *Henry Vaughan: a Life and Interpretation* (1947).
11. This and the previous paragraph owe much to Stevie Davies's *Henry Vaughan* (1995).
12. Thanks to Julia Smith, author of *Traherne* (forthcoming), for this information.
13. Traherne's pursuit of original innocence chimes neatly with the ancient

Welsh/British heresy of Pelagianism that influenced both Traherne and Vaughan in the seventeenth century – a sixth century Welsh heresy denying Original Sin. Pelagus's Welsh name was Morgan.

14. Wanting to comprehend them within the national church: these included Sir Edward Harley, Thomas Barlow, Thomas Good, and Sir Orlando Bridgeman.

15. *TLS* Sep 14 1984 p.103.

18 January 1766: Rousseau and Radnorshire

1. Sir John Vanbrugh's play *Aesop*.

2. The Welsh eighteenth century has been brilliantly recorded by Prys Morgan in *The Eighteenth Century Renaissance* (1981) and 'The Hunt for the Welsh Past in the Romantic Period' in Hobsbawm and Ranger, *The Invention of Tradition* (1983); also Gwyn A. Williams, 'Romanticism in Wales' from Roy Porter and Mikulas Teich, *Romanticism in National Context* (1988).

3. All letters from 'Six Lettres inedites de J-J Rousseau' by G de Beer in *Bulletin de la Societe et archeologie de Geneve* XIII, 1966, pp.297-307.

4. *Archaeologica Cambrensis* 1873, series 4, p.410.

5. Denis Diderot – see de Beer, p.50.

6. *Reveries d'un Promeneur Solitaire* in its original French title.

7. *Modern Language Notes* vol. 60, May 1945, 'Wordsworth's Tour of the Wye'.

8. Price also cooperated with Wordsworth, who frequented the March, on the design of a Leicestershire garden. Today Price's own great garden is in ruins. A US/Canadian air force hospital camped there during the war, following which a DP camp was set up for demobbed Polish military personnel, then closed down and demolished with the house in 1958. Where Price once showed off his great garden, conifers now flourish.

9. Price's 1797 book is entitled *Thoughts on the Defence of Property*.

10. Herbert Wright, 'The Associations of T.L. Peacock with Wales' *Essays & Studies* Vol XII 1926 pp.24-46.

11. Article in *Cornhill* cited in *Peacocks in Paradise* p.116.

12. Johnston, *Hidden Wordsworth* p.274, in 1791.

13. 1810, 1824 and 1828.

14. Gwyn A.Williams *Madoc*, p.189 et seq.

15. Prys Morgan p.84.

16. 1971 *TRS* p.10: Oliver, however, doubts he ever set foot in the county.

Autumn 1937 and Summer 1870: Estrangement and Belonging

1. W. Plomer, *The Autobiography*, 1975, p.284.

2. Peter Alexander, *William Plomer, a Biography*, (1989), p.232.

3. *Autobiography*, p 373.
4. The theme of suicide in the Marches could have earned a chapter in itself: in an area of strong kinship, those who fall out of its grip fall into despair.
5. *Cornwall Journal*, p.63.
6. Her family name survives in the British engineering company, Guest, Keen and Nettlefold.
7. *Gweledigaethau y Bardd Cwsg* was its title in Welsh.
8. See 'People of the Black Mountains', *Planet* 65 (Oct/Nov 1987), p.11 cited *TRS* 2004, p.27.
9. As A.L. Rowse well understood.
10. See W.H. Howse, *Radnorshire*, p.87.
11. Suggett, p.6.
12. David Lockwood, *Francis Kilvert* (1990) pp.65-7.
13. See Mark Bostridge, 'Life on the Wing', *Guardian* Sat review 19 Jan 2008 p.22: "To his everlasting regret, though, he allowed the typescript of the full diary to go missing. Initially, this was not a matter of great concern".

1905: Sacred Space
1. http//www.tate.org.uk/research/tateresearch/tatepapers/06autumn/daniels.htm#is6note20.
2. http://www.badarchaeology.net/spiritual/earth.php.
3. http://www.stonesofwonder.com/ley2.htm.
4. T.J Hughes, *Wales's Best One Hundred Churches* (2006).
5. see *Legendary Poems from the Book of Taliesin* pp.503-4 for some references (à propos Uthr, Arthur's father).
6. The railway signalman at Pandy, Henry Williams was, it is curious to reflect, father of the three-year old future critic Raymond Williams.

Solitude and Community
1. See *TRS*, 1992, Nicholas Murray, 'Bruce Chatwin's Radnorshire' pp.13-16.

Seers and Remembrancers
1. Opening poem in the limited edition *Six Poems* (1997).
2. *Poetry Wales* ed. Meic Stephens, R.S. Thomas Number, Spring 1972. Vol 7 no 4, Roland Mathias, 'Philosophy and Religion in the Poetry of R.S. Thomas'.
3. Written 1966-8.
4. Sam Adams (ed.), *The Collected Poems of Roland Mathias* (2002) p.175.
5. Adams writes of this visit and of his growing involvement with Mathias in *Moment of Earth, Poems & Essays in Honour of Jeremy Hooker*, edited

by Christopher Meredith (2007). Thomas Jeffery Llewelyn Prichard, 1790-1862, is the subject of a monograph by Sam Adams in the Writers of Wales series (2000).

6. Dr Jason Walford Davies writes that "Thomas probably came across the stanza in John Cowper Powys's article 'Welsh Aboriginals' in the influential periodical *Wales* in 1943 when he was at Manafon, Montgomeryshire (an article subsequently collected in *Obstinate Cymric* [1947]). But it is equally possible that Thomas heard it as part of the oral tradition at Manafon. ...The critic M. Wynn Thomas, interestingly, has suggested that Thomas echoes the stanza in his poem 'A Welshman in St James' Park': letter to the author.

Now

1. 'An Abstract Sort of Joy', *Guardian*, 11 September 2008.
2. Curiously Jonathan Williams in his great county history also describes the common people of Radnorshire as possessing "health without medicine and happiness without affluence".
3. But see Nigel Heseltine's *Tales of the Squirearchy* (1946) which pokes fun at the landed gentry of Montgomeryshire.
4. Anna Haycraft aka Alice Thomas Ellis lived both in Camden Town and Pennant Melangell. My contention is that her three Welsh novels – *The Sin-Eater, Birds of the Air, Unexplained Laughter* – are her best. See Peter J Conradi, 'Alice Thomas Ellis: Kinder, Kirche, Küche' in *Image and Power: Women in Fiction in the Twentieth Century* eds G. Cunningham and S. Sceats, (1996) pp.149-62.
5. See Meic Stephens, *A Semester in Zion* (2003) p.76.
6. Reprinted in *TRS* 1982, vol 52. 'A Country Childhood' and 'Far Away: Not Long Ago'.
7. See Peter J Conradi, 'Iris Murdoch and Wales', *TRS*, 2005.
8. http://news.bbc.co.uk/1/hi/wales/mid/7423835.stm.

Publisher's Acknowledgements

Seren gratefully acknowledges The Estate of Roland Mathias for permission to quote 'Cascob' from *The Collected Poems of Roland Mathias* (University of Wales Press, 2002) and The Estate of R.S. Thomas and Orion Publishing for permission to quote or quotes from: his translation 'Let the stranger, if he will' from *The Mountains* (1968); 'To a Lady' from *No Truce With the Furies* (1995); 'For Alice' from *Six Poems* (1997); 'The Sign-post' and 'The Bright Field' from *Frequencies* (1978) and 'The Small Window' from *Not That He Brought Flowers* (1968). Most of the poems are to be found in the *Collected Poems* (Orion, 2000).

The Author and Illustrator

Peter J Conradi is the author of the much-praised *Iris Murdoch: A Life* and *Going Buddhist*. His *A Writer at War: Iris Murdoch 1939-45* comes out with Short Books early in 2010 and he is currently writing a life of Frank Thompson for Bloomsbury. In addition to his writing Conradi has taught at South Bank University, University of East Anglia and Jagiellonian University in Krakow. Now Prof Emeritus at the University of Kingston, and Honorary Research Fellow at University College London, he divides his time between London and Radnorshire, where he walks, gardens, co-edits the *Transactions of the Radnorshire Society* and is a Trustee of the Bleddfa Centre for the Creative Spirit.

Simon Dorrell is a garden designer, author and artist. The co-owner of Bryan's Ground, he also designed the Burton Court and Hampton Court gardens in Herefordshire. He is the Art Director of the magazine *Hortus*, and a contributor to many books, including *The Penguin Book of Garden Writing*. His ink drawings were made using a 0.13mm nib, and are reproduced at their original size.

Index